HEARING MANY VOICES

Dialogue and Diversity in the Ecumenical Movement

Dale T. Irvin

**UNIVERSITY
PRESS OF
AMERICA**

Lanham • New York • London

Copyright © 1994 by
University Press of America®, Inc.
4720 Boston Way
Lanham, Maryland 20706

3 Henrietta Street
London WC2E 8LU England

Library of Congress Cataloging-in-Publication Data

Irvin, Dale T.
Hearing many voices : dialogue and diversity in the
ecumenical movement / Dale T. Irvin.
p.   cm.
Includes index.
1. Ecumenical movement.   I. Title.
BX8.2.I76   1993   270.8'2—dc20   93–27910 CIP

ISBN 0–8191–9261–9 (cloth : alk. paper)
ISBN 0–8191–9262–7 (pbk. : alk. paper)

to

Victoria Lee Erickson

Contents

Acknowledgements

In a closing chapter of his 1938 *Out of Revolution* appropriately entitled "Farewell to Descartes," Eugen Rosenstock-Huessy proposed a new principle for the post-modern world of the third millennium: *respondeo etsi mutabor*, I respond although I will be changed. Here, at the beginning of a book dealing with response, dialogue, and change among the Christian churches of the world close to the end of the second millennium of the common era it is fitting that I acknowledge some of the people who have enabled me to respond and be changed. In a variety of ways they have embodied for me personally the ecumenical imperatives that will be explored in the pages that follow, keeping alive my hopes for a new church and world. With them I must share credit for whatever of value these pages offer. The errors and shortcomings of the book are of course my own.

First of all I would like to thank the many students in my classes at New York Theological Seminary over the last several years who have challenged me to respond. While they are too numerous to mention individually by name, I would be remiss if I did not acknowledge the immense contributions they have made to my understanding of difference and to my commitments to change. New York Theological Seminary is a unique institution doing ecumenical theology on a local level in the midst of the global reality of this metropolitan reality. Much of what I have learned about living with an openness to being transformed has been taught to me in its classrooms by students.

In the same breath I would also like to thank my faculty colleagues at NYTS for the support and nurturance experienced in our community. I owe special debts of gratitude to three persons in particular, Professors H. Dean Trulear, Angela Askew, and Keith Russell, for the many hours of conversation, critique, and camaraderie they have provided. The entire faculty at NYTS truly embodies the fullest meaning of that calling, sharing in its abundance of gifts and abilities.

James Melvin Washington, Professor of Church History at Union Theological Seminary, New York, has sparked countless insights and enabled numerous moments of intellectual comprehension for me over the years. For his extraordinary intellectual abilities, generosity of heart, love of the church, and intense commitments to the endeavors of the mind I am deeply thankful.

Professor Melanie A. May, Dean of the Program for the Study of Women and Gender in Church and Society at Colgate Rochester Divinity School provided critical comments and encouragement at a crucial point in the life of this study. For this, but also for the leadership she has provided globally to the ecumenical movement, to advancing the causes of women in church and society, and to increasing appreciation for the diversity of women's voices I am grateful.

Professors Larry Rasmussen, Christopher Morse, and Kosuke Koyama of Union Theological Seminary, New York, have kept the ecumenical conversation alive for me in a variety of contexts. The Rev. Sarah Hicks of the Majority Baptist Church, St. Albans, New York, shared with me impressions and materials she gathered at the Seventh Assembly of the WCC in Canberra, Australia in 1991. J. Richard Butler and the Rev. Luis Barrios both read an earlier draft of this manuscript and provided helpful comments. Seth Kasten of the Burke Library at Union Seminary provided assistance with research whenever I called on him for help. A good portion of the research for this book was completed in the Missionary Research Library housed within Burke Library at Union. I am thankful for the time and efforts being spent in preserving this outstanding ecumenical resource.

Among others I would acknowledge for their gifts of friendship and collegiality I only mention Ada Marie Isasi-Diaz, Augustine Musopole, Renee Leslie Hill, Bill Pindar, Doug Irvin, Joan Speaks, Koo Choon Seo, Bernard Quick, Sr. Rosina Araba Ampah, Chet Burger, and Irene Monroe. Norman Wilkerson belongs to this company of friends and colleagues. He is no longer with us in this life, and although I severely miss his intellect and sensitivity I know that he appreciates the contents of these pages.

Douglas and Andrew Irvin-Erickson are two of the most wonderful people in my life. They have endured much to see this study completed. Often they have helped me to see the world in a different light, challenging me in an intimate way as the embodied presence of the future. They have taught me that dialogical living knows no boundaries of age or perspective. To them I am especially thankful.

Finally, my deepest gratitude is reserved for Victoria Lee Erickson to whom this book is dedicated. Above all others she has been the one who has taught me about committed living, faith, dialogue and hope. For her joyous spirit and courage, for the contributions she has made to my own intellectual journey, and for the contributions she has made to this particular study I dedicate to her these pages.

Preface

The ecumenical movement among the Christian churches of the world this century has been one of the most important events in the history of world Christianity. Its effects have touched virtually every church in the world, even those that have refused to participate fully. Yet despite registering such pervasive influence, the ecumenical movement remains poorly understood by many people, partially because it encompasses such a complex, multifaceted array of projects that represent a diversity of theological agendas. Ecumenism resists simple characterizations or singular definitions.

We can however identify several major themes and accomplishments over the history of the last century, providing a basis for developing an interpretation of the meaning of ecumenism for today. One of the goals of the movement has been the search for the renewal of the historical project of Western Christendom, pursued under the banner of unity and mission. But it is the thesis of this book that this is only a part of the ecumenical story, for there have been significant forces and voices within the movement that have resisted such unity, pointing instead toward diversity and solidarity. Over the course of the last century the ecumenical movement has repeatedly embodied such contending voices dialogically.

In order to hear the many voices the following chapters will examine the several trajectories of ecumenical history institutionalized within the World Council of Churches, the single most important instrument of ecumenism this century. The first chapter explores M. M. Bakhtin's conception of dialogue in order to shed light of the dialogical experience of ecumenism as it has come to expression in the World Council of Churches. Succeeding chapters explore the dialogue among multiple voices in the three major ecumenical trajectories of faith and order, life and work, and missions. A final chapter examines the implications for a wider ecumenical movement.

Throughout the book I am arguing for remembering a more diverse ecumenical past and for constructing a more diverse ecumenical future for churches of the world. The end result of ecumenism this century has arguably been more diversity rather than either greater unity or greater uniformity in world Christianity. The greater diversity of faith and practice is finally a sign of life in the Christian movement today. Some might even say it's a sign of the renewing work of the Spirit.

Chapter 1:

A Dialogical Affair

It is quite possible to imagine and postulate a unified truth that requires a plurality of consciousnesses, one that in principle cannot be fitted within the bounds of a single consciousness, one that is, so to speak, by its very nature *full of event potential [sobytiina]* and is born at a point of contact among various consciousnesses.
--Mikhail Bakhtin[1]

Christ has made us His own, and He is not divided. In seeking Him we find one another. Here at Amsterdam we have committed ourselves afresh to Him, and have covenanted with one another in constituting this World Council of Churches. We intend to stay together.
-- from the inaugural "Message of the Assembly," Amsterdam 1948

1. Ecumenical Unity, Ecumenical Diversity

The ecumenical movement of the twentieth century represents one of the most significant occurrences in the history of world Christianity. For more than a century Christians from churches from across the world have been participating in conferences, programs, and study projects that have become institutionalized as the ecumenical movement. There is hardly a church in the world that has not been affected in some manner by the spirit and concrete achievements of ecumenism. Virtually every church and Christian community has to some degree responded to the ecumenical imperative.

Yet after a century of discussions, debates, conferences, and programs many remain unsure of just what ecumenism means, or what the ecumenical movement is all about. When asked, most people in the churches respond that it is a project seeking to overcome differences among Christians so to unite the churches of the world into one. Yet the same people will often use the term 'ecumenical' to describe someone who is respectful of differences among denominations or who appreciates the diversity of Christian points of view, rather than someone who advocates eliminating differences. Sometimes the term is used to describe joint programs or services involving Christians from several denominations, at other times to describe Christians and non-Christians working or worshipping together.

Within the religious community in North America many have come to the conclusion that the search for the unity of the Christian church has ended in failure; and indeed it does appear at least in part that the sectarian spirit of denominationalism and separatism among Christians is making a strong comeback at the end of the twentieth century.[2] Yet in a growing number of congregations one encounters a vital (if largely undocumented) ecumenism that is flourishing as members who have come from different denominations and traditions learn to worship and work together. Increasingly lay people reject strong denominational and confessional identification, or seek out churches that identify themselves as simply 'non-denominational.' In response a growing number of church leaders have become *de facto* ecumenists. In order to minister more effectively they have had to develop a sensitivity to the broader range of Christian spirituality and identities.

The term 'ecumenical' for many in the U.S. is still associated primarily with the more theologically liberal wing the of Protestant churches, to the point of obscuring the participation and contributions of Roman Catholic, evangelical Protestant, and Orthodox churches.[3] There have been significant new institutional forms of ecumenism among conservative Evangelicals, Pentecostals, and Charismatics in recent decades that have been overlooked by those who believe the winds of ecumenism have blown over. We could go on to expand upon the ecumenical significance of the many interfaith organizations that have emerged across North America at the community level, or discuss the ecumenical character of the numerous parachurch organizations which many people in the churches -- lay and ordained -- support and participate in. But if ecumenism in its broader reaches is flourishing, why then do we tend to hear that the ecumenical movement is in trouble, or even in crisis?

The answer to this question might lie in part in the identification of ecumenism with its more visible structural forms and instruments. For most Christians in North America the ecumenical movement has been institutionally identified with the World Council of Churches (WCC) and the National Council of Churches of Christ USA (NCCCUSA), and to a somewhat lesser degree with the traditionally dominant Protestant churches that are members of these Councils, the so-called 'mainline' churches. A number of conservative and anti-institutional winds have been blowing through churches in North America in recent decades, directly affecting many of these ecumenical bodies.[4] The willingness of several national Protestant church bodies identified with the ecumenical cause to become embroiled in controversy over social issues has added to the negative publicity that has been directed toward national and international ecumenical structures. To many it appears that there has been a general abatement in ecumenical excitement that has followed in the wake of gains made in the 1960s, following the Orthodox entrance into the WCC in 1961 and the reforms in the Roman Catholic Church set in motion by Vatican II after 1965. For whatever reasons, there appears to be at least the sense of ecumenical retrenchment among many in the churches.[5]

Much of the criticism of the ecumenical movement in recent years has come from conservative critics on the political-ecclesial 'right.' Yet at the same time the ecumenical movement has been criticized from the 'left' as well, as being too conservative, too entrenched in a middle-class European/American ethos, and dominated by a Eurocentric patriarchal agenda. The fact that criticism has come from both sides of the politico-ecclesial spectrum suggests more than an ecumenical irony. The diversity of perspectives concerning what the ecumenical movement is, and is seeking to accomplish, points toward one of the fundamental truths concerning the nature of the movement itself, one that will occupy us throughout this study. Simply put, it is that the ecumenical movement is, and has always been, a multifaceted affair encompassing different historical, political, and theological agendas which resist easy integration or synthesis within a single coherent framework. Criticism of the ecumenical movement from any particular perspective can only be partially correct insofar as it reflects only a part of the truth. The ecumenical movement is by definition a complex, multifaceted project encompassing a diversity of agendas and resisting singular definition.

In the following chapters we shall explore several of the major ecumenical trajectories of this century, paying particular attention to the on-going tension between unity and diversity. It is the thesis of this book that one of the major objectives of the ecumenical movement has been the search for the renewal of the historical project of Western Christendom, carried out under the joint mandate of the unity and mission of the church. But that can only be part of the ecumenical story, for there have been significant forces and voices within the ecumenical movement that have resisted and opposed such unity in support of diversity and solidarity. These voices of resistance have most often been non-European/American, and have over the course of the century forged an ever-sharper critique of Eurocentric notions of unity.[6] The search for the reconstruction of a unified world church such as that achieved under the Emperor Constantine in the fourth century of the Christian era has been a significant objective of the ecumenical movement. But it is one that has been identified by others within the same ecumenical movement as being a project of European/American ecclesial domination. The ecumenical movement has been criticized by some as being a white, European/American, patriarchal project. But at the same time the critique of the white, bourgeois, patriarchal character of ecumenical theology has arisen from within the structures of the movement itself and not just from beyond them, and it too legitimately lays claim to being deemed the meaning of 'ecumenical.'[7]

We can see then that the current uncertainty about the future of the ecumenical movement does not arise from a lack of direction or identity.[8] Uncertainty arises instead from the fact that there are several conflicting understandings of both, within the one movement. Its multifaceted character makes the ecumenical movement resistant to simple definition or categorization. Differing and even opposing perspectives and commitments often meet within its common arena in ways that defy total synthesis, integration, or consensus. Yet it is my contention that these contradictions are not fatal to the movement as some might suppose. Far from it, they are the generating source for its life and practice.

It is precisely in the ecumenical movement's role as the theological meeting ground of churches and traditions that these contradictions have emerged within it. The external contradictions that exist between and among the churches and theological traditions of the world are internal to the ecumenical movement, because it is by definition their meeting place. By its very nature, noted Kosuke Koyama at a 1984 WCC symposium held in Cartigny, Switzerland, the ecumenical movement is a gate. That means it is a meeting place for difference, a reality 'in-between' traditions, cultures and religions.[9] It is thus a place for dialogue and diversity. It is a movement taking place always at a cross-roads, but it is also a movement seeking to create cross-roads, a place for exchange, collision, controversy, and discord. It is, in short, a hot spot.

In a subsequent letter reflecting upon the 1984 Cartigny symposium, Werner Simpfendörfer depicted his own sense of the ecumenical action which must flow from its nature as a movement at the crossroads. Ecumenism means, he pointed out, to be "in transit."

> For me the basic significance of Cartigny is that it left the safe ground of ecumenical definitions, affirmations and conclusions and dared to enter the 'transit lounge' of the ecumenical movement, to expose itself to the risks of dead-end roads, to unfinished business, in one word to the crisis of the ecumenical movement. ... If ecumenical hope is once more to turn into ecumenical action, we must accept the challenge of transit, face the judgment and wait upon the Spirit to create a new people.[10]

Simpfendörfer is certainly not alone among participants as well as critics of the ecumenical movement when he observes that the movement is in crisis. But if it is the very essence of ecumenism to be in passage, to be in the transit lounge, then ecumenism is by its very nature to be in crisis. Ecumenism is by definition unfinished business. The crisis which it faces is not that of being a dying movement, but that of living between the safe ground of its accomplishments, conclusions, and affirmations of the past and the choppy waters of passage which lie in front of it in its future.[11] Crisis, in other words, is the permanent vocation of ecumenics.[12]

In the course of its history over the past century the ecumenical movement has found itself repeatedly to be in crisis.[13] The issues, contexts, and institutional locations have changed over time. Often the theological stakes have been significantly different. At times there have been attempts to conceal the crisis, and the temptation to rest content with achieved accomplishments has been powerful. But then the call to be 'in transit' is heard, the challenge "to face judgement and wait upon the Spirit" is responded to, and the hopes for the creation of a new people spring alive. This is why after more than a hundred years of multiple and continuing dialogues, when the churches of the world remain as divided as they were at the beginning of the century, the ecumenical hope is still not dead. It is why the emergence of new forms of ecumenism apart from the older existing organizations on local, region, and international levels (when and should these occur) does not so much represent its demise as new signs of life. The *praxis* of ecumenism is found wherever boundaries are broken, cross-roads are reached, new imperatives begin to be heard, and Christian communities become 'in transit.'

2. Understanding Dialogue

From what has been said so far it is obvious that the *praxis* of dialogue is central to the ecumenical experience. For more than a century, as representatives of churches from around the world have participated in conferences, symposiums, and various cooperative projects they have been engaged in this process of dialogue. The major textual productions of the ecumenical movement -- the reports and statements from conferences, symposiums, commission meetings, and visitations -- are often explicitly dialogical in their structure and contents, representing differing points of view or commitments side by side within their pages. Written by committees, reports and conference statements often hold together within their paragraphs and pages contradictions and tensions that are reflective of their historical production. Many of the secondary texts of the ecumenical movement -- the books, articles and papers, covering particular topics or the sweep of the ecumenical movement as a whole -- are dialogical in the manner in which they seek to engage other texts or experiences.[14] The very word 'ecumenical' embodies a dialogue. Attached to it and even contained in it are the various voices and concerns of its participants over the decades.

When we consider how central the *praxis* of dialogue is to ecumenism, it is surprising to note how minimal the attention paid to the meaning of dialogue has been within ecumenical discourse. Several important methodological studies or 'how to' statements on dialogue have emerged from ecumenical circles, and frequently books on the ecumenical movement state the importance of dialogue as a practice.[15] But by and large the theoretical basis for understanding dialogical experience has been lacking, or has been inadequately assumed in the movement. For the most part there has not been a great deal of attention paid either to dialogue as a method or as a way of being ecumenical. Too often dialogue has been perceived as a means to an end; but from what has been noted above, it can also be seen to be constitutive of the vocation of ecumenism.

Part of the problem I believe rests with a general lack within ecumenical circles of adequate philosophical models for understanding dialogue and diversity. Too often ecumenical discussions assume theological and philosophical models of dialogue that assume closure and resolution of contradictions to be the final goal. Consensus is taken to mean singularity of intent and meaning, and the unity of faith is presumed to lie at the end of a process in which contradiction and conflict are finally overcome. In these instances dialogue is seen as a means toward an ultimate end which is the sublimation of difference and diversity. Dialogue then will be no longer necessary once the end -- unity -- is achieved.

Yet over the course of a century the ecumenical experience has pointed in precisely the opposite direction. Now, at the end of a century of global ecumenical conversations and action, we see more divisions and diversity among the churches of the world, not less.[16] While agreement and consensus have been reached in some areas or concerning some theological matters, new divisions and differences have emerged concerning others. Quite often the process of ecumenical dialogue has revealed points of conflict that participants previously had not addressed. At times the process of dialogue has actually facilitated new differences among churches and Christian ecclesial communities.

At this point I believe a better theoretical understanding of the nature of dialogue would significantly increase our understanding of the dialogical nature of ecumenism itself. Needed within the ecumenical movement is a more adequate understanding of its own dialogical existence, and the imperatives that emerge from a dialogical understanding of the world. To this end I propose to examine briefly some of the theoretical explorations into the meaning of dialogue undertaken by the late Russian literary critic, Mikhail Bakhtin. Bakhtin's insights can provide an important foundation for understanding the dialogical nature of the ecumenical movement, both in its programs and in the texts these have given rise to. His insights into the dialogical character of human experience can provide a richer and fuller grasp of ecumenism today.

Born in 1895 and educated in the classics and philology, Bakhtin carried out his first studies in Russia in the midst of a circle of friends concerned with literature, philosophy, religion and politics. He survived the repression of the Stalinist years to be rediscovered in the 1960s in Russia, and since his death in 1975 has received growing attention outside his homeland.

Bakhtin situated his own understanding of philosophy, language and experience over against the prevailing philosophical and linguistic schools of his time. His criticism of these existing schools was that they

> have all postulated a simple and unmediated relation of speaker to his unitary and singular 'own' language, and have postulated as well a simple realization of this language in the monologic utterance of the individual.[17]

Unitary models of language which postulate an individual speaker of the language, he argued, are the result of, and reflect, socio-historical forces toward unification and centralization of the "verbal-ideological" and material world, in his case of European societies.

> Unitary language constitutes the theoretical expression of the historical processes of linguistic unification and centralization, an expression of the centripetal forces of language.[18]

Language, he argued, is always "ideologically saturated." As a system of linguistic norms and generative forces, a common unitary language gives expression to and reflects particular ideological processes of socio-political and cultural centralization.

These centripetal forces are not all that can be said however for language (and by implication for socio-political and cultural life) according to Bakhtin. The forces of unitary language struggle to overcome the multiplicity of what he calls the "heteroglossia" of language. At the same time as forces for unitary language are at work for centralization, new systems of stratification are taking place, both on the level of dialects but also on the level of socio-ideological formation (class, profession, or even generation). The philosophical and linguistic models of unitary language themselves, and the centralizing forces of language with which they are saturated, are but instances in a growing stratification of linguistic, socio-political, and cultural life, he argued. Stratification, centralization, decentralization -- all are occurring at once in a dynamic process of heteroglossia.[19]

In other words, every moment of speaking, every act of utterance is an instance in which opposing centrifugal and centripetal forces are both at work. This for Bakhtin holds true for the entire range of experience, which is thoroughly infused with language. There is never any such thing as a unitary moment, for each moment always occurs at intersections of social and historical forces. As such, every moment is both at a point of historical convergence and at a point of historical divergence. Consequently the historical life of language is "a contradiction-ridden, tension-filled unity" of multiple meanings, a polyphonic dialogue:

> The living utterance, having taken meaning and shape at a particular historical moment in a socially specific environment, cannot fail to brush up against thousands of living dialogic threads, woven by socio-ideological consciousness around the given object of an utterance; it cannot fail to become an active participant in social dialogue. After all, the utterance arises out of this dialogue as a continuation of it and as a rejoinder to it -- it does not approach the object from the sidelines. [20]

For Bakhtin, in every instance of speaking, we are not only located socially and historically within a dialogue. Our utterances themselves are dialogized from within. In every instance of speaking we are responding to something that was said before, using words that were used before, taking a stance in relation to one that was taken before. We are immersed in the context of language or heteroglossia which is characteristic of social life. At the same time we are anticipating what will be said, using words which will probably be used again, offering directives for the future. From within our words the centrifugal forces of heteroglossia emerge offering "loopholes" to the givenness of language and experience.[21] Dialogue insures the unfinalizability of history and the openness of the future.

Dialogue occurs in a number of different modes for Bakhtin. The ones he examined most thoroughly in his writings on Dostoevsky and Rabelais were those of the dialogue within a written text (novel or story) and the dialogue between author and her or his text. In both instances the dialogue extends to the reader of texts as well, leading Bakhtin to the interactive character of understanding and response. He recognized the material dimensions of textual and uttered dialogue, both the material world in which it is 'imprisoned' (the stones or paper that 'contain' written texts, the structures and systems of sound which 'contain' spoken texts) and the social world of real people who are speaking, writing, and reading. Distinguishing between the world that creates a text and the representation of the world which a text accomplishes, he argued that there is dialogue across the boundaries between texts and contexts, and that every text is also a context.[22]

Seeing the fullness of the dialogical character of all language and reality enabled Bakhtin to discern that words themselves are fully dialogized from within. Within religious systems the manner in which this dialogue is carried out regarding particular sacred words is through methods for transmitting and interpreting them. But all words bear along their history and multiple contexts, their varied meanings and understandings among their users and even across languages. The possibility/impossibility of interpretations and translations of words, utterances, and texts from one language to another is related to the dialogical character of language itself.

Through all of these modes Bakhtin recognized the unfinalizability of meaning which is characteristic of dialogue. No single statement of meaning is ever possible regarding a moment of dialogue, no single intention or purpose can be discerned within it. The separate thoughts, words, sentences, and languages which converge in any instance of dialogue cannot be united into one statement or system of meaning, for there is no monological truth in dialogue. He observed:

> It is quite possible to imagine and postulate a unified truth that requires a plurality of consciousnesses, one that in principle cannot be fitted within the bounds of a single consciousness, one that is, so to speak, by its very nature *full of event potential [sobytiina]* and is born at a point of contact among various consciousnesses.[23]

Bakhtin's understanding of dialogue can help shed light on the experiences and purposes of the ecumenical movement. Indeed, it would be possible in a broader sense to define the ecumenical dimension of the Christian churches as their dialogical character, and to perceive the ecumenical movement as an expression of the dialogical character of Christian faith itself. In this sense ecumenism represents the permanent openness of Christian faith it its own future, to the future of the world, and to God. The manner in which the centripetal and centrifugal forces are operative at the same time prevents us from construing a unitary model for ecumenics, and from reducing the ecumenical movement to a single purpose or series of events. Instead, we would see the ecumenical movement as a site for dialogue.

Participants in this dialogue do not always agree on why they are even together, much less on single purpose or goal toward which they are journeying. "From the very beginning," writes Ernst Lange, in his reflections on the meeting of the Faith and Order Commission in 1971 in Louvain, Belgium, "the ecumenical movement has never really been certain of its goals. The main reason for this is that quite different and even conflicting motives have been operating."[24] Lack of agreement (which is a common experience in the ecumenical movement) is sometimes perceived to be a sign of weakness, ambiguity, or lack of commitment on the part of the churches. In Bakhtin's understanding of dialogue however, the tension-filled unity and disunity of ecumenical discourse and experience are not indicative of the weakness, but of strength in the movement. If unified truth requires a plurality of consciousnesses and voices, so that it in principle cannot be fitted into the bounds of a single consciousness or ascribed to a single voice, church, or even tradition, then the diversity of voices speaking to each other and even against each other in ecumenical dialogue holds far more potential for truth than many credit today to the ecumenical movement.

Some ecumenists have proposed a universal council of Christians meeting to agree upon a common statement of faith and practice as the ultimate goal of the movement. While discussions of such a universal council were more common thirty years ago among ecumenical leaders, the conciliar objective still continues to generate excitement and hope. We can see however that the conciliar model of unity is substantially altered when viewed in light of Bakhtin's conception of truth not being capable of being fitted into a single consciousness. Most advocates of a universal council foresee uniformity of faith and practice being its end. Bakhtin would have noted that such is never the case for any dialogical experience. Within the confines of such a council no single voice or perspective could unambiguously hold the truth. Different interpretations and meaning would arise among its immediate participants, to say nothing of those who were unable or refused to attend. Even were common formulations of faith to be reached, along the lines perhaps of the ecumenical creed that emerged from the councils at Nicaea (325) and Constantinople (381), the understanding and eventual interpretation of this creed would proceed along multiple dialogical trajectories for the churches involved. New, and in a number of cases, explicitly oppositional interpretations would no doubt be put forth by those Christians who had refused to attend such a council, or by those who were in attendance but witnessed their own perspective being silenced. As was true for the creed that was agreed to in 381 at Constantinople, no less than is true for even such a recent event as

Vatican II, a diversity of meanings emerges from conciliar events due to their inherent dialogical character.

No such council by itself could contain the fullness of truth in its formulations. Whatever unity it achieved would not be final or closed, but would instead be immediately the ground for further dialogical diversity and even disunity, due to the centrifugal forces that are at work in history and in language. A genuinely universal council that seeks to speak for all Christians would, in Bakhtin's terms, be a dialogized event of convergence and divergence. While all might even come to agree to the formulations of language that would issue from such a council, the meaning and interpretation of such formulations would be already in the moment of their production be plural, multiple, and contradictory. To such a council participants would bring their already dialogized understandings of faith; from it they would undoubtedly carry further dialogized understanding and practice.

We can see this dialogical process at work in the manner in which different meanings and interpretations have attached themselves to terms, concepts and statements in the ecumenical movement. Aram Keshishian has explored the multiple meanings of 'conciliar' that have emerged in ecumenical discussion, for instance, while Lange has charted different meanings of 'renewal.'[25] Particular statements or reports have often received different and even unreconcilable interpretations, by those who participated in their production as well as by those who later read them. The multiplicity of meanings that are contained in the saturated language of ecumenism give rise to misunderstanding as often as they give rise to understanding, resulting in a significant level of indeterminacy in interpretation.

In short, the ecumenical movement is a dialogical social and historical process taking place in and among churches of the world. The conferences, symposiums, statements, study projects, consultations, and assemblies that have occupied its agenda have institutionalized this process since the beginning of the current century, all the while concretizing and accelerating interaction among churches. Yet even now the full meaning of the ecumenical movement remains unrealized, for ecumenical history is by its very definition open-ended and unfinalizable. It is a polyphonic event that can not be reduced to a single narrative. It is an event born of the plenitude of perspectives of world Christianity and alive still with multiple possibilities.

3. The Multiplicity of Meaning

We can see then that the word 'ecumenical' embodies a dialogue that remains inconclusive and open-ended. The range of programs described as ecumenical encompasses projects that often appear to be at odds with one other. Inter-religious dialogue, evangelism, and missions, for example, are all contained under the ecumenical umbrella. One finds the term used to describe movements for political liberation as well as discussions that are strictly ecclesial in nature. To some observers ecumenism should be confined to describing intra-Christian affairs, but for others the ecumenical horizon must encompasses other religions and ideologies as well. The diversity of projects covered under by term is one reason why the word 'ecumenical' still "does not trip lightly from English lips," as Norman Goodall noted in 1961[26]. In over a half-century of common usage it has not achieved stable meaning.

As I noted at the beginning of the chapter, for many people in the churches in North America the goal of the ecumenical movement is the visible unity of the Christian churches of the world. This has indeed been, and remains, a central purpose articulated by the Constitution of the WCC. Although the Council defines itself as a fellowship of churches, having no ecclesiastical authority on its own, it functions as a forum for theological discussion among the various Christian communions in the world and thereby works toward the reunion of separated churches as an expression of its ecumenical character. Christian unity in this case has generally been pursued through the formulation of doctrinal consensus represented in statements to which all participant churches could agree. Among the doctrinal differences matters of ministry and sacrament have seemed to many Christian leaders to be the most significant issues dividing the churches; over the course of this century addressing them has emerged as the focus for discussions of matters pertaining to faith and order.

One of the more celebrated milestones in this ecumenical search for unity was the document entitled *Baptism, Eucharist and Ministry (BEM)* which was approved for transmission to the churches by the Commission on Faith and Order of the World Council of Churches at its 1982 meeting in Lima, Peru.[27] *BEM* represents more than a decade of ecumenical discussion and dialogue within the Commission on Faith and Order concerning the different understandings of sacraments and ministry that divide the churches of the world. Its text and commentary sought to provide a means by which various separated churches could recognize their own ministry and sacraments within a larger theological expression. Different understandings were brought together side by side in the text, with accompanying commentary highlighting commonalities and differences. The overall goal of *BEM*, as for much of the work of Faith and Order, is to achieve doctrinal convergence among the separated churches, which is perceived within many Christian traditions as being a necessary prerequisite for full ecclesial communion.

Understanding 'ecumenical' to mean 'ecclesiastical consensus' recalls the meaning of *oikoumene* (the Greek word from which we derive 'ecumenical') that emerged among the ancient churches following the conversion of the Roman Emperor Constantine the Great in 314 A.D., and in the ensuing councils that were called under Roman imperial aegis. The political-cultural meaning of *oikoumene* (literally the 'inhabited earth') of the Apostolic period, which coincided with the world of human culture known to the writers of the Second Testament (understood predominantly but not exclusively as the world of Greco-Roman culture), gave way to an ecclesiastical understanding of *oikoumene* represented by the hierarchy of the church and often under imperial domination. So historian Robert Grant points out

> Some of the earliest witnesses call the council [at Nicaea in 325 A.D.] "ecumenical," but the term means no more than "Roman-imperial." What the council actually represented was the area [of the eastern half of the Roman empire] formerly controlled by Licinius.[28]

Willem A. Visser't Hooft, the first General Secretary of the WCC, has suggested that for Orthodox churches the collapse of the Byzantine Empire in the fifteenth century removed the "political overtones" of the word 'ecumenical' at least as far as the Orthodox are concerned. "But the full consequences of this change in significance were destined to appear only at a much later date."[29] Islamic conquest brought to an end official linkage between the hierarchy of the Church and imperial power in the Byzantine empire, although close relations between Church and political rulers were to continue in the East in some situations, in Russia for instance, until the beginning of the twentieth century.[30]

Beyond the imperial political meaning of being ecumenical, the Orthodox Church tradition teaches there is a mystical unity which is not dependent on overt coercion, but is the inner working of the Holy Spirit. The inner experience of unity of love and obedience is closely related for the Orthodox churches to the formal unity of Creed and Tradition. The unity of Creed and Tradition in turn requires for the Orthodox adherence to the doctrinal standards of the seven Ecumenical Councils of the ancient churches, which more than the unity symbolized in the bishops or in the Patriarch of Constantinople (called the Ecumenical Patriarch) remain the basis for its claim to possessing the universality of *Una Sancta*.[31] For the Orthodox churches more so than for any other of the major Christian traditions engaged in the movement 'ecumenism' has meant striving for the restoration of the unity that was achieved in the seven ancient Ecumenical Councils.

For this reason there has been a certain amount of uneasiness voiced by Orthodox theologians over some of the assumptions and directions of the modern ecumenical movement. Orthodox participants at the first World Conference on Faith and Order held at Lausanne, Switzerland, in 1927 voiced their concern regarding the conference's method which, in their view, allowed for differences in meaning and understanding regarding matters of doctrine. Explaining the Orthodox decision to abstain from voting in favor of most of the conference's final reports, Archbishop Germanos, Metropolitan of Thyateira stated, "we desire to declare that in our judgement the most which we can now do is to enter into co-operation with other Churches in the social and moral sphere on a basis of Christian love."[32]

A shift in the Orthodox Church's stance began to be evident during the early 1960s, beginning with the New Delhi Assembly in 1961 when the Russian Orthodox Church joined the World Council officially, and Orthodox theologians since then have generally been willing to explore doctrinal differences even though the prospects for unity with Roman Catholic and Protestant churches remain considerably distant. It is important to note here that while the Orthodox churches might originally have been more willing to cooperate on matters of service and practical ministry, the discussion of doctrinal unity has always been central to the ecumenical movement for them. So Theodore Stylianopoulos, responding to *BEM*, notes that:

> The Orthodox did not necessarily have to join in the work of Faith and Order or they could have joined only as observers. Yet the underlying desire for unity, the predilection of many Orthodox to discuss theology, as well as changing perceptions about the possibilities of unity have led many Orthodox in the last decades to *insist* that the World Council place theology and issues of unity at the center of its agenda, as we all know.[33]

A similar horizon of meaning for ecumenism as a movement for unity is encountered in official documents issued by the Roman Catholic magisterium in the wake of Vatican II. The term generally was little used by Catholic theologians during the first half of this century, but since the 1960s it has become a common Catholic designation for what is described as a movement toward the reintegration of separated Christian communities. The Vatican Council's "Decree on Ecumenism" *(Unitatis Redintegratio)* opens with the statement, "The restoration of unity among all Christians is one of the principle concerns of the Second Vatican Council."[34] The process by which this restoration is to be realized, the road to which Christian unity will be achieved again, is one of dialogue, says the decree. *Unitatis Redintegratio* calls for dialogue with both Eastern Orthodox and Protestant communions who are described as separated Christians. Restoration and unity take shape concretely in a movement toward reintegration of separated Christians into the Roman communion. "For it is through Christ's Catholic Church alone, which is the universal help towards salvation, that the fullness of the means of salvation can be obtained."[35]

The presence within the Catholic Church of the Apostolic successor to Peter is determinative for reunion, according to official Roman Catholic teaching. The unity of the church is symbolized by the presence of the Bishop of Rome who, as Peter's successor, is the chief pastor of the whole church. Further, unbroken succession is the fundamental symbol for historical continuity. Hence the ecumenical task is reintegration of separated Christians into the Church in which the unity of the faith has been preserved.

In interpreting the Council's decree, Roman Catholic theologian Karl Rahner contrasted ecumenical theology with controversial theology.[36] Amplification of dogmas and clearer exposition of particular theological positions are the immediate tasks of ecumenical dialogue, obtaining the removal of theological obstacles to concrete unity, argued Rahner. While this reunited church of the future will be marked by a relative pluralism in theological expression, it will stand in "legitimate, historical continuity" with the Roman Catholic Church of the present and hence with "the Church of our beginnings."[37] Ecumenism aims toward an ecclesiastical consensus, achieved through dogmatic formulations which are historically and theologically continuous with the past.[38]

A comparison of Roman Catholic and Orthodox understandings of universality reveals ambiguities regarding the meaning of the Church's ecumenical character. For both communions the historical dimensions of catholicity or fullness reside in the Church's unbroken hierarchical continuity with the Apostles. Continuity and catholicity for the Roman Church are strongly asserted to be in the person of the successor to St. Peter. Orthodox theologians, on the other hand, generally regard the Roman form of catholicity as being too juridical, and claim a more mystical understanding through Tradition. According to Orthodox teaching, Catholicity is not guaranteed through visible communion with the Bishop of Rome, but rather through the reception of the seven Ecumenical Councils and the "*consensus Traditionis.*"[39]

Both churches assert their unbroken continuity with the church of the Apostles. Yet they have broken communion with each other. Both continue to participate in theological dialogues with separated communions (including with each other), dialogues that are described as being ecumenical and in search of Christian unity. But both communions at the same time claim to represent fully the unity of the Ecumenical Church. Undergirding the latter concept of ecumenical in both traditions are totalizing historical claims to universality which are often in tension and even in crisis with each other, and with other non-universal historical claims regarding ecclesial life.

At the end of the nineteenth century a different meaning of ecumenical came into usage through several Protestant missionary conferences. In the World Ecumenical Conference of the Methodist Churches, first held in 1881, and again in the Ecumenical Missionary Conference held in New York in 1900, the word 'ecumenical' was primarily an international geographical designation. The Ecumenical Missionary Conference, held in New York in 1900, defined itself so not because it claimed to represent the one universal church, nor even the various separated churches, but because it proposed to encompass "the whole area of the inhabited globe."[40] The usage designated an orientation toward the world community, rather than a comprehensive ecclesial tradition.

It is in the series of missionary conferences held in the USA, England and Germany in the second half of the 19th/early 20th century, Visser't Hooft argues, that we find an initial conjoining of a desire for "world-wide unity of the Church of Christ, which transcends national and confessional differences,"[41] and a program for "world-wide missionary outreach of the Church"[42] that would give rise to one of the more common meanings of 'ecumenical' in this century: the search for the *unity* and *mission* of the churches. By far the most important of these 'ecumenical missionary' conferences held at the beginning of the twentieth century was the World Missionary Conference, in Edinburgh, Scotland, in 1910. Most histories of the ecumenical movement in the twentieth century cite Edinburgh 1910 as the beginning, thereby providing for the ecumenical movement a genealogy rooted in the missionary movement of the nineteenth century. Histories of the WCC usually draw several trajectories from the World Missionary Conference in 1910 to the official formation of the WCC in 1948 at its inaugural Assembly in Amsterdam, Holland.[43]

According to the dominant historiography, three streams of distinctive ecumenical movement flowed from Edinburgh 1910: the International Missionary Council; the Universal Conference on Life and Work; and the World Conference on Faith and Order.[44] The theological problem that drove these movements forward, and together, was the conjoining of the missionary task with the obligation to work toward Christian unity.   "These twin poles of unity and mission have characterized what has come to be referred to as 'the ecumenical movement.'"[45]   This historical narrative, with its three distinctive streams or trajectories, has been represented as an uninterrupted lineage despite the occurrence of a number of ruptures that suggest a more complex historical narration, and despite the presence within the WCC of churches whose historical identity is not bound to the Western Protestant missionary expansion.[46]

During the second half of the 20th century the dominant meaning of 'ecumenical,' and of the phrase 'ecumenical movement,' came generally to be associated with the WCC which formed in 1948 through the merger of Faith and Order and Life and Work. Problems regarding the meaning of ecumenism surfaced early within the World Council itself, resulting in the publication by the Central Committee of the WCC of a study document, "The Calling of the Church to Mission and Unity," following its meeting in Rolle, Switzerland, in 1951.[47]

"The Calling" acknowledged that there was confusion among churches concerning the theological relationship between two tasks, both understood to be ecumenical: a missionary obligation and an obligation to unity. At that time there were still two separate but closely related organizational structures which were carrying on ecumenical work among Protestant churches of the world, the WCC and the International Missionary Conference (IMC). The WCC, composed primarily of representatives from European/North American ecclesiastical bodies (the non-European churches were at this time usually not yet regarded by North Atlantic churches as 'independent' and thus were not members of the WCC), was becoming identified as the embodiment of the obligation to unity. The IMC, on the other hand, was constituted by representatives of boards, agencies and national councils. It included mission boards and councils from regions of the globe other than those of European/American civilization which were still being labeled in the 1950s by the paternalistic designation 'younger churches.' Its focus had been on the extension of Christianity among peoples who were not Christian, through 'foreign' missions or missionary penetration by European/North American churches into areas of the world which were not historically part of Western Christendom. But, noted the "Calling," the WCC and the IMC both engaged in activities for missions and unity, even though each was primarily active on one or the other front. Within a decade this organizational dichotomy would be eliminated through the merger of the IMC into the WCC, in 1961 at the New Delhi Assembly of the Council. After 1961 the two obligations would be carried out within a single institutional framework.[48]

In 1951 "The Calling" noted that among some sectors of the church, most notably among students, a general belief had taken hold that the missionary era of Christian history had come to an end, and had been succeeded by an ecumenical age.[49] Through the 1950s the tension between missions and ecumenics would grow. At the same time there would be increasing criticism of ecumenism that was confined within the horizons of the churches. The roots of this latter tension between church-centered and world-centered ecumenism also reached back to the opening decades of the twentieth century, when the quest for the unity of the churches had led to the convening of Faith and Order, while the quest for the renewal of the churches' mission within modern industrial society had led to the formation of the movement called Life and Work.

The Universal Christian Conference on Life and Work which convened in Stockholm, Sweden, in 1925, gathered representatives from Western churches in search of a collective response to social, political, and moral questions confronting European civilization of that day. The path of ecumenism that Life and Work pursued in its early years was that of collective witness and service before the 'world' (conceived then primarily as the world of Western industrial society). The aphorism that the principal architect of Life and Work, Archbishop Söderblom of Sweden, suggested as the motto for the Stockholm Life and Work

Conference in 1925, "Dogma divides, service unites," was characteristic of this early form of ecumenism through service. It was soon apparent however even to Söderblom that service and doctrine could not be easily separated. "The policy of ignoring theological differences was soon abandoned as Life and Work set up its own Theological Commission to reach agreement on understandings of the Church, of the world, and of the Kingdom of God, without which there could be little service.[50]"

In the decades that followed 1925, doctrinal aspects of ecumenical social witness would receive considerably more attention. At the same time there was among leaders of the movement an increasing awareness of the challenges to Western churches of alternative ecumenical visions posed by Western secularization and modern political ideologies. In a 1952 editorial in *Theology Today*, addressing the impact of secular and totalitarian ideologies, John A. MacKay wrote, "In a sense and to a degree not true of any previous epoch in history, our age is ecumenical in character." In response to the demands of history he argued, the task of the church was to bring within its scope of ministry the whole world, which has been made one in the modern age through technology, the modern unifying ecumenical force. "Technology did in the twentieth century what Greek culture and Roman law had done two thousand years before."[51]

By the 1950s the manner in which the reappraisal of the 'world' was confined to the social world of the Western or North Atlantic churches likewise began to be addressed in ecumenical discourse. Alternatives to ecclesiocentric and Western social ecumenisms received articulation in the 1950s among 'Third World' churches that were living in the midst of rapid social change. By the 1960s the call for political liberation and historical transformation had been heard throughout the ecumenical movement.[52] In the rupture that political and liberation theologies would eventually achieve, a new understanding of the concept of 'world' emerged. For liberation theologians the ecumenical world was the world of the marginalized and oppressed of the modern era. In liberation theology ecumenism made an explicit option for the poor who inhabit and constitute the world. In contrast to that form of ecumenism understood to mean ecclesial unity, liberation theologies over the last several decades have articulated a challenge to pursue "the recreation or reconstruction of the ecumenical movement on the basis of a class option for the poor."[53] Following Gustavo Gutierrez's insight that "In a continent like Latin America...the main challenge does not come from the nonbeliever but from the *nonhuman*," this new ecumenism often leads to unecclesiastical places.[54]

To the political liberative meaning in the last decade has been added an ecological concern for the wider world of creation. The convergence of these concerns found institutional expression in the program of the World Council on Justice, Peace and the Integrity of Creation (JPIC). JPIC sought through a conciliar process to bring the churches of the world into a joint commitment (or covenant) to work toward a common witness that would make connections across these issues. The JPIC world convocation that was held in Seoul, Korea in 1990 renewed the hopes for many that the churches of the world -- Orthodox, Protestant, and Roman Catholic, from North and South -- could reach a common global confession along the route of Christian *praxis*. The deep divisions that were manifest at Seoul; the resistance among even many of the participating churches to committing themselves to the covenantal process JPIC called for; and the failure of other sectors in the ecumenical movement to respond positively to the possibility of united Christian voice addressing contemporry global problems bring us again to the diversity and even fragmentation of the ecumenical quest.[55]

In considering these multiple definitional understandings of ecumenism it begins to appear that the horizon of ecumenism is a receding one. What appeared to be an all-encompassing ecumenical method or project from the perspective of Edinburgh, Amsterdam, or Geneva, can in turn be seen to have too narrow a compass when viewed from Puebla, Addis Ababa, or New Delhi. To some the horizon of ecclesial unity is too narrow. To others the horizon of liberation theologies is too horizontal. For some ecumenism can only extend to the perimeters of the Christian movement. For others, such as Raimundo Panikkar, Christians must pursue an "ecumenical ecumenism" that emerges from dialogue with other religious traditions and faiths, a larger, more catholic ecumenism that would be more "faithful to the call of Christ within history."[56]

From examining these various ways of understanding the meaning and goal of being ecumenical we are driven to conclude that the full reality of the ecumenical movement cannot be reduced to any one perspective or platform. There are further meanings that continue to reside within the word 'ecumenical' itself. These will continue to emerge so long as there are representatives and participants from the different living communities or communions engaged in the dialogical process of ecumenical articulation. We have seen that no single definition has emerged from the movement as a whole which can be said to encompass all of the experiences and understandings of those participating. Some have called this a crisis. I would rather call it the sign of a critical dialogical process at work, giving birth to a new reality for Christian communities in the world today. The multiple meanings and associations that we encounter along the ecumenical path point us back to the realization stated above that the ecumenical movement is an open-ended project, and that the word 'ecumenical' embodies dialogue in the transit lounge.

4. Focus on the WCC

In the concluding pages of this chapter I will examine the reasons why, given the range and diversity of the ecumenical movement, this book will focus specifically on the historical experiences associated with the World Council of Churches. The multiplicity of meaning we have discovered in the word 'ecumenical' would appear at first glance to be at odds with a study that is focussed institutionally and even ideologically on the WCC. One obvious reason for taking the WCC as the institutional focus for this study is that given the parameters of a single book, some boundaries are necessary. It would be impossible to cover all dimensions of twentieth century ecumenism in a single text. The widely divergent themes found within Roman Catholic, Evangelical, and Pentecostal forms of ecumenical relationships; the various levels of national, regional, and local movements; and even the distinctive contours of ecumenical liberation theologies all would need to occupy separate volumes.

Noting the limits of this particular study is not to minimize the broader institutional locations for ecumenism that exist. Indeed, they have been recognized even from within the institutional framework by some who have been significant contributors to the life of the WCC. One of the major theorists of ecumenical missions for instance, Hans Hoekendijk, noted the significance of the 1966 Wheaton Declaration by conservative evangelicals, an ecumenical theological tradition which has still not been fully integrated into the World Council, although clearly there is a greater openness to Evangelical and Pentecostal participation in the World Council today.[57] A number of Protestant and Orthodox church leaders who participated in World Council events were invited to serve as official observers at the Roman Catholic council, Vatican II, during the 1960s. Since 1965 ecumenical relationships between the Roman Catholic church and the WCC, and between Rome and other churches, has continued to be manifested in a concrete way through official Roman Catholic representation on the Commission for Faith and Order, this despite Rome's rejection of an invitation to full membership in the WCC and its recent reluctance to participate in several other major ecumenical programs.[58]

Despite these considerations, the WCC warrants special attention because it has held a privileged role within the ecumenical movement of the twentieth century. A number of important studies have made the methodological assumption that the history of the ecumenical movement resides institutionally within the organizational framework of the WCC and its predecessor structures.[59] Other scholars have been more careful not to reduce the ecumenical movement to the institutional life and thought associated with the World Council, for as Kathleen Bliss noted, "The ecumenical movement is other than, and greater than, the institutions and organizations which have become its chief expression."[60] Yet Bliss is correct in calling the WCC and its related institutions the ecumenical movement's "chief expression." The tendency in theological and historical scholarship has been to define the ecumenical movement of the twentieth century by the organizational structures and councils that have composed the World Council of Churches. While not encompassing the complete historical reality of ecumenism, the history of the WCC has served metonymically to represent the history of the ecumenical movement of the twentieth century as a whole.[61]

For this reason focussed consideration of the WCC is necessary if we are to gain a better understanding of the historical consequences of the movement. It has been within the arena of the WCC and its affiliated bodies that we find the language and categories of modern ecumenism being constructed. This is the place where the dialogue is taking place most often and most intentionally. It is where one finds ecumenically relevant parameters of meaning being forged. Within this institutional framework dialogue has taken place most concretely, creating the multiplicity of meanings we will be exploring in the coming chapters. The WCC thus provides us something of a bounded multiplicity that allows us in this study to assume something that could be called the modern ecumenical tradition, institutionalized in the WCC.

Given the institutional focus on the WCC, we must next address the question of ecumenical continuity versus discontinuity. This question has become particularly significant as the WCC and the movement for which is has been the privileged instrument have undergone the ruptures and generational shifts that characterize their history. In light of the changes that have taken place over the years, and the ever-present uncertainty concerning its future, we must raise questions concerning the continuity of dialogue in the WCC. This was the very question that Hans Jochen Margull sought to answer over thirty years ago. Margull called for a more scientific articulation of ecumenical theology, a difficult proposition given the course of ecumenical discussions that had blossomed over the half-century preceding him. Concerned about the vast quantity of ecumenical work which had seemed to appear suddenly, Margull was more worried about the passage of a generation of ecumenists. He sought to insure the continuity of the discussion for the new generation by educating them in the ecumenical past. While he recognized that the future of ecumenical theology remained open-ended, determined only by the achievements produced by participants, he argued that reflection upon the ecumenical past could be the only adequate basis for rigorous ecumenical work.[62] Hence for Margull historical study of the ecumenical movement superceded systematic study of ecumenics.[63] The absence of a coherent theological reflection on the totality of ecumenical theology was addressed by what at least appeared to him to be a coherent historical movement which ran from Edinburgh to Amsterdam. Margull in effect displaced theological questions by asserting the singular historical identity of this ecumenical movement, requiring of participants in the discussion that they walk the same road from Edinburgh through Amsterdam.[64]

Concerns about the passage of a generation of ecumenists have appeared almost as often as have declarations of a crisis. Often they have found expression as an anxiety regarding the passing on of the 'ecumenical memory.' Such a concern is explicitly identified by the former General Secretary of the WCC, Emilio Castro, for instance, in his "Foreword" to the book by Marlin VanElderen, *Introducing the World Council of Churches*.[65] In another recent WCC publication entitled *The Teaching of Ecumenics* Alan Falconer has expanded on this perceived problem of passing on an ecumenical memory. Knowledge of the history of any particular community is essential for the identity of that community, Falconer argues. "Through an examination of its history, the identity of a community also becomes apparent to those who have not taken part in its past, thus enabling them to understand the community better, and to be confronted by its perspectives and values."[66] Knowledge of ecumenical history is therefore essential to maintaining the ecumenical movement (or 'community'), including its values and perspectives. The documents and texts which have emerged from and surround the significant events in ecumenical history are the primary sources which contain the memory of ecumenical history. From them students of ecumenics, which is to say the next generation of the community, derive their "common memory."

The concept of "a 'common memory' of the ecumenical movement," Falconer says, was stressed by Jose Miguez Bonino in a 1986 report to the Executive Committee of the WCC entitled, "The Concern for a Vital and Coherent Theology." According to Falconer, Bonino suggested that the result of a better articulation and appropriation of such a common memory would be twofold: on the one hand, participants "will be able to act more cohesively"; and on the other, "the identity or vision of ecumenicism will become more apparent to those who have not yet committed themselves to it." In other words, the unity and mission of the ecumenical movement itself depend upon the articulation of a common memory. Falconer goes on to quote Bonino:

> The modern ecumenical movement has run for almost one century. The WCC is close to its fortieth anniversary. It is not such a long history, but it is already too long for us to rely on a *spontaneous* living memory. How, then, to "rememorate", to make the past present and effective in our daily work? There have been changes but also continuities and "metamorphosis" in this history. For a body like the WCC to maintain an organic and not merely an institutional continuity, it needs constantly to re-read and re-live its common past.[67]

The problem of "rememorating" the past was raised in a critical manner by Bonino in the Cartigny symposium of 1984 referred to above, in relation to what he perceived to be the two forms of *oikoumene* experienced today. At Cartigny, Bonino argued that an "oikoumene of domination" was characteristic of ecclesial relations, analogous to that of international economic relations. "Do we not know to what extent the shape of the relations between the churches of the centre and those of the periphery is determined by the religious, institutional, bureaucratic or psychological needs of the former?"[68]

Bonino continued, "We all know, however, that this is not the whole truth. There is, thank God, another reality." This other reality, the "oikoumene of solidarity," could be found in the generous help and support expressed by certain communities from the north for grass-roots groups of the south, for instance. Furthermore, this other reality could be found in the history of the World Council. "It would also be difficult to exaggerate the role that the WCC has played in freeing the Latin American churches for a new understanding of their mission and in awakening and enabling the people to become a ferment in the life of their communities," he argued.[69]

So we see again that the ecumenical experience encompasses contradictions, and the ecumenical memory is multifaceted and complex. The task of "rememoration" includes deciding which memories to recall or make effective in the present. Re-reading and re-living the common past raises important questions regarding the multiple agendas, tasks, understandings, and commitments that are contained in the ecumenical memory, which in turn raises fundamental questions regarding the goals of the ecumenical movement itself. The practice of "rememoration" is caught up in a larger process of critical ecumenical dialogue.

Exploring the historical dialogical identity of the ecumenical movement leads me to question singular or unitary conceptualizations. In the following chapters I will examine the dialogical character of each of the three streams of the "official" history[70] of the ecumenical movement that flow from the World Missionary Conference held in Edinburgh, 1910, into the World Council of Churches: Faith and Order, Life and Work, and the International Missionary Council. I will argue that the ecumenical movement has in part attempted the renewal of the Western theological project of 'Christendom,' or 'the Christian West.' The unitary historical identity which Hans Margull and others have invoked when speaking of an ecumenical memory suggests a model of unity which recalls the mythical past of a unified Christendom. It invokes (consciously or unconsciously) the European memory of an age in which there was supposedly one unified Catholic church, and in which this church was bound up with dominant social and cultural order. Only the peoples of Europe belonged to Christendom, and when its renewal has dominated the ecumenical agenda, imperialistic relationships have been reproduced.

The next three chapters will examine therefore the history by which the ecumenical movement has rendered account of its own identity.[71] This historical identity is an inscribed memory that is reproduced in historical studies, theological texts, and social practices. It has taken on the appearance of an internal coherence which bridges historical disjunctions, a coherence Visser't Hooft has gone so far as to describe as a sign of the Spirit.[72] My thesis is that there are also centrifugal forces present in the ecumenical movement that are at work against the centripetal memory of Christendom. In the course of the next three chapters I will be examining these historical forces in each of the three streams, seeking to uncover the historical identity that is being constructed dialogically in each sector of the ecumenical arena. In doing so I am assuming that incoherence can also be a sign of the presence of the Spirit, more so even than the false coherence of imposed unity. I will therefore look for the discontinuities, ruptures, and contradictions that are part of the 'official' ecumenical memory. A critical examination of the historical and theological texts raises fundamental questions concerning the singularity of the movement. The official history of the ecumenical movement locates it around an axis whose twin poles are unity and mission, its agenda responsive to the crisis in Western Christendom. Examining the discontinuities, tensions and ruptures suggests a different meaning and identity for the WCC as well as for the ecumenical movement as a whole however, best characterized as a dialogical struggle between the centripetal forces of dominant churches and the centrifugal forces of "subjugated knowledges" which are also ecumenical but in a different manner.[73]

Notes

1. Quoted by Gary Saul Morson and Caryl Emerson, *Mikhail Bakhtin: Creation of a Prosaics* (Stanford: Stanford University Press, 1990), p. 236 (emphasis and brackets original).

2. The studies sponsored by the Commission on Faith and Order of the National Council of Christ in the USA in the have proven to be particularly productive through the 1980s, engaging representatives from a range of church traditions in theological studies on the apostolic faith in the North American context, on Jesus Christ, and on the Holy Spirit. See Thaddeus D. Horgan, ed., *Apostolic Faith in America* (Grand Rapids, Mi: Wm. B. Eerdmans Publishing Co., 1988); David T, Shannon and Gayraud S. Wilmore, eds., *Black Witness to the Apostolic Faith* (Grand Rapids, Mi: Wm. B. Eerdmans, 1985); Paul Fries and Tiran Nersoyan, eds., *Christ in East and West* (Macon, Ga: Mercer University Press, 1987); and Theodore Stylianopoulos and S. Mark Heim, eds., *Spirit of Truth: Ecumenical Perspectives on the Holy Spirit* (Brookline, Ma: Holy Cross Orthodox Press, 1986). For an example of the ecumenical dialogue projects of a particular denomination, see Joseph A. Burgess, ed., *Lutherans in Ecumenical Dialogue: A Reappraisal* (Minneapolis: Augsburg Press, 1990).

3. See for instance Dale Irvin, "John R. Mott and World-Centered Mission," *Missiology: An International Review*, 12/2 (April, 1984), pp. 155-164. The contemporary organizational structure for furthering evangelical ecumenism is the Lausanne Committee for World Evangelization, stemming from the Lausanne Congress of 1974. See J. D. Douglas, ed., *Let the Earth Hear His Voice: International Congress on World Evangelization, Lausanne, Switzerland* (Minneapolis: World Wide Publications, 1975); and Edward R. Dayton and Samuel Wilson, eds., *The Future of World Evangelization: The Lausanne Movement* (Monrovia, Ca: MARC, 1984).

4. Several better-known incidents of negative reporting in the 1980s were "The Gospel According to Whom?" on the CBS-TV program *60 Minutes*, Jan. 23, 1983, and Rael Jean Isaac's article, "Do You Know Where Your Church Offerings Go?", in *Readers Digest*, also in January 1983. *Reader's Digest* again in February 1993 published an attack on the WCC under the title, "The Gospel According to Marx." See Theodore A Gill, Jr., "The Reader's Digest and the World Council of Churches," *Ecumenical Trends* 22/3 (March 1993).

5. See Thomas Sieger Derr, *Barriers to Ecumenism: The Holy See and The World Council of Churches on Social Questions* (Maryknoll, NY: Orbis Books, 1983), esp. pp. 1-24.

6. See Jose Miguez Bonino, "A 'Third World' Perspective on the Ecumenical Movement," *Ecumenical Review* 34/2 (1982), pp. 115-124. For a general appraisal of radicalism within the ecumenical movement between 1948 and 1968 (prior to the Uppsala Assembly of the WCC) see the chapter by David L. Edwards, "Signs of Radicalism in the Ecumenical Movement," in *The

Ecumenical Advance: A History of the Ecumenical Movement, Volume 2 1948-1968, Harold E. Fey, ed., Second edition (Geneva: World Council of Churches, 1986). The full history of the North American black churches in the ecumenical movement has not yet been written, but a start is made by William Watley, *Singing the Lord's Song in a Strange Land* (Geneva: WCC, 1993). It is important to point out here that black churches have played significant roles at all levels of the ecumenical movement. On the ecumenical character of developments in Black theology since 1966, see Gayraud S. Wilmore and James H. Cone, eds., *Black Theology: A Documentary History, 1966-1979* (Maryknoll, NY: Orbis Books, 1979, second ed. 1993); and also James H. Cone, *Speaking the Truth: Ecumenism, Liberation, and Black Theology* (Grand Rapids, Mi; Wm. B. Eerdmans Publishing, 1986), esp. Part II, pp. 83-157. Regarding Black Baptist participants in the ecumenical movement, see Pearl L. McNeil, "Baptist Black Americans and the Ecumenical Movement," *Journal of Ecumenical Studies* 17/2 (Spring 1980), pp. 103-117.

7. Manuel Quintero writes in the *WSCF Journal*, August 1990, "The [World Student Christian] Federation had experienced a profound ideological conversion since the late 50s.... As a consequence of this conversion, the language and thinking of the Eurocentric era was abandoned and the reality of the Third World - with its problems, injustices and hopes - become the essential concern for the WSCF witness and ministry." (p. 23) For a fuller depiction of the WSCF's transformation, see Alan McLean, *A Relevant Minority: Historical Glimpses of the WSCF* (Geneva: WSCF, 1981).

8. For an insightful exploration of current uncertainties in the ecumenical movement, and it paradigmatic shifts undergone in recent decades, see Konrad Raiser, *Ecumenism in Transition: A Paradigm Shift in the Ecumenical Movement?* (Geneva: WCC, 1991).

9. In Thomas Wieser, ed., *Whither Ecumenism? A Dialogue in the Transit Lounge of the Ecumenical Movement* (Geneva: WCC, 1966), p. 96.

10. *Ibid.*, p. x-xii.

11. The *oikoumene* symbol of the boat on the waters which is often associated with the ecumenical movement and is the official logo for the World Council of Churches intentionally depicts this metaphor of launching out onto troubled waters. See Charles C. West, *The Power to Be Human: Toward a Secular Theology* (New York: Macmillan Publishers, 1971), p. 15, for an interpretation of the symbol. Philip Potter, past-General Secretary of the World Council of Churches, in an interview in 1978 affirmed the image of the ecumenical boat but noted that the waters have become more choppy today (*What in the World is the World Council of Churches* [Geneva: WCC, 1978], p. 1).

12. The word, "crisis" in English shares a common Greek root with "critique," and means judgement as well. Thus Simpfendörfer's call to "face the judgement and wait upon the Spirit...."

13. See W. A. Visser't Hooft, *The Genesis and Formation of the World Council of Churches* (Geneva: WCC, 1982), pp. 27- 29, for instance; also Visser't Hooft, *Has the Ecumenical Movement a Future?* (Belfast: Christian Journals Ltd, 1974).

14. See Ernst Lange, *And Yet it Moves: Dream and Reality of the Ecumenical Movement*, Edwin Robinson, trans. (Belfast: Christian Journals Ltd./Geneva: WCC, 1978), p. 123. ff. on "ecumenical methodologies." See also Raiser, *Ecumenism in Transition*, pp. 13-23

15. Reports and studies on ecumenical and interfaith dialogues are too numerous to list here, but I would point out the importance of the *Journal of Ecumenical Studies* as an on-going site for multiple dialogical projects. Regarding the method of dialogue, see Leonard Swidler, "The Dialogue Decalogue: Ground Rules for Interreligious Dialogue," *Journal of Ecumenical Studies* 20/1 (Winter 1983), pp. 1-4; and more recently, the article by Peter Neuner, "Dialogue, Intrafaith," *Dictionary of the Ecumenical Movement*, Nicholas Lossky et al, eds. (Geneva: WCC / Grand Rapids, Mi: Wm. B. Eerdmans Publishing Co., 1991), pp. 287- 291. For a study of dialogue in the Faith and Order movement, see Kuncheria Pathil, *Models in Ecumenical Dialogue: A Study of the Methodological Development in the Commission on "Faith and Order" of the World Council of Churches* (Bangalore: Dharmaran Publications, 1981).

16. See for instance the exponential number of new churches, denominations, and ecclesial movements founded in recent years around the world, catalogued by David Barrett, ed., *The World Christian Encyclopedia* (New York: Oxford University Press, 1982).

17. Mikhail M. Bakhtin, *The Dialogic Imagination: Four Essays*, Michael Holquist, ed. (Austin: University of Texas Press, 1981), p. 269.

18. *Ibid.*, p. 270.

19. *Ibid.*, p. 272.

20. *Ibid.*, p. 276-277.

21. See Morson and Emerson, *Mikhail Bakhtin*, p. 159ff.

22. Bakhtin, *The Dialogic Imagination*, p. 253.

23. Quoted by Morson and Emerson, *Mikhail Bakhtin*, p. 236 (emphasis and brackets original). For a full study of Bakhtin's understanding of dialogue, see also Michael Holquist, *Dialogism: Bakhtin and his World* (London: Routledge, 1990). Michael Gardiner, *The Dialogics of Critique: M. M. Bakhtin and the Theory of Ideology* (London: Routledge, 1992), explores the political dimensions of dialogics

24. Lange, *And Yet It Moves*, p. 107.

25. *Ibid.*, pp. 108-110.

26. Norman Goodall, *The Ecumenical Movement: What It Is and What It Does* (London: Oxford University Press, 1961), p.2.

27. *Baptism, Eucharist and Ministry* (Geneva: World Council of Churches,

1982), p. viii. For commentary and an introduction to BEM, see Max Thurian, ed., *Ecumenical Perspectives on Baptism, Eucharist and Ministry* (Geneva: WCC, 1982); *Baptism, Eucharist and Ministry 1982-1990: Report on the Process and Responses* (Geneva: WCC, 1990); Jeffrey Gros, ed., *The Search for Visible Unity* (New York: Pilgrim Press, 1984); and Michael Kinnamon, *Why It Matters: A Popular Introduction to the Baptism, Eucharist and Ministry Text* (Geneva: WCC, 1985).

28. Robert M. Grant, "Religion and Politics at the Council at Nicaea," *Journal of Religion* 55/1 (1975), pp. 5.

29. Willem A. Visser't Hooft, "The Word 'Ecumenical' -- Its History and Use," *A History of the Ecumenical Movement, 1517-1948*, Ruth Rouse and Stephen Charles Neill, eds. (Geneva: WCC, 1986), p. 737.

30. John Meyendorff, *The Orthodox Church: Its Past and Its Role in the World Today* (Crestwood, NY: St. Vladimir's Press, 1981), p. 88, points out that Islam's conquest of the Byzantium empire brought about a change in the political character of the Orthodox hierarchy, but did not remove the political overtones. The Islamic rulers invested the Greek hierarchy and the jurisdiction of the Patriarch of Constantinople in particular with a greater degree of ecclesial power than they had exercised under the Roman Emperors. "In his role as *millet-bachi*, 'head of the Christian nation,' or 'ethnarch' in Greek, the patriarch was now virtually the regent of an enslaved people."

31. Constantin G. Patelos, ed., *The Orthodox Church in the Ecumenical Movement: Documents and Statements, 1902-1975* (Geneva: WCC, 1978), p. 226 provides the Orthodox understanding of *Una Sancta* succinctly: "[There is] One Undivided Unbroken Tradition of the Church. And according to our teaching, the Eastern Tradition ... is the Holy Tradition of the Church of Christ itself."

32. *Ibid.*, p. 81.

33. Gennadios Limouris and Nomikos Michael Vaporis, eds., *Orthodox Perspectives on Baptism, Eucharist, and Ministry* (Brookline, Mass: Holy Cross Orthodox Press, 1985), p. 115, emphasis original.

34. Austin Flannery, ed., *Vatican Council II: The Conciliar and Post Conciliar Documents* (Northport, New York: Costello Publishing Co., 1980), p. 452.

35. *Ibid.* See also Heinrich Stirnimann and Lukas Vischer, eds., *Papsttum und Petrusdienst* (Frankfurt am Main: Verlag Otto Lembeck, 1975); Willem A. Visser't Hooft, "WCC-Roman Catholic Relations: Some Personal Reflections," *Ecumenical Review* 37/3 (1985), pp. 336-344.

36. Karl Rahner, *Theological Investigations* XI (New York: The Crossroad Publishing Co., 1974), p. 32.

37. Rahner, *Theological Investigations* XVII (New York: The Crossroad Publishing Co., 1981), pp. 195-196.

38. Rahner, *Theological Investigations* XI, pp. 3-23.

39. Patelos, *The Orthodox Church in the Ecumenical Movement.*, p. 229.

40. Quoted by Visser't Hooft, "The Word 'Ecumenical,'" p. 737.

41. *Ibid.*, p. 738; cf. p. 735.

42. *Ibid.*, p. 735.

43. See David M. Paton, ed., *Breaking Barriers: Nairobi 1975, The Official Report of the Fifth Assembly of the WCC* (London: SPCK/ Grand Rapids: Wm. B. Eerdmans, 1976), p. 5. See also "Ecumenical Diary," *Ecumenical Review* 32/2 (1980), p. 193: "The Melbourne Conference stands in a long line of world mission conferences which began in 1910."

44. Brown, "Ecumenical Movement," pp. 18-19.

45. *Ibid.*, p. 18.

46. See the letter from His Holiness Abuna Theophilus, Patriarch of Ethiopia, at Nairobi, 1975, in Paton, ed., *Breaking Barriers*, p. 155.

47. "The Calling of the Church to Mission and Unity," *Theology Today* 9/1 (1952), pp. 13-19. See also Günther Gassmann, *Konzeptionen der Einheit in der Bewegung für Glauben und Kirchenverfassung 1910-1937* (Göttingen: Vandenhoech und Ruprecht, 1979), p. 56-57.

48. Leslie Newbigin wrote following the New Delhi Assembly: "Mission and unity are two sides of the same reality, or rather two ways of describing the same action of the living Lord who wills that all should be drawn to Himself." And later in the same essay: "No movement is entitled to the use of the word ecumenical which is not concerned that witness be borne to the Gospel throughout the whole earth, and which is not committed to taking its share in bearing that witness." "The Missionary Dimension of the Ecumenical Movement," *Ecumenical Review* 14/2 (1962), pp. 208, 214.

49. "The Calling of the Church to Mission and Unity," p. 14.

50. Darril Hudson, *The Ecumenical Movement in World Affairs* (London: Weidenfeld and Nicolson, 1969), p. 82. Hudson wrote on p. 4: "[The Continuation Committee of the World Conference on Faith and Order] busied itself with seeking Christian unity through a discussion of liturgy and dogma, avoiding the task of helping formulate a social ethic, a task more relevant to the world."

51. John A. Mackay, "Ecumenical: The Word and the Concept," *Theology Today* 9/1 (1952), p. 1.

52. See Margaret Nash, *Ecumenical Movement in the 1960's* (Johannesburg: Ravan Press, 1975), pp. 6-7; 351-55.

53. Juan Antonio Franco, "WSCF in Latin America and Class Ecumenism," *WSCF Journal* 3/1-2 (1981), p. 88.

54. Quoted in Rosino Gibellini, ed., *Frontiers of Theology in Latin America* (Maryknoll: Orbis Books, 1979), p. x. Concerning the new kind of ecumenism see Gustavo Gutierrez, *A Theology of Liberation: History, Politics and Salvation* (Maryknoll: Orbis Books, 1973), p. 278.

55. See D. Preman Niles, ed., *Between the Flood and the Rainbow:*

Interpreting the Conciliar Process of Mutual Commitment (Covenant) to Justice, Peace and the Integrity of Creation (Geneva: WCC, 1992).

56. Raimundo Panikkar, *The Unknown Christ of Hinduism: Towards an Ecumenical Christophany* (Maryknoll: Orbis Books, 1981), p. 66; and Panikkar, *The Intrareligious Dialogue* (New York: Paulist Press, 1978), p. 3.

57. Hans Hoekendijk, "Evangelization of the World in this Generation," *International Review of Missions* 59/1 (1970), p. 26. For a challenge to the ecumenical movement from an evangelical Holiness perspective, see Donald W. Dayton, "Yet Another Layer of the Onion: Or Opening the Ecumenical Door to Let the Riffraff in," *Ecumenical Review* 40/1 (1988), pp. 87-110.

58. See Paul M. Minus, Jr., *The Catholic Rediscovery of Protestantism: A History of Roman Catholic Ecumenical Pioneering* (New York: Paulist Press, 1976); Thaddeus D. Horgan, ed., *Walking Together: Roman Catholics and Ecumenism Twenty-five Years after Vatican II* (Grand Rapids: Wm. B. Eerdmans, 1992); and John J. McDonnell, *The World Council of Churches and the Catholic Church* (Lewiston,NY: The Edwin Mellen Press, 1985). Rome's reasons for withdrawing from participation in the 1990 Seoul world convocation on Justice, Peace, and the Integrity of Creation relate directly to its uneasiness with the open questions concerning the conciliar process employed by the project, as well as by the presence of non-ecclesial 'movements' participating in the convocation. See Niles, *Between the Flood and the Rainbow*.

59. Hudson, *The Ecumenical Movement in World Affairs*, p. 4.

60. Kathleen Bliss, "Lay Reflections on Oikoumene," *The Sufficiency of God: Essays on the Ecumenical Hope in Honour of W. A. Visser't Hooft*, Robert C. Mackie and Charles C. West. eds. (London: SCM Press, 1963), p. 172.

61. The report from Issues Group II in the Vancouver Assembly of the WCC in 1983 articulated this relationship concisely: "The ecumenical movement is more than the World Council of Churches, and it is not limited to any one Christian World Communion or church....The World Council of Churches is a privileged instrument of the ecumenical movement." David Gill, ed., *Gathered for Life: Official Report, VI Assembly, World Council of Churches* (Geneva: WCC/Grand Rapids: Wm. B. Eerdmans Publishing Co., 1983), p. 51. On the meaning of the ecumenical movement being found within the WCC, see Eugene Carson Blake, "Uppsala and Afterwards," *The Ecumenical Advance*, p. 436; Geoffrey Wainwright, *The Ecumenical Moment: Crisis and Opportunity for the Church* (Grand Rapids: Wm. B. Eerdmans Publishing Co., 1983), p. 202. Examples of metonymic reduction include: Robert McAfee Brown, *The Ecumenical Revolution: An Interpretation of the Catholic-Protestant Dialogue* (Garden City, NY: Doubleday & Co., 1967), pp. 3-47, as well as his more recent article, "Ecumenical Movement," in *The Encyclopedia of Religion*, Vol. 5, M. Eliade, ed. (New York: MacMillan Publishing, 1987); Norman Goodall, *The Ecumenical Movement*; Ruth Rouse

and Stephen Charles Neill, *A History of the Ecumenical Movement, 1517-1948*; Harold E. Fey, *The Ecumenical Advance: A History of the Ecumenical Movement, 1948-1968* (Geneva: WCC, 1986). Contemporary Roman Catholic theology includes the history of the Second Vatican Council and the discussions between Rome and the WCC within this inner history of the ecumenical movement. See, for example, George H. Tavard, *Two Centuries of Ecumenism* (London: Burns and Oates, 1960); and Yves Congar, *Essais oecumeniques: Le mouvement, les hommes, les problemes* (Paris: Le Centurion, 1984), p. 76-80.

62. Hans Jochen Margull, "Oekumenische Diskussion," *Baseleia: Walter Freytag zum 60. Geburstag,* Jan Hermelink and Hans J. Margull, eds. (Stuttgart: Evangelische Missionsverlag, 1959), p. 415.

63. *Ibid.,* p. 417.

64. *Ibid.,* p. 416.

65. Wieser, *Whither Ecumenism,* "Introduction."

66. Alan D. Falconer, "Significant Events in the Ecumenical Movement," *The Teaching of Ecumenics,* Samuel Amirtham and Cyris H.S. Moon, eds. (Geneva: WCC, 1987), p. 5.

67. *Ibid.*

68. Weiser, *Whither Ecumenism?,* p. 27.

69. *Ibid.,* p. 28.

70. Concerning the term "official," see Emilio Castro, "Preface to the Third Edition," *A History of the Ecumenical Movement 1517-1948,* Rouse and Neill, eds.

71. See Johan Huizinga, "A Definition of the Concept of History," *Philosophy and History: Essays Presented to Ernst Cassirer,* Raymond Klibansky and H. J. Paton, eds. (Oxford: Clarendon Press, 1936), p. 6-7.

72. "Thus is it shown again that the *cause of ecumenism is indivisible,* that, as the Decree on Ecumenism of the Second Vatican Council said, *there is one ecumenical movement,* and that the spiritual gift of the active desire for unity, as all spiritual gifts, is given for the common good of the whole People of God." W. A. Visser 't Hooft, "The General Ecumenical Development since 1948," *The Ecumenical Advance,* Fey, ed., p. 17 (emphasis added).

73. Michel Foucault, *Power/Knowledge: Selected Interviews and Other Writings 1972-1977,* Colin Gordon, ed. (New York:

Chapter 2:

Community and Diversity in Faith and Order

For just as the body is one and has many members, and all the members of the body, though many, are one body, so it is with Christ. For in the one Spirit we were all baptized into one body -- Jews or Greeks, slaves or free -- and we were all made to drink of one Spirit. --I Corinthians 12:12-13

However, the heritage handed down by the apostles was received differently and in different forms, so that from the very beginnings of the Church its development varied from region to region and also because of differing mentalities and ways of life. --*Unitatis Redintegratio*, 14

One head cannot hold a consultation. --Asante Proverb

1. Intending to Stay Together

The opening message from the World Council of Churches' Sixth Assembly in Vancouver, Canada in 1983 placed the Vancouver Assembly "in a succession which began at Amsterdam in 1948 with the commitment to stay together."[1] The reference was to the final report from the constituting Assembly of the WCC in 1948, in which 351 official delegates representing 147 Protestant and Orthodox churches affirmed, "We intend to stay together."[2] These delegates had gathered to inaugurate a project called the World Council of Churches. Their commitment to staying together represented in some measure a commitment by their churches to develop a more comprehensive framework for common Christian witness and action.

What the framework is to be, and what precisely constitutes the meaning of being together in a World Council, continue to be questions that the ecumenical movement struggles to resolve. Clearly the search for unity has been a central goal of the ecumenical movement. It is a goal often identified not only as the primary reason for the existence of the Commission on Faith and Order, but for the existence of the World Council itself. At the same time the search for unity in the ecumenical movement has had an ideological function as well, in so much as the legitimate diversity of Christian faith and practice have been subordinated to the quest for unity and consensus. Staying together has involved a continuing dialogue within the Faith and Order movement, and within the World Council as a whole, around questions of the unity and the diversity of Christian faith.

Eleven years prior to the Amsterdam inaugural Assembly two separate inter-church organizations had made the decision for merger which would result in the formation of the World Council. The Universal Christian Council for Life and Work and the World Conference on Faith and Order, meeting in the summer of 1937 in Oxford and Edinburgh respectively, approved a provisional plan for a World Council of Churches which had been worked out earlier in 1937 by a joint committee of the two bodies.[3] Both of these organizations had come into existence during the first quarter of the twentieth century, holding their initial conferences in Oxford, 1925 (Life and Work) and in Lausanne, 1927 (Faith and Order). Both had brought together leaders from Protestant and Orthodox communions (The participation of the Roman Catholic church was actively sought for both Faith and Order and Life and Work movements, and in the formation of the World Council, but Rome declined to participate.) With the decision to merge invitations were sent out to those churches that had been invited to Oxford and Edinburgh, and a Provisional Committee was formed to guide the construction of the World Council. The international turmoil caused by the World War was to delay the actual formation of the Council in its inaugural Assembly for more than a decade, however.

The 1938 invitation sent to the churches identified the purpose of the World Council as being a vehicle and an expression of Christian unity. The WCC was to be a consultative body representing the churches across national and confessional boundaries in response to the need to present a unified Christianity before an un-Christian world. But unity was not just a practical concern; the very nature of the Church required the manifestation of unity before the world, and so the Council was to be in some sense an expression of, as well as a means toward unity.

It was to be a highly qualified means and expression nevertheless. In an accompanying memorandum issued by the Archbishop of York, England, William Temple, the consultative relationship of the World Council to the churches was strongly emphasized. The Council "exists to serve the churches, not to control them," he explained regarding the proposed Constitution of the WCC. Neither the Assembly nor the Central Committee was to have constitutional authority or power over any of the constituent churches. "Not only has the Council no power to legislate for the participating churches; it is also forbidden to act in their name except so far as all or any of them have commissioned it to do so.[4]" Whatever authority the Council did have would be "in the weight which it carries with the churches by its own wisdom."[5]

The purpose of the Council as being to serve as an expression and a means of cooperation and unity among churches, and not in any manner to legislate or control the constituent churches, was again expressed in the report from Amsterdam. These initial attempts to clarify the manner in which the Council was structurally related to the churches did not resolve the question of the ecclesiological status of the World Council, however. The Central Committee of the WCC meeting in Toronto in 1950 was forced to take up the issue again, issuing to the churches for study and comment a statement on "The Church, the churches and the World Council of Churches."[6]

Sub-titled "The ecclesiological significance of the World Council of Churches," the Toronto Statement pointed out that the imprecision regarding the ecclesiological definition of the WCC was reflective of the imprecision of the various churches themselves regarding the definition of the nature of the church. The plurality of ecclesiologies held by the member churches of the World Council resulted in the World Council having to formulate its own ecclesiological significance "without using the categories or language of one particular conception of the Church."[7] What the Statement did in effect was to use the ecclesiological categories and language of several of the church traditions constituting the World Council. The Statement embraced within it the debate concerning the meaning of unity, and the direction of the ecumenical movement insofar as the churches were concerned. Rather than attempting to offer a simple ecumenical statement upon which all member churches could agree, it offered a series of negations and then affirmations regarding the WCC.

At the top of the list of "What the World Council of Churches is not" was that of being either a "superchurch" or "the Una Sancta of

which the Creeds speak." The rejection of the WCC being a
"superchurch" responded to concerns about the loss of autonomy in
church decision-making. The reference to "the Una Sancta" was an
attempt to address Orthodox concerns regarding the ambiguity implied
in the terminology of a "council." The World Council was not to be
confused with a united Church which would be the result of a universal
Christian council, even if in the years to come the WCC was to call for
just such a universal Christian council.[8] Left open in the Toronto
Statement, and in succeeding WCC discussions, was whether the World
Council itself should be superceded by a united Church resulting from
a universal council. As far as the Toronto statement was concerned,
however, the WCC was not going to seek to press churches into unity
decisions nor to negotiate church unions. The Council could only
provide churches with an opportunity to meet with one another and to
promote study and discussion of Church unity.

Thus within the Council dissenting and even contradicting points of
view regarding the nature of the true Church and the role of the WCC
in relation to the Church were welcomed. "There is room and space in
the World Council for the ecclesiology of every church which is ready
to participate in the ecumenical conversation and which takes its stand
on the Basis of the Council, which is 'a fellowship of churches which
accept our Lord Jesus Christ as God and Saviour'".[9] According to the
Toronto Statement, no single conception of the nature of the church can
be called the "ecumenical theory." "The whole point of the ecumenical
conversation is precisely that all these conceptions enter into dynamic
relations with each other."[10] No church is required to consider its own
conception of the church as being relativized by membership in the
World Council, nor does membership require of any church acceptance
of a specific doctrine regarding church unity.

On the other hand, the Toronto Statement went on in an affirmative
vein, almost all Christian churches have recognized that membership in
the body of Christ extends beyond their own particular church body.
While churches in the World Council do not necessarily have to regard
other churches as being true or full churches, membership does suggest
that churches recognize *vestigia ecclesiae* or traces of the truth in other
churches. "These elements are more than pale shadows of the life of
the true Church," the Statement explained, venturing beyond its earlier
caution against opting for one ecclesiology over others. A particular
ecclesiology was in fact offered as the positive basis for the World

Council, an ecclesiology which the authors of the Statement discerned as being implicit if not explicit in the ecumenical movement that had given rise to the World Council: "The ecumenical movement is based upon the conviction that these 'traces' are to be followed. The churches should not despise them as mere elements of truth but rejoice in them as hopeful signs pointing towards real unity.[11]

Such unity was based on the common recognition of the Lordship of Jesus Christ, and thus was manifest christologically. But the Statement did not leave the question of visible unity there lest the World Council be charged with advancing a purely spiritualized conception of invisible unity. It offered an eschatological conception of visible unity, the "real unity" toward which the signs and traces point. The concrete results of living toward unity would be practical solidarity and a growing together into the body of Christ. Whatever unity had already been experienced in the ecumenical movement was only a foretaste of what was to come. The discrepancy between the eschatological truth that there is only one true church of Jesus Christ, and the contemporary situation in which churches are not living in unity and solidarity, creates "a holy dissatisfaction with the present situation."[12] In this way the Statement succeeded in discerning a particular ecclesiology, an eschatological one, implicit throughout the ecumenical movement and even among those churches which claimed to embody the fullness of truth but who were nevertheless willing to enter into sincere ecumenical dialogue with other church communities. The Statement implied that the realm of truth is greater than any particular church embodied on its own. By membership in the World Council, churches were acknowledging in some sense that they each have a positive task to fulfill in a larger realm of the church universal. "That task is to seek fellowship with all those who, while not members of the same visible body, belong together as members of the mystical body. And the ecumenical movement is the place where this search and discovery take place."[13]

The Toronto Statement set forth a fundamental vision of the World Council as being a fellowship or *koinonia* of churches (leaving unresolved the question of how far such fellowship extended and accompanying questions such as those of intercommunion). Through it the Central Committee sought to articulate what the commitment to staying together did and did not seem to imply, at least at that stage of the ecumenical journey. Explicitly addressed to the member churches, the Statement emphasized that the ecumenical movement was by definition a movement of the churches. The fellowship of the ecumenical movement was to be a fellowship among churches separated by geographical, historical, and confessional boundaries but brought into dialogue and common life through the World Council of Churches.

One of the critical factors that became apparent in the discussion surrounding the Statement (and remains a problem for the WCC to this day) is that for all of the talk about the ecumenical movement belonging to the churches, the 'we' who spoke together at Amsterdam in 1948 were not the churches themselves but representative church delegates sent to form the World Council. Even those delegates who held hierarchical office or positions of leadership within their particular communions were unable at Amsterdam to speak authoritatively for their churches. While officially representing the churches, the delegates and the World Council they inaugurated could not compel the churches as a whole toward unity and fellowship. After forty years of existence the World Council has still not been able to compel its member churches, through either the weight it carries in its own wisdom or through any other means, to achieve the visible unity of being one universal Church of Christ. The *koinonia* among the ecumenical leadership and among participants in ecumenical events might perhaps serve as a sign, an incentive, and even a foretaste of the ecumenical fullness of unity and solidarity among the churches. But then Lange wonders if "The ecumenical movement is a sort of daydream indulged in by the few on behalf of the many."[14]

The question which emerges at this point is just what fellowship the member churches of the WCC seek, with one another and through their representation in the World Council. Presumably the member churches as churches do indeed desire some manner of unity, toward which the Toronto Statement said the WCC works. But precisely what unity means and what form it takes remains unresolved. Ecumenical experience since 1948 suggests consensus or convergence are not what the churches seek, otherwise the accomplishments in this direction would be much greater. A truly universal council does not appear to be any more feasible for the multiple Christian churches of the world at the end of the second millennium of the Christian era than it did a century ago. Whatever the various churches in the World Council intend and proclaim through their membership and participation (and the motives remain plural), it would appear that the various churches and ecclesial communities of the world which elect to remain officially represented within the circle of fellowship of the World Council at the same time chose against the unity of belonging to one church of Jesus Christ. The twin forces of centripetal and centrifugal movement appear to be operative in the ecumenical movement among the churches and within the World Council still today.

"Being together" and "staying together" nevertheless continue to be important aspects of the dialogical experience of the ecumenical movement. The World Council continues to be an important arena for discovery through confrontation, discussion, and at times even mutual celebration. Without claiming any form of binding authority the WCC does claim to embody a heritage of being a movement toward visible unity. And the unit within the World Council which is most often identified with the search for visible unity is the Commission on Faith and Order. Faith and Order's perceived mandate before and after 1948 has been, and continues to be, to call the churches to visible unity. As a Commission with its own By-Laws, and with membership from churches that are not a part of the World Council (Roman Catholic and Pentecostal communions for instance), Faith and Order has a distinctive identity within the overall structure of the World Council. For many it is at the very heart of the ecumenical movement. It has become, according to Günther Gassmann, Director of the Secretariat of the Commission on Faith and Order, "an indispensable instrument of the churches by constantly pointing to and serving the centre of the ecumenical vocation: the quest for the visible unity of Christ's church."[15] It would appear at first glance that the Faith and Order movement, and its current incarnation in the Faith and Order Commission of the World Council of Churches, represents the centripetal force within the ecumenical movement. Yet, as we shall see, such a characterization is too simplistic even of such a project dedicated to the task of visible unity.

2. Faith and Order, and the Quest for Visible Unity

The formation of the World Council of Churches from 1937 to 1948 was brought about through the integration and deepening of two interchurch movements. Closely related to these at the time of the formation, and eventually integrated into the World Council in 1961, was a third organization whose origins were also in the first quarter of the twentieth century: the International Missionary Council (IMC). Until its integration into the WCC at the Third Assembly in New Delhi the IMC had been working closely with the WCC through a Joint Commission and through numerous points of contact among the leadership and participants in the two movements.

There were several reasons for the IMC not being initially part of the WCC, among them the structural representation in the IMC of missions boards and regional councils, and the fact that non-Europeans had achieved a greater level of representation in the IMC than in either of the two bodies forming the WCC which many were concerned not to lose. A third reason (one that continued to be challenged by both the IMC and WCC through the 1950s) concerned the differing goals of Faith and Order and Life and Work movements on the one hand, and the IMC on the other. The former, it appeared to many, were concerned primarily with the unity of the divided churches of Christendom. The latter was concerned with the mission of the churches beyond Christendom. While this simple division of labor was challenged even prior to the integration of the WCC and the IMC, the general characterization of the separate tasks of unity and mission as belonging to separate organizations seemed at least reflected in the existence of two ecumenical organizations representing various Protestant and Orthodox communions from around the world.

Unity and mission were in fact much more closely related even in the period prior to 1948 than the existence of two separate organizations would seem to imply. The work of the three interchurch movements prior to 1948 were related through common participants, themes, and structures. As noted in the first chapter, historians of the ecumenical movement have often traced all three movements directly or indirectly to the World Missionary Conference which met in Edinburgh, Scotland, during June of 1910.[16] Tracing the official "ecumenical memory" of the WCC (and thereby of the larger ecumenical movement of this century) to a common point of origin in turn gives subtle ideological support to claims of a common ecumenical identity. It is not insignificant that this common origin secures for the ecumenical movement a Western "missionary identity."[17]

The conference that gathered in Edinburgh in 1910 was initially conceived by Protestant missionary leaders in North America and England as a third decennial Anglo-American missionary conference, following up on two earlier conferences held in London, 1888, and in New York, 1900.[18] German and Scandinavian missionary participation was minimal in the 1888 and 1900 conferences, but increased in the 1910 conference due primarily to the organizational participation of *Der Ausschuss der deutschen evangelischen Missionen.*[19] Earlier missionary gatherings in India, Japan, China, Africa, Latin America, and the Middle East had provided Europeans and North Americans an opportunity to share information and provide mutual support. (These regional missionary conferences were also occasions for and expressions of the emerging indigenous consciousness of churches under Western Protestant missions). National mission conferences had also taken place in Germany, England and North America. Organizers of Edinburgh 1910 sought to build upon this institutional base (the Roman Catholic and Orthodox communions were not invited to attend), and expand the resources "for the effective prosecution of the missionary task."[20]

This missionary task at the turn of the century was summarized succinctly by the "watchword" of the World's Student Christian Federation (WSCF) organized in 1895: "the evangelization of the world in this generation."[21] The participation of two of the early leaders of the WSCF, John A. Mott and J. H. Oldham, in the planning of the 1910 conference, is depicted by historians of the ecumenical movement such as Hogg and Latourette as having brought not only their organizing skills, but the experience of the WSCF itself to bear upon the Edinburgh conference.[22] Mott had already organized a number of international student conferences, including the WSCF's seventh world student conference 1907 which met in Tokyo. But the Federation's theological base in nineteenth century revivalism and individualistic pietism, coupled with organizing methods which established conference agendas by planning committees in advance and focused discussion on mission theology, served to keep the theological dialogue of the 1910 gathering within a relatively narrow range.[23]

One of the fundamental principles the planning committee adopted for the World Missionary Conference was the exclusion of "questions of doctrine or Church polity with regard to which the Churches or Societies taking part in the Conference differ among themselves."[24] It was on this basis that Anglican bishops were persuaded to participate in the conference. The effect of the conference, however, was to generate among at least some participants a desire for greater doctrinal and ecclesial unity. That, according to Tatlow, is what lead Bishop Charles H. Brent, missionary bishop of the Philippines and a delegate from the Protestant Episcopal Church in the United States, to propose at the General Convention meeting in Cincinnati in October of 1910 that a Joint Commission be appointed to convene a world conference on faith and order.[25]

Thus Edinburgh proved to be as significant for what it had excluded as for what it had accomplished. Edinburgh's exclusion of questions concerning unity is situated by the dominant forms of ecumenical historiography as the basis for the initiatives which led to the founding of the movement for church unity in Europe and North America following 1910. The historical relationship of the World Conference on Faith and Order (which Brent was eventually to succeed in organizing) to Edinburgh 1910 is one of conjunction through disjunction. This ironic relationship is crucial for the historical self-understanding of the Faith and Order movement, and for the relationship church unity has to missions and the larger ecumenical movement in general. It was at Edinburgh, in the midst of the discourse of mission, that the need for unity was revealed, a need which was linked for Brent with his experience as a missionary bishop in the Philippines. Tatlow records this sentiment of Brent's: "we missionaries have moments of deep depression when the consciousness sweeps over us that it is little short of absurd to try to bring into the Church of Christ the great nations of the Far East unless we can present an undivided front."[26]

For Brent, as well as for other missionaries, the desire for unity was coupled with the mission proclamation, a connection reflected in the "Final Report" of the First World Conference on Faith and Order, Lausanne, 1927. The report from Section I, "The Call to Unity," noted that, "At home and abroad sad multitudes are turning away in bewilderment from the Church because of its corporate feebleness."[27] It was the desire for unity that was furthered by Edinburgh. The connection between the absence of unity and the presence of world mission mandated for Brent the initiation of a separate movement for unity; but it also linked the World Conference on Faith and Order with the World Missionary Conference of 1910, "always and rightly" so according to Tatlow.[28]

The Protestant Episcopal Church did appoint the Commission Brent proposed. On the day before this decision, October 18, 1910, a similar action was brought before another U.S. denominational body, the Disciples of Christ, by their President. And again a third coinciding decision is noted by Tatlow as occurring on October 18, 1910: "The National Council of Congregational Churches in the United States, on the very same day and quite independently, appointed a special commission to consider any overture" for church unity.[29] The effect of these surprising coincidences creates a sense of a grass-roots and diversified movement for church unity initiated one decade into the twentieth century.

The actual work of planning for Faith and Order did not reflect quite so broad or spontaneous a base, however. The immediate action of the Protestant Episcopal Commission was to contact leaders of the Anglican communion in Great Britain and Ireland. Then, in 1913, a meeting of representatives from fifteen other Protestant churches and one representative of the Russian Orthodox Church was convened by the Commission of the Protestant Episcopal Church. Prior to the War the Anglican influence upon the Faith and Order movement is significantly more than any other denomination. So, according to Tavard, "It has often been said that the very idea of 'Faith and Order' is Anglican."[30]

The Anglicanism that Brent and the Joint Commission exemplified bore the stamp of his North American context. Both the sense of mission and the tradition of unity that were brought to bear upon the planning for the Faith and Order conference were shaped by this context, argues Gassmann.[31] Understanding them sheds light on some of the early directions of the Faith and Order movement. First, the U.S.A. was becoming increasingly conscious of itself as a world power at the end of the nineteenth century. Missionaries from the U.S.A. reflected aspects of this new sense of international importance and power that was manifested in U.S. government policies and actions. By the end of the War in 1917 this had translated into an idealism concerning U.S. leadership in the world. There was also in North America a Protestant tradition of searching for unity, expressed in Campbell's movement for a "nondenominational" Christianity, for example, as well as in the work of such leaders as S. S. Schmucker and in the founding of the Federal Council of Churches of Christ in America in 1908.[32]

The Protestant Episcopal Church had given its distinctive Anglican and American sense of unity expression in the Chicago conference of 1886. Where other proposals for unity would focus on a minimal confessional basis (Campbell) or on social endeavors (Federal Council), the Anglican proposal called for unity on the basis of the four essentials of Scripture, Nicene Creed, two sacraments, and a historic episcopate.[33] The Chicago conference in turn had served as the basis for the Lambeth Conference and the "Quadrilateral" statement which defined the Anglican understanding of the practical basis for unity among Christian churches.[34] The Anglican position which was brought to the work of Faith and Order was in favor of full unity, not federation.[35] The initial conferences sought clarification of issues which separate communions, but the work of Faith and Order as an inter-church movement has been on behalf of the unity of separated churches.[36]

Prior to the first meeting of the Joint Commission in 1913, the Protestant Episcopal Church sent a deputation to meet with the Anglican Church of Great Britain and to secure support for the proposed World Conference. A second deputation secured participation by free churches in Great Britain in 1914, the same year in which an initial invitation was sent to the Vatican. After the War of 1914-1918, with initial planning for the Conference already underway, a deputation successfully met with and gained the participation of Orthodox churches in the Middle East and Europe; met with representatives of the Vatican but failed to gain the official participation by the Roman Catholic Church; met with success among French and Scandinavian Protestant Churches; but failed even to meet with German churches.[37] The organizational structure and the theological terms in which the conference preparations were being set were suspicious to the Germans. Tatlow notes that in Europe as a whole there was a strong feeling "that the Faith and Order movement was an Anglican imperialist move."[38]

Suspicions were found among Orthodox participants in the movement for Faith and Order as well. The Encyclical of Joachim III in 1902 had raised the question of Orthodoxy's present and future relationship to Protestants and Catholics; behind this lay a long history of Protestant and Catholic proselytism and aggression directed against Orthodox communities.[39] However, following the reception of the Joint Commission delegation by the Holy Synod in Constantinople, 1919, the Ecumenical Patriarch issued an important Encyclical in which he called for a *koinonia* of churches parallel to the League of Nations.[40]

The members of the Joint Commission had invited Orthodox participation in the planning conference in Geneva, 1920, and their invitation was accepted. Metropolitan Germanos of Seleukia explained to the Geneva Conference that the Commission's invitation had coincided with an initiative from within Orthodoxy itself.[41] Professor Alivisatos spoke directly of Orthodoxy's deep concern for the unity of the church, and saw unity as the goal of the proposed conference.[42] At the World Conference on Faith and Order itself which met in Lausanne, Switzerland in 1927 a statement from the Orthodox participants read to the conference by Metropolitan Germanos reported that the Orthodox representatives "recommended that before any discussion of the reunion of the Churches in faith and order, a League of Churches should be established for their mutual co-operation in regard to the social and moral principles of Christendom."[43]

The separate Orthodox statement at Lausanne in 1927 was necessitated by the conclusion that the basis for the Conference Reports "are inconsistent with the principles of the Orthodox Church."[44] The primary Orthodox objection was to the methodology adopted by the conference which allowed separate and conflicting meanings to be set side by side in the final report -- "the basis of compromise between what in our understanding are conflicting ideas and meanings."[45] The alternative basis for ecumenical understanding set forth by this statement is one of "co-operation with other Churches in the social and moral sphere on a basis of Christian love,"[46] and continued participation in discussions concerned with dogmatic unity and questions of theological meaning, a position which could be argued as substantially depicting the state of world ecumenism still at the end of the century.

Despite their presentation of separate statements, and their lingering uneasiness with this "comparative" methodology which characterized the early work of Faith and Order, the Orthodox churches have remained consistent participants in the movement through the present. The unbending dogmatic basis for the Orthodox position on questions of Faith and Order is the basis upon which Orthodoxy itself rests: the Tradition of the undivided Church of the Seven Ecumenical Councils and of the first eight centuries. This includes the Scriptures, the teachings of the ancient Church's theologians, the decisions of the Seven Councils, and the liturgical life of the ancient undivided Church.[47]

Orthodox dissent has been registered consistently against the approach to reunion that has been taken by the ecumenical movement not only in Faith and Order, but often in the World Council as a whole. At the Evanston Assembly of the WCC in 1954, for instance, the Orthodox delegation rejected the Report of Section I, on Faith and Order, specifically because the Report called for repentance by the churches on account of their disunity. The Report had stated that past divisions "have been caused, and are perpetrated, to a large degree, by sincere concern for the gospel."[48] Such concern, however, in the lives of sinful human beings, results in sinful divisions within the true church; the church reflects the historical brokenness and dividedness of human existence. The Orthodox response to the Report, on the other hand, asserted strongly its emphasis upon the presence of the Kingdom of God in the Church as present reality, and not only future hope. The Church lies beyond judgement (and hence beyond repentance) even as its members are liable to sin and error.

> [W]e reject the notion that the Church herself, being the Body of Christ and the repository of revealed Truth and the "whole operation of the Holy Spirit," could be affected by human sin. Therefore we cannot speak of the repentance of the Church which is intrinsically holy and unerring.[49]

The problem of disunity was said to be a Protestant problem; the path for ecumenical renewal was the return of the Protestant churches to the full faith of the ancient, undivided Church. Their return to a common past would not be "static restoration of old forms."[50]   The original basis for discussion of unity within the Anglican communion, the Quadrilateral, has been criticized on precisely this point, that it was a static position, incapable of development or of encouraging further explication.[51] The Orthodox perspective, on the other hand, envisioned a dynamic recovery which did not demand rigid uniformity. The one true faith is capable of various expression because it is "mysterious in its essence and unfathomable adequately in the formulas of human reason."[52]   The concept that the Orthodox theologians have rejected, however, is the notion that the church is fundamentally a historical entity, and that its achievement of unity remains a historical task.

The deep, underlying tensions between Protestant and Orthodox participants in the Faith and Order movement have also been manifest in relation to missions. At the Geneva planning conference in 1920, the issues of Protestant missionary efforts and Bible distribution among Orthodox communities were raised by Professor Alivisatos.[53]   Such Protestant missionary activity did not cease through the mid-century, prompting an Orthodox objection to the integration of the International Missionary Council into the World Council in 1961. Integration was in fact achieved only after a statement against proselytizing was adopted.[54] Despite such statements, and a greater sensitivity on the part of the World Council as a whole concerning the place of the Orthodox church within it, tension has continued, most recently manifested in Orthodox reaction to a number of the theological and social positions held in some sectors of the ecumenical movement. The difference is not only a matter of mission, but of the understanding of the nature of the churches themselves, their unity, diversity, and extension. Theodore Stylianopoulos has located that tension succinctly "between, on the one hand, the *implied* ecclesiology of the World Council of Churches and [the *Baptism, Eucharist and Ministry* text] which is so loud, and, on the other hand, the *explicit* ecclesiology of the Orthodox Churches constituting the one, holy, catholic and apostolic Church which is so silent in the ecumenical arena."[55]

Citing the 1982 *Sophia Consultation* as evidence of a more general Orthodox reaction against the Protestant ecclesiological domination of the WCC,[56] and Protestant unfamiliarity with the Orthodox position which leads repeatedly to Orthodox surrender, Stylianopoulos suggested a Pan-Orthodox Ecumenical Commission through which all Orthodox involvement in the WCC could be coordinated.[57] Recognizing the tremendous benefits the Orthodox Church has received from its participation in the World Council, he nevertheless confirmed the judgement of the Orthodox delegates at New Delhi in 1961 who stated: "The ecumenical problem as it is understood in the current ecumenical movement, is primarily a problem of the Protestant world. The main question, in this setting, is that of 'Denominationalism.'"[58] The statement, "The Church, the Churches and the World Council of Churches," which was accepted by the Central Committee at Toronto in 1950, declared that "no Church is obliged to change its ecclesiology as a consequence of membership in the World Council."[59] Nevertheless, Stylianopoulos argued, Protestant ecclesiology, without being clearly articulated as a Protestant understanding of the church, has subtly shaped Faith and Order.

> The overwhelming tone, literature and vision of the World Council as a "conciliar fellowship" both presupposes and seeks to give practical expression to a Protestant ecclesiology, *one that simultaneously holds to the historical divisions and also the spiritual unity of all the Christian churches.*[60]

The Orthodox uneasiness with certain forms of ecclesiology, methodology, and even theology that have been expressed in the ecumenical movement may indeed be an uneasiness with an ecumenical context that is predominantly Protestant. A recurring assumption within the World Council, reflected even in the Toronto statement (despite its disclaimer), that ecclesiology encompasses twin dimensions which can be described as historical and spiritual, has appeared to the Orthodox to be a particularly Protestant notion. Despite the general Protestant flavor of such conceptions of the church, however, the problem Orthodox theologians have confronted is not so much that of Protestant ecclesiology as it is that of historical relativity.[61]   The Orthodox theologians have given clearer expression to what is for other Roman Catholic and even Protestant theologians an uneasiness with the manner in which the ecumenical movement has provided a forum for change, fostered theological innovation, and legitimated new forms of contextual theology that appear to some to be syncretistic. Historical relativity is a principle presupposed by a dialogical *praxis* that embraces difference, self-limitation, and the multiplicity of historical expressions of faith.

Historical relativity has lurked in the background of much of the ecumenical discussion concerning unity since the beginning of the century. The First World Conference on Faith and Order, in Lausanne, Switzerland in 1927 succeeded in identifying several of the major historical and confessional differences among churches. At Lausanne, and again at the Second World Conference on Faith and Order held in Edinburgh, Scotland in 1937, the common faith of all Christians in Jesus Christ had at least implicitly served as the basis for agreement among delegates.[62]   The method which was adopted for actual conversations at Lausanne and Edinburgh was a comparative one however. Different positions were articulated in the discussions without significant attempts made toward arriving at a common confession of faith (despite lingering expectations by some that these conferences would work toward achieving the confessional unity of one true church). The final reports from the sections stated differences without attempting to solve them. It was not until the Third World Conference on Faith and Order held in Lund, Sweden in 1952, (called now by the Faith and Order Commission of the WCC), that the comparative method was superceded. At Lund the Faith and Order movement sought to go beyond merely a comparative methodology, noting:

> We have seen clearly that we can make no real advance toward unity if we only compare our several conceptions of the nature of the Church and the traditions in which they are embodied....We need, therefore, to penetrate behind our divisions to a deeper and richer understanding of the mystery of the God-given union of Christ with His Church. We need increasingly to realise that the separate histories of our Churches find their full meaning only if seen in the perspective of God's dealing with His [sic] *whole* people.[63]

The comparative methodology had highlighted differences in doctrine and confession. In doing so it had highlighted the presence of separate histories among Christians who claimed at least in a spiritual sense to be members of one community, the 'Church.' The existence of these different histories was most apparent in the area of ecclesiology, where the historical reality of the diverse institutional existence of the churches was difficult to ignore. Delegates at Lund affirmed that there was an intimate relationship between Christology and ecclesiology in terms of concrete existence.[64] The final statement from the 1952 conference asserted that all agreed there was some form of historical continuity between the Church and the risen Christ, assured by the action of the Holy Spirit through the present. This "apostolic continuity" was a continuous institutional (historical) existence which more or less was said to characterize all confessional traditions.[65] Discontinuities in the forms of schism and heresy were said to be responsible for separating Christians from one another, pluralizing this historical line.[66] The ecumenical task Lund sketched for the future of Faith and Order was to locate behind or beneath the diversity a common tradition which is already given through our unity in Christ, and which would be capable of drawing the various confessions into fellowship again. In the multiplicity of confessional and historical identities, the Faith and Order movement after Lund sought a common tradition.

The relationship between historical diversity or relativity, and theological continuity with the past, was taken up explicitly in a study pursued between Lund and the Fourth World Conference on Faith and Order held in Montreal, Canada in 1963. Conducted by a committee on the Theological Commission on Tradition and Traditions, the study was pursued in two sections, one North American and the other European. (The confinement of 'traditions' and 'Tradition' to these twin contexts of a post-European Christendom is of course highly significant). Preliminary results of both sections of the commission were published together in 1961 as "The Renewal of the Christian Tradition," with a final report from the study emerging from the Montreal gathering.[67]

Unlike the European section, which took up first the Reformation concern for the relationship between Scripture and Tradition, the North American section developed a line of discussion from comparative ecclesiology to historical relativity. Out of Lund had come "a dawning realization of the importance of historical understanding as context for doctrinal dialogue," the North American section report noted.[68] The comparative project had set diverse theological perspectives side by side, raising the issue of doctrinal or denominational relativity. While particular ecclesial traditions each might claim in some manner to contain within themselves the fullness of truth, brought together in the comparative process their particularity was inescapable. Within the comparative framework various traditions in effect served to limit each other's claims to representing the truth unequivocally, and to reveal the historical character of all dogmatic convictions. The method had in effect relativized the various ecclesial traditions confessions. "All of this suggests that there is a corollary in church history to the principle of historical relativism in general historiography."[69] For this reason, the North American report suggested, dogmatic discussions needed to be pursued with the aid of historical methodologies. "In short, the ecumenical movement stands in urgent need of some sort of ecumenical historiography."[70] Exploring dogmatic disagreements within the framework of critical historiography, a hermeneutics of tradition (*denominational hermeneutics*) would emerge to set disagreements in their historical context, and refer them to their origins and intentions.

But historical relativity would seem, as a matter of principle, to exclude the possibility of locating one integral, essential tradition, or the Tradition, within the many traditions. While historical relativity could clarify the many, and perhaps even serve a critical function in exposing false absolutes, it would in itself ultimately undercut the basis of ecumenical study and action, argued the report. The fact that there is such a reality as Christian communities suggests that there is "*some* sort of identity and continuity in space and time," and this identity is related to the basis for the World Council of Churches itself.[71] This unitary referent in the diverse traditions is Tradition, the report asserted. If as a historian the Christian must recognize the relativity of traditions, as believer she or he must remain committed to belief in one, holy, catholic, and apostolic church.

> As a member of the company who confess Jesus Christ as Lord...the historian finds himself [sic] intuiting the Christian Tradition in, with and under the manifold of church traditions.[72]

There is a "real presence" of Tradition within the traditions. The (plural) traditions are historical phenomenon; Tradition, on the other hand, is "the divine origination, maintenance and prolepsis of the people of God...."[73] The one Tradition is not unrelated to history, but is in fact bound to or hidden within the concrete phenomenal histories of existing churches. Thus, it was argued in the North American section report, the church does not come into being in a new national or cultural contexts spontaneously, but is transplanted. The relationship of foreign missions to the *actus tradendi* was implied to be analogous to that of traditions to Tradition.

The North American report distinguished between the process of traditioning and the reproduction of cultural forms. It criticized the identification of the Gospel with particular cultural forms in the West, noting the ambiguity both of the "indigenization" of Christianity in Western culture and more recently in non-Western cultures. Each new tradition must be in continuity with the human community which is its own immediate context or environment, but it must also be in continuity with "the Christian community in all ages and places...."[74] The continuity with the whole Christian community, however, was decisive for locating the one Christian Tradition, for the historical location of the Tradition is the total heritage of the Christian past. Only in the historical past of the Christian church can be located the Tradition.

Implicit in the report was the assumption that this past is predominantly the history and heritage of the European Christianity. The confessions or creeds which could be said to give doctrinal form to this one Tradition, even those commonly called "ecumenical," belong to the history of the European church (which is also the heritage of the dominant Protestant churches of North America). The Western historical past is implicitly the privileged vehicle for the deposit of apostolic faith. While the history of the churches of the West was not said to be synonymous with the one Tradition, that Tradition was located in the history of these churches.

As noted above, the European section of this study took a different route, considering first the relationship between Scripture and tradition, which located the discussion primarily within the historical context of Roman Catholic-Protestant dialogue. The immediate focus upon tradition or *paradosis* raised a number of theological issues related to various Roman Catholic, Protestant and Orthodox beliefs. When the study turned to "systematic" consideration of the problem however, it too found itself confronting the problem of historical consciousness. "The more the metaphysical thought of earlier centuries has been superseded by a 'historical' way of thinking, the more has the relation between Christianity and history become a problem," it claimed.[75]

The European report also acknowledged that Christianity is

inseparably bound to history, and that historical causality of necessity impinges upon the discussion of tradition. The absolute significance of Christianity does not disappear into a process of historical relativity, however, for Christianity is bound to one definite historical moment of *kairos* the Europeans argued, that of Jesus Christ. The historical life of the church bears this moment along in its *depositum fidei*, employing earthly words and deeds. The connection between these human words and deeds, which are the vehicle, and that which is borne along, which is the Word of God, is given not of necessity however but by the Holy Spirit as an act of grace. Thus the study shifted the burden of *paradosis* (literally 'handing over,'or 'traditioning') from the human vehicle of traditions of the churches to the work of the Holy Spirit. At the same time the European section report was able to reconcile the multiplicity and divergences of Christian traditions with the existence of one true Tradition. Quoting Daniel Jenkins, it stated: "No church can be so completely confident of its own ability to interpret and obey the Spirit that it can assert without qualifications that its own particular historical tradition is entirely free from the same weaknesses and that it has nothing to learn from others."[76]

While it presented the relationship between traditions and the Tradition more dialectically, more critically, the European report nevertheless continued to locate the eternal *kairos* only in relationship to the particular *chronos* of the European historical past. Unexamined in either section report was the *manner* in which Christian communities are continuous with the apostles. It was implied that the multiple histories of the churches are joined somewhere in the past to one continuous historical line. In the American discussion of the two-fold continuity, between the Christian community and its context and between a Christian community and the community in all ages and places, the former continuity suggested the particularity of the church while the later denoted its catholicity. Continuity in this historical dimension, "the catholicity of time,"[77] has continued to be pursued by Faith and Order since the Lund conference in its search for consensus (or more recently, convergence).

Several major studies undertaken by the Faith and Order Commission after the New Delhi Assembly in 1961 and the Montreal Conference in 1963 pursued the possibility of historical convergence or locating a common ecumenical past in the early Christian era. An on-going Faith and Order study on "Scripture and Tradition," and the discussion in

Montreal regarding the diversity and unity of the churches depicted in the New Testament, sharpened questions regarding the difficulties of locating a unified biblical faith. At the same time a Faith and Order study group made up of Orthodox and non-Orthodox ("western") representatives began a joint examination of "The Significance of Patristic Study for Ecumenical Discussion." The contemporary ecumenical importance of the post-apostolic church was discerned at New Delhi when the Assembly voted to recommend a study of the conciliar process through the early centuries of the Christian era.[78] The search for a common ecumenical history behind the separated histories has been continued through several different Faith and Order studies, including the current study program on the "Apostolic Faith."[79]

The focus that quickly emerged for the studies of the conciliar process of the early Christian churches was the Nicene- Constantinople Creed of 381. Already at Lausanne in 1927 the common profession of the Nicene creed by many of the churches present had been noted. But especially in the work of Faith and Order toward visible unity since the early 1970s, the Nicene Creed has emerged as an important point for centripetal convergence or even consensus among the churches. Presumably, for instance, it would be the Nicene Creed that the representatives of the churches would profess together at the opening of a truly universal or ecumenical council.[80] For the Faith and Order movement the Nicene Creed has symbolized a point of historical convergence and unity behind the churches of the ecumenical movement today, since supposedly it "is part of the historical heritage of all contemporary churches."[81]

The problem of the historical particularity of the Nicene Creed and of the councils of the early Christian era were already apparent to the initial Faith and Order study on "The Importance of the Conciliar Process in the Ancient Church for the Ecumenical Movement" however. The report which was received and approved by the Faith and Order Commission meeting at Bristol, England, in 1967 had already limited the conciliar process which would become the focus of the Faith and Order program "primarily to the type of ecumenical councils of the Christian Roman Empire." The report continued, "They deserve particular attention insofar as they have taken a very determinative position in the history of the church."[82] It is critical here that we recognize the hegemonic direction that is being pursued in this quest for a modern ecumenical council. The ancient ecumenical councils had been called by Roman emperors who had assumed responsibility for the church. They were imperial events, unifying the churches under imperial power. The problem of the social and political particularity of the councils called by Roman emperors affects their ecumenical importance today. So even the 1967 report notes:

> It was already evident when churches which lay outside the boundaries of the empire or which were in opposition within the empire rejected the imperial councils for political, as well as theological and religious, reasons. *Subsequent history has brought the problem much more clearly into the foreground in a way that could not have been seen at the beginning of the Christian empire. After this has been recognized, we can no longer simply return to the example of the first Ecumenical Councils.*[83]

The ecumenical councils of the early Christian era represent the centripetal forces of consensus among the ancient Christian churches as well as for today. But they were at the same time occasions for dissent and disunity, for the decisions of no ancient council were accepted by all the churches of that period. For the dissenting voices (often but not always labeled 'heretics' or 'schismatics') they were not adequate models of conciliarity. The Nicene Creed, perhaps the best the symbol of ecumenical unity achieved by the councils, was not, and is not today, without its dissenting voices holding out against it serving as the basis for visible unity.

The problems of the historical particularity of the Nicene Creed indicates a more general problem with the very conception of the conciliar process as it has emerged in the Faith and Order movement toward visible unity. The same problem of the particularity of one cultural expression of faith serving as the ecumenical standard, or of one church or group of churches controlling the ecumenical center, is raised by historical consideration of the *oikoumene* envisioned by the ancient councils or by the domination of the modern ecumenical movement by churches of the North Atlantic political community.

The early Christian movement rejected social and cultural boundaries for its faith; the biblical story of the Ethiopian eunuch and the traditions of apostles who traveled to Armenia, Persia and India demonstrate an awareness of a larger *oikoumene*. However the conversion of the Roman Empire brought with it a new ambivalence; *oikoumene* "was appropriated by the church itself, or more specifically, by the church whose theology had been formed in encounter with Hellenic philosophy and whose centres of power were those of the beleaguered Roman Empire."[84] In other words, the theology which was articulated in the encounter between the story of the death and resurrection of Jesus of Nazareth and Greco-Roman culture was a theology which belonged to a particular context. The ambivalence of its particular expression being asserted as representing the universal faith arose from the politics and culture of imperialism which emerged in this experience of the ancient councils. As Charles C. West has argued:

> The ecumenical creeds (Apostolic, Nicean, Athanasian) and the first seven ecumenical councils expressed this ambivalence. On the one hand they defined the teaching of the church by using and transforming the categories of Greek thought. For these formulations they claimed ecumenical validity which has more or less been authoritative for the churches in Europe, their diaspora in the Americas and elsewhere, and their missions throughout the world. On the other hand, however, these creeds and councils produced a schism in the church to which the non-Chalcedonian of Egypt, Ethiopia, India and the Middle East still bear witness today.[85]

Cultural imperialism would seem to be inherent in the efforts to reconstruct the unity of the church on the basis of a common Tradition, or through convergence in ministry and sacraments. Taking the Creed of 381 as a confessional center offers a centripetal model of unity, one which undergirds the historical and cultural domination by North Atlantic churches claiming direct linguistic, geographic, and institutional continuity with the ancient churches. Not to recognize the danger of a singular model of unity, or seeking to establish unity on the basis of creeds articulated by churches within the ancient culture symbolically (ideologically) identified with the modern West (or 'Europe') effectively maintains the cultural domination of Western Christendom.

Ecumenical discussions concerning the catholicity of the church, and continuity with the ancient Tradition, have too often avoided cultural hermeneutics of the sort practiced by Charles West in the passage quoted above. In the Faith and Order discussions prior to 1968 sociological and cultural analyses were most often considered to be "non-theological." The report from Section I of the Evanston Assembly of the World Council, 1954, sharply contrasted a sociological analysis of unity with a theological one, thereby masking social and cultural dimensions of doctrine.[86] Yet we have seen that the North American section report of the study on "Tradition and the traditions" raised these 'non-theological' factors explicitly in its recognition of historical relativism. Likewise, the European section report gave evidence of a more critical historical consciousness impinging upon Tradition.

Questions concerning the relationship to faith of social, cultural, and gender diversity within and among churches were not absent from Faith and Order deliberations even early in the movement. Nor have they been removed from the contemporary discussions regarding unity. On the contrary, questions concerning the diversity of faith, and challenges to the political, cultural, and ecclesiological domination of the *oikoumene* have been persistent in Faith and Order deliberations -- even if they have received marginal attention. These voices of diversity have been no less concerned for the *koinonia* of churches and communities in the global setting. Unfortunately the meaning of *koinonia* has been characteristically experienced as a centripetal force within the Faith and Order movement, and within the World Council in general.[87] This tendency can be seen in the preparatory document for the Fifth World Conference on Faith and Order in Santiago de Compostela, Spain, in August of 1993, whose theme is "Towards Koinonia in Faith, Life and Witness." The preparatory statement (called "the Dublin Text") offers no positive account of diversity.[88] Centrifugal tendencies are deemed by it only as being negative and divisive. There is hardly a reference in the Dublin Text to the considerable movements of contextual theologies that have grown up across the world over the last half-century, a silence which is inexplicable given the attention Faith and Order has paid to them in the recent past. From the perspective of the Dublin Text, *koinonia* appears to be exclusively a matter of unity, despite the positive value of diversity that is being extolled in numerous contextual theologies around the world today.

3. The Solidarity of 'Reconciled Diversity'

The problem which has emerged in the Faith and Order quest for visible unity of one universal church is that of the ideological function of unity. In turning toward the conciliar process of the first four centuries, and in seeking ecumenical convergence historically in the common recitation of the Nicene-Constantinople Creed, Faith and Order has invoked the political memory of Christendom. The *oikoumene* which is invoked in this memory is not that of the six continents, but as Irmgard Kindt-Siegwalt has recently pointed out, "the former world of the Roman Empire in New Testament times."[89] It is a memory which has served, and continues to be deployed on behalf of, the ideological legitimation of North Atlantic political and cultural domination, a function which can only be ignored in the ecumenical movement at the risk of legitimating domination.

The close relationship between the visible unity of one true church confessing a common creed and the political memory of imperial Christendom raises critical questions concerning the ideological character of consensus sought by Faith and Order. To say this is not to question the theological validity of the doctrines articulated at Nicaea, Constantinople, or Chalcedon. Nor is it to question the importance to the Christian faith of such doctrines as the Holy Trinity, or even the particular soteriology and ecclesiology which emerged from the ancient councils. To raise the ideological meaning of unity and consensus as articulated by Faith and Order is to recognize that formulations of doctrine and practice in the early centuries as well as today represent local theologies related to particular social and cultural contexts. To raise the question is at the same time to seek to discern the political processes of legitimation and suppression which went on then and now, concealing diversity and suppressing difference.

The visible unity of ideological consensus toward which the councils called by the Roman emperor labored resulted in processes of exclusion (of so-called heresy) and enforced conformity (often concealed within concepts.of orthodoxy). The ideological function of consensus within the ecumenical movement of the present century has likewise too often served the *oikoumene* of domination shaped within the crucible of the modern political era. But just as in the early centuries of the Christian era the political suppression of ecclesial difference was not complete, so in this century the ecumenical movement has not been monolithic in its quest for unity. Just as the theological situation of the churches during the early centuries of the Christian era remained diverse, so the diversity of theological voices of the excluded political and ecclesiastical 'others' of modern Christendom have been heard in the ecumenical movement. The discourse on unity and the ideological quest for consensus have only been partially successful. The essentially heterogeneous nature of the Christian churches and communities in the contemporary ecumenical situation has irrupted in discontinuous and even disruptive voices, even within Faith and Order.

These voices of the excluded 'others' of modern ecumenical Christendom are the voices of those who have been marginal to and within the dominant North Atlantic churches: the voices of non-European peoples, of women, of the poor. While their existence within the Faith and Order movement has often been relegated to the margins (and consigned to the footnotes of ecumenical texts) they remain inscribed within the movement ineradicably.[90] Often disqualified from being theological (especially in earlier Faith and Order texts where they were often relegated to the category of being "non-theological"), these voices of the ecumenical 'others' within the movement have been as resistant to systematic ordering as they have been to exclusion.[91] They are the voices of "all in each place" that the New Delhi Assembly spoke of, the women and men in diverse ecclesial communities across the six continents.   Through them the Faith and Order movement has experienced moments of opening up to the *oikoumene* which lies beyond the margins of a visible unity centered around a common creed. Through them we also can begin to discern the *oikoumene* in which all can truly act and speak together in the unity of solidarity.[92]

Such a moment of opening up beyond the margins occurred at the First World Conference on Faith and Order in Lausanne, 1927, when six of the eight women listed as delegates to the Conference issued a call to the Conference to acknowledge their presence. Claiming not to wish to raise any discussion on the subject of women in the church, they proceeded to do just that: "we believe that the right place of women in the Church and in the councils of the Church is one of grave moment, and should be in the hearts and minds of all."[93] The gifts of women to the unity of the whole church were to be found in and beyond the margins constructed by an exclusively male leadership. A similar voice in and beyond the margins, in this case that of the non-European 'other,' was heard at Lausanne when the Rev. H. Sumitra of India during one of the sessions urged the Conference to be centered "not so much on the Church of the past, as on the Church in its entirety, past, present, and future...." This would enable the Conference to recognize the new developments which were taking place in the churches of the East, he argued. "For we believe that in the Church in the mission field [that is, beyond the boundaries of Western Christendom], the Spirit is revealing to us truths that are perhaps obscure in Christian lands."[94]

One of these moments of convergence at the margins at Lausanne in 1927 took place during a series of public presentations not formally part of the deliberations of the Conference, held at the Cathedral. The program for the evening of August 14 on "The Necessity of Christian Unity for the Missionary Enterprise of the Church" consisted of two presentations, one by Vedenayakam Samuel Azariah, Bishop of Dornakal, India and the other by the Rev. Professor Timothy Tingfang Lew of Bejing. Chairing the discussion for the evening was Bishop John Hurst, of the Florida Conference of the African Methodist Episcopal Church and one of two AME Bishops at Lausanne.

During their lectures both Bishop Azariah and Professor Lew criticized the existing confessional and denominational divisions of Christendom as belonging to the Western heritage and therefore being irrelevant to the churches in the East. "The divisions of Christendom do not appeal to the Christians in these lands," asserted Bishop Azariah. "Christians in India, for instance, did not have a share in creating them."[95] Overcoming confessional and denominational divisions was a nationalist imperative for the Indian churches. The theme was echoed by Professor Lew in his lecture, which began by making reference to the call for a united church made by the Shanghai National Christian Conference of China in 1922. At the conclusion of his presentation Lew articulated the ecumenical vision from the margins of Lausanne, a vision of a truly universal church which embraced the cultural and historical heritage of humankind beyond that of Western churches.

> The peoples in the Far East have their own spiritual and religious inheritance, which is in some aspects different from that of the Western nations. Their inheritance helps them to understand the purpose of God in Jesus Christ in their own way. It may give them a certain insight and understanding which the West has not yet seen. There is among the Chinese Christians now a felt command of God to interpret Christianity in terms of the spiritual inheritance of the Chinese race. They believe that such interpretation, when made together with their own spiritual experience, should find a wider expression. It does not belong to them alone, but should become the possession of the whole Church universal.[96]

At Lausanne the multiple voices marginal to the dominant Western churches were joined at several instances. The presence of an African-American Bishop presiding at a session in which an Indian Bishop and a Chinese Professor presented was perhaps one symbolic instance of this convergence. Another instance was expressed in the body of Lew's presentation, where he stated that an increasing number of Chinese Christians opposed barriers to the full ministry of women.[97] Nor where these voices absent from the main course of the Conference deliberations. The final report from Section I of Lausanne, "The Call to Unity," in its third and fourth paragraphs, acknowledged the presence of these ecumenical voices. The fourth paragraph addressed specifically issues which would continue to occupy the ecumenical movement, regarding the place of women and youth in the churches:

> Some of us, pioneers in this undertaking, have grown old in our search for unity. It is to youth that we look to lift the torch on high. We men have carried it too much alone through many years. The women henceforth should be accorded their share of responsibility. And so the whole Church will be enabled to do that which no section can hope to perform.[98]

Here, at its beginning, the Faith and Order movement had heard something of the ecumenical impatience which would continue to grow through the rest of the century. The third paragraph of "The Call to Unity" from Lausanne in 1927 had stated, "Already the mission field is impatiently revolting from the divisions of the Western Church to make bold adventure for unity in its own right." Still "The Call" left unchallenged the dominant relationships among the churches of the world at that time. While the envisioned future was one in which Western and non-Western churches would "labour side by side until our common goal is reached," the "we" who spoke in paragraph three "of the Churches represented in this Conference" were ones who "cannot allow our spiritual children to outpace us." Nevertheless, whether through the *praxis* of women or the truths of the non-Europeans, at Lausanne the voices from beyond the margins offered a greater unity, a greater truth, than that which was possible within the dominant discourse of the North Atlantic churches.

At the Second World Conference on Faith and Order in Edinburgh, 1937, and through the period of the formation of the World Council, the Faith and Order movement struggled primarily to clarify its identity and purpose in relation to other sectors of the ecumenical movement, and to the dominant churches represented within it. The effects of this struggle were evident in the partial independence Faith and Order maintained as a Commission in the World Council, as well as in the content of the studies and discussions it undertook during the 1950s. At the same time Faith and Order retreated to relative silence regarding concerns of women, youth, and non-Europeans, concerns that were often labeled "non-theological."

Already at the Edinburgh Faith and Order Conference in 1937 the effect of social and cultural factors on ecclesiastical divisions had been recognized. At Lund in 1952 prominent consideration was paid to these so-called "non-theological" factors affecting divisions. Considered primarily to be obstacles to unity, such factors were to be judged in light of the standard of Jesus Christ. Lund's christological focus and new methodology of seeking to "penetrate" more deeply behind the historical diversity of the churches led it to minimize non-theological or relative factors. The general direction of the ecumenical quest for church unity during this period, evident both at Lund and at the first two Assemblies of the World Council, lay in proclaiming the unity God had already given the churches in Jesus Christ, a unity experienced as well as expressed by the ecumenical movement, then "working and praying for the shortening of the days of our separation, in obedience to Him in whom we affirm ourselves to be one."[99]

But even at Lund the voice from the margin was heard to challenge the easy categorization of social, political, and cultural factors as non-theological. Bishop Lakdasa De Mel, of Sri Lanka (then Ceylon) preached the first sermon (there were two) at the opening worship service on Friday evening. Taking as his text John 15.26-7, the bishop spoke as a "representative of the Younger Churches who is deeply grateful for all that the missionaries have done for us," to urge those from the dominant churches of the North Atlantic community to attend to their "possessiveness in two spheres."

> In the material, there is the temptation to cling to property or institutions long after the local Church has passed the stage of adolescence. In the spiritual, there is the temptation to excessive fear that syncretism will corrupt our faith and cause fresh divisions. The parent Churches seek to build us up into a pattern -- either the first four centuries, the thirteenth, or the sixteenth. We must learn from all these, but such patterns are partly dated and inadequate. We must look to the future, to a Church which includes territories and peoples then unknown to Christendom, and therefore to a future capable of a fullness and a wholeness hitherto unimagined.[100]

Bishop De Mel refused the tendency to render culture and social issues non-theological, and thus distinguishable from the more essential issues of theological unity. He joined the two spheres of institutional and theological domination ("possessiveness") and spoke from beyond the margins of Christendom against them both. The doctrinal standards to which the Faith and Order movement would eventually turn in its quest for visible unity were already criticized by bishop De Mel at Lund as being "partly dated,"and "inadequate" for the churches in Asia. Churches of the North Atlantic, he went on to assert, "must resist the temptation to measure everything by their own standards," for "unprecedented situations cannot be dealt with in every detail by the precedents of church history."[101]   The future toward which De Mel looked was an open one, "hitherto unimagined" and unprecedented. It was a future beyond the conceptions of unity dominating the ecumenical discourse of Faith and Order through this period.

It was precisely in search of the precedent of "Tradition" (hidden or visible) that Faith and Order engaged in its studies prior to Montreal in 1963. At the same time, however, the historical study of the early churches and of tradition were exposing the political and ecclesiastical pressures that helped shape what otherwise could be taken to be an uncritical ecumenical consensus. The continuity of the experience of modern Churches of the North Atlantic with the first centuries of church history was becoming more difficult to assert in the ecumenical movement without qualification. At the same time another continuity such as was voiced in the "Tradition and traditions" study, the continuity of churches and ecclesial communities with particular local contexts that do not belong to the *oikoumene* of the dominant North Atlantic community, provided a basis for bringing a more historically differentiated consciousness to bear upon the unity discussion.

The twin movements within Faith and Order, toward a historical center and toward an open historical future, were both evident in the deliberations of its Commission Meeting in Bristol, England, in 1967. Both the unity and the diversity of the churches' beliefs and practices were articulated in the study papers and discussion at Bristol. Moreover at Bristol the theological meaning of history emerged more clearly than in any previous Faith and Order setting, leading to discussion of the unity and diversity of human historical experience and of the relationship of history to faith.

One of the studies received at Bristol, "God in Nature and History," drew together the results of several earlier Faith and Order studies on creation and the relationship of Jesus Christ to human history. "God in Nature and History" asserted the universal character of history in the modern era as a given for the modern world, and sought to reflect upon the ecumenical meaning of universal history. Confidently the study declared that the God of biblical faith was revealed in the arena of human history, so that the historical process of the unification of humankind in the modern era needed to be comprehended in the context of the biblical witness to the unity of humankind. This biblical conviction was summarized: "So God's history must sooner or later give birth to the conception of universal history, in the sense that all groups, tribes, nations, imperia, races, and classes are involved in one and the same history."[102] And its contemporary ramifications were drawn:

> So long as in the West Christianity was identified with a special 'Christian culture', limited to Europe, no more could the germs of universality in the Christian message bear fruit either. *The universalizing and unifying of history started in the ages of mission and colonialism, and is now in this generation penetrating human minds everywhere as never before.*[103]

The universal historical intentions of the biblical message, according to the study, thus provide theological justification of mission and colonialism, or of the domination of the modern era in general. "Universal history" served as an ideological force supporting the historical as well as theological dominance of the North Atlantic (European) cultural community.

At the same time Bristol suggested a different vision of historical unity, however, one which was beginning to become more pronounced within ecumenical discourse elsewhere as well.[104] In the study section on "Creation, New Creation and the Unity of the Church" several lacunae in ecumenical theology were enumerated in relation to the theology of creation. The one most pertinent for the development in Faith and Order of a more adequate understanding of the historical and cultural diversity of humanity was the observation of the lacuna between the unity of the churches and the unity of humankind, or of the world. The scope of truly ecumenical unity was not limited to the church, this study asserted. The biblical hope for a "new creation" did not refer to the church but to the whole of humankind.

In respect to the universal dimensions of biblical faith the "Creation" study shared several common assumptions with the "God in Nature and History" project. But the conclusions drawn by the "Creation" study were significantly different, for here the relationship between church unity and the unity of the world was reversed:

> Church unity is not an end to be pursued for its own sake. Nor is it an object which the Church should try to attain as a preparation for more effective mission to the world. The Church cannot expect to be fully reconciled to God as a first stage in the restoration of creation, before the world itself, as a second stage, comes to be summed up in Christ. The unity of the Church is not a separate object of eschatological hope; a fully and perfectly united Church will be a united world, and *vice versa*.[105]

The conclusion drawn by the authors of the "Creation" study stand in sharp contrast to the dominant ecumenical discourse concerning unity:

> Church unity must be a by-product of the reconciliation of the world. The Church can therefore hope for unity to the degree that it directs its efforts outward, away from its internal concerns and towards the needs of mankind [sic] in general.[106]

The direction toward unity in which this study pointed was neither that of consensus regarding the conciliar past, nor convergence of faith and order among the churches today. It was outward, in a movement opening toward the world in the fullness of its contemporary political, social, and cultural diversity. This trajectory within the Faith and Order Commission was taken up explicitly at the Uppsala Assembly under the heading, "Unity of the Church - Unity of Humankind," and continued as an ongoing Faith and Order study into the 1980s.[107] Strengthened by the 1968 Assembly's profound encounter with the social/cultural reality of the modern world, the discussion of unity and renewal moved from an ecclesiastical context to a historical one. In doing so it took as the frame of reference for ecumenical Christianity "humankind in all its ambiguous global interdependence."[108]

At the 1971 Louvain meeting of the Faith and Order Commission, which was almost entirely occupied by the concern for the unity of humankind, these two trajectories for ecumenical unity emerged in sharp contrast. The Orthodox theologian John Meyendorff, for instance, in a paper given in connection with the "Unity of The Church - Unity of

Humanity" project, criticized what he perceived to be a shift from theology to anthropology in recent ecumenical statements. He argued that *koinonia* exists only in the church, where it is centered on the eucharist. In response to the paper, both José Miguez Bonino and John Gatu presented their own sharp criticisms. For Miguez Bonino, the eucharist-centered unity Meyendorff proposed sought a place outside the conflicts of the world; for Gatu, the anthropological approach enabled him to enter into the religious and cultural realities of contemporary Africa, a way which he identified as that of Jesus.[109]

Further studies and conferences after Louvain took up the ecumenical trajectory of unity which leads beyond the church, into the world and the diversity of humanity. In the process fuller realization of the reality of pluralism and of the heterogencity of the ecumenical voices within the Faith and Order movement gave rise to a new ecumenical methodology which has come to be called "inter-contextual."[110] After 1968 the impact of liberation theology within the ecumenical movement as a whole but also in theological work of Faith and Order began to be felt. In a statement submitted to delegates at the Nairobi Assembly, 1975, resulting from the "Unity" study, the bold suggestion was made that the struggles for liberation brought to light a solidarity which could better serve the churches in their search for unity.

> An ecclesiastical unity which would stand in the way of struggles for liberation would be a repressive unity, hindering the just interdependence which Christians are called to serve. We are learning that church unity can be a "unity in tension."[111]

Solidarity with the world came to mean primarily solidarity with those who were suffering from historical forms of oppression within the ecumenical movement. The quest for justice among human communities, and in the community of women and men, emerged as distinctive focal points for dialogue and conversation among various participants in the ecumenical movement. A major impetus toward empowering the voice of women within the WCC as a whole was the 1974 Consultation in Berlin.[112] Even within Faith and Order the voice of women, and the task of renewal of community between women and men in the church, began to be heard with a clarity previously unknown within the ecumenical movement.[113]

Despite these gains made in the 1970s and into the 1980s by contextual theologies the dominant ecumenical theme of the Faith and

Order movement has continued to be the search for convergence in the visible unity of the one true church. The impact of the contextual methodology has been found among the confessional discussions where a model of "reconciled diversity" has been articulated. With the publication of the *BEM* text following the Lima meeting of the Faith and Order Commission in 1982, and through the process of response and reception among the churches, convergence in visible unity has been reasserted as the ecumenical center. This theme has functioned as an ideological focus of sorts for Faith and Order through the 1980s, as it has given its major attention to the "Baptism, Eucharist and Ministry" and "Apostolic Faith" studies.[114] While the other trajectory (or even trajectories) have remained, they have existed in tension with the on-going "ecumenical center" of Faith and Order. So Gennadios Limouris has observed that the "Unity of Humanity" study needs to be brought to bear upon "Baptism, Eucharist and Ministry" and "Towards the Common Expression of the Apostolic Faith Today"

> to remind them of the seriousness of contextualizing. This study should also raise significant questions about the importance of "culture" on credal formulations and of "community" on eucharist and ministry.[115]

Miguez Bonino's and Gatu's responses at Louvain in 1971, or the voices of women and men engaged in the conversations around sexism and community, or the call for solidarity and liberation which has become increasingly stronger in other sectors of the World Council and in the ecumenical movement in general, have emerged not from the internal Faith and Order conversations over the last seventy-five years. They have had a different genesis, and a different social/cultural context. They suggest an ecumenical movement beyond that of the churches of Western Christendom. The last two decades have witnessed a sharper awareness within Faith and Order of issues of social and cultural liberation, although it has often had an origin outside Faith and Order. The ecumenical conversation which has emerged through these voices is constantly moving across the proscribed boundaries of ecumenical discourse, and often subverting them in the process.

Yet, as Melanie May has pointed out, it is a "coherent conversation" that has emerged in and through the wider diversity of the ecumenical movement.[116] The "reconciled diversity" of the de-centered ecumenical reality calls for solidarity without demanding uniformity; recognizes the importance of difference without seeking to determine its dialogical meaning; and accepts the risk of living toward an unprecedented future. In a de-centered community of churches each undergoes baptism into the spirituality of its own cultural and historical experience.[117] The community which emerges from this experience of difference and diversity is that of wholeness in which we begin "hearing one another to speech."[118] Its memory is too great, too diverse, and too wondrous to belong to the possession of one class or group or even community. For the ecumenical truth requires multiple communities to hold it. And the ecumenical conversation engages a diversity of voices.

Amidst the diversity of this larger ecumenical experience the central work of Faith and Order remains an important contribution. The texts Faith and Order has worked to generate have played an important role in the larger ecumenical dialogue as one voice in a larger conversation. The adequacy of these texts for speaking to as well as responding to the other voices in the conversation remains itself a subject of critical and on-going ecumenical dialogue.[119] The dialogue which has been taking place within Faith and Order is also a dialogue which has been going on between Faith and Order and other sectors or communities within the World Council and the larger ecumenical movement. The dialogue, tension, and even struggle between the ecumenical 'center' and de-centered ecumenism which has taken place within the Faith and Order movement is also a dialogue, tension, and struggle which has taken place elsewhere within the World Council. Examining the trajectory of ecumenical social witness, through the course of the Universal Council for Life and Work and the Church and Society studies of the World Council, as well as in other programs in the WCC, reveals some of these other voices within the World Council.

Notes

1. David Gill, ed., *Gathered for Life: Official Report,VI Assembly, World Council of Churches* (Geneva: WCC, 1983), p. 1.

2. Willem Adolf Visser't Hooft, ed., *The Message and Reports of the First Assembly of the World Council of Churches* (London: SCM Press, 1949), p. 13.

3. W. A. Visser't Hooft, "The Genesis of the World Council of Churches," *A History of the Ecumenical Movement, 1517- 1948*, (third edition), Ruth Rouse and Stephen Charles Neill, eds. (Geneva: WCC, 1986), p. 703.

4. W. A. Visser't Hooft, *The Genesis and Formation of the World Council of Churches* (Geneva: WCC, 1982), p. 109.

5. *Ibid.*

6. The text of the statement can be found in *ibid.*, p. 112- 120.

7. *Ibid.*, p. 113.

8. Norman Goodall, ed., *Uppsala Report 1968: Official Report of the Fourth Assembly of the World Council of Churches, Uppsala, July 4-20, 1968* (Geneva: WCC, 1968), p. 17.

9. Visser't Hooft, *Genesis and Formation*, p. 114-15.

10. *Ibid.*

11. *Ibid.*, 118.

12. *Ibid.*, p. 116.

13. *Ibid.*, p. 117.

14. Ernst Lange, *And Yet it Moves: Dream and Reality of the Ecumenical Movement*, Edwin Robinson, trans. (Belfast: Christian Journals Ltd./Geneva: WCC, 1978), p. 21. Lange comments later, p. 72, on the ambiguity which is evident in ecumenical leadership: "An ecumenical maximalism and a denominational minimalism continue unreconciled side by side in the soul of one and the same church leader."

15. Thomas F. Best, ed., *Faith and Order 1985-1989: The Commission Meeting at Budapest 1989* (Geneva: WCC, 1990), p. 3.

16. See Rouse and Neill, eds., *A History of the Ecumenical Movement*, pp. 216, 324, 345-349, and 727; William Richey Hogg, *Ecumenical Foundations: A History of the International Missionary Council and Its Nineteenth-Century Background* (New York: Harper and Row, 1952), p. 98f; Geoffrey Wainwright, *The Ecumenical Moment: Crisis and Opportunity for the Church* (Grand Rapids: Wm. B. Eerdmans Publishing Co., 1983), p. 1; Norman Goodall, *The Ecumenical Movement: What It Is and What It Does* (London: Oxford University Press, 1961), pp. 8-9; John A. Mackay, *Ecumenics: The Science of the Church Universal* (Englewood Cliffs, NJ: Prentice Hall, 1964), p. 108; "Ecumenical Diary," *Ecumenical Review*, 32/2 (1980), p. 193 for examples.

17. See David M. Paton, ed., *Breaking Barriers: Nairobi 1975, The Official Report of the Fifth Assembly of the WCC* (London: SPCK/ Grand

Rapids: Wm. B. Eerdmans Publishing Co, 1976), p. 17; Thomas F. Best, ed., *Faith and Renewal: Reports and Documents of the Commission on Faith and Order, Stavanger 1985, Norway* (Geneva: WCC, 1985), pp. 3, 17-20.

18. Hogg, *Ecumenical Foundations*, p. 101.

19. *Ibid.*, p. 68f; Karl-Heinz Dejung, *Die ökumenische Bewegung im Entwicklungskonflikt 1910-1968* (Stuttgart: Ernst Klett Verlag, 1973), p. 25, points out that significant theological differences emerged at Edinburgh between Anglo-American and German participants, particularly related to understandings of eschatology and of the Kingdom of God.

20. Hogg, *Ecumenical Foundations*, p. 104.

21. See John R. Mott, *Evangelisation of the World in this Generation* (New York: SVM, 1901); for criticism of Mott by Warneck and others, see Hans O. A. Mayr, *Einheit und Botschaft: Das ökumenische Prinzip in der Geschichte des Christlichen Studentenweltbundes, 1895-1939 mit einen Ausblick bis zur Gengenwart* (Unpub. Ph. D. Dissertation, University of Tübingen, 1975), pp. 18, 50-54, 160.

22. Hogg, *Ecumenical Foundations*, p. 111f; Kenneth Scott Latourette, "Ecumenical Bearings of the Missionary Movement and the International Missionary Council," *A History of the Ecumenical Movement*, Rouse and Neill, eds., p. 356.

23. See Ruth Rouse, *The World Student Christian Federation: A History of the First Thirty Years* (London: SCM, 1948); and Mayr, *Einheit und Botschaft*, p. 158f.

24. Hogg, *Ecumenical Foundations*, p. 112.

25. Tissington Tatlow, "The World Conference of Faith and Order," *A History of the Ecumenical Movement*, Rouse and Neill, eds., p. 406f.

26. *Ibid.*, p. 426.

27. Lukas Vischer, ed., *A Documentary History of the Faith and Order Movement 1927-1963* (St. Louis, Missouri: The Bethany Press, 1963), p. 28.

28. Tatlow, "The World Conference of Faith and Order," p. 405. See also Günther Gassmann, *Konzeptionen der Einheit in der Bewegung für Glauben und Kirchenverassung 1910-1937* (Gottingen: Vandenhoeck & Ruprecht, 1979), p. 11.

29. Tatlow, "The World Conference of Faith and Order," p. 408.

30. George H. Tavard, *Two Centuries of Ecumenism* (London: Burns and Oates, 1960), p. 99.

31. Gassmann, *Konzeptionen der Einheit*, p. 13.

32. See Samuel McCrea Cavert, *On the Road to Christian Unity: An Appraisal of the Ecumenical Movement* (New York: Harper and Row, 1961), p. 28.

33. Gassmann, *Konzeptionen der Einheit*, p. 23.

34. See Randall T. Davidson, ed., *The Five Lambeth Conferences, 1867-1908* (London: SPCK, 1920). At Lausanne, 1927, A. C. Headlam,

Bishop of Gloucester reduced the four points to three: unity of faith, union of sacrament, and union in ministry. See H. N. Bate, ed., *Faith and Order: Proceedings of the World Conference Lausanne, August 3-21, 1927* (New York: George H. Doran Co., 1927), pp.332-333. These three can be reduced to faith and order.

35. *Ibid.*, p. 31. See also the Hans-Georg Link, "Introduction: Towards Unity in the Faith," *Apostolic Faith Today: A Handbook for Study*, Hans-Georg Link, ed. (Geneva: WCC, 1985), p. 2.

36. In spite of Brent's assertion at Lausanne that their purpose was clarification and not achieving a united church, suspicions to the contrary lingered. "Some of the Americans thought that the Conference aimed at achieving a plan for a united church before it dispersed, and some of the Orthodox were never disabused of the same idea." Tatlow, "The World Conference on Faith and Order," p. 423.

37. *Ibid.*, p. 417.

38. *Ibid.*

39. Constantin G. Patelos, ed., *The Orthodox Church in the Ecumenical Movement: Documents and Statements 1902-1975* (Geneva: WCC, 1978), p. 30; and Nicolas Zernov, "The Eastern Churches and the Ecumenical Movement in the Twentieth Century," *A History of the Ecumenical Movement*, Rouse and Neill, eds., p. 649f.

40. Patelos, ed., *The Orthodox Church in the Ecumenical Movement*, p. 43.

41. Tatlow, "The World Conference on Faith and Order," p. 418.

42. Vasil T. Istavridis, "The Work of Germanos Strenopoulos in the Field of Inter-Orthodox and Inter-Church Relations," *Ecumenical Review* 11/2 (1959), p. 295.

43. Patelos, ed., *The Orthodox Church in the Ecumenical Movement*, p. 79.

44. *Ibid.*

45. *Ibid.*, p. 80.

46. *Ibid.*, p. 81.

47. *Ibid.*, p. 85.

48. Vischer, ed., *A Documentary History of the Faith and Order Movement*, p. 136.

49. Patelos, ed., *The Orthodox Church in the Ecumenical Movement*, p. 95. Theodore Stylianopoulos suggests in response to *BEM* that *metanoia* is indeed a permanent vocation of the Orthodox Church, contrary to the above quotation; but it is a concrete challenge to submit to the divine will, and hence a call to the Orthodox to become more Orthodox. See his article, "The Question of the Reception of BEM in the Orthodox Church in the Light of its Ecumenical Commitment," *Orthodox Perspectives on Baptism, Eucharist, and Ministry*, Gennadios Limouris and Nomikos Michael Vaporis, eds. (Brookline, Mass: Holy Cross Orthodox Press, 1985), p. 110.

50. Patelos, ed., *The Orthodox Church in the Ecumenical Movement.*, p. 98.

The quotation is from the Orthodox Statement at New Delhi, 1961.

51. Gassmann, *Konzeptionen der Einheit*, p. 31.

52. Patelos, ed., *The Orthodox Church in the Ecumenical Movement*, p. 98.

53. Istavridis, "The Work of Germanos Strenopoulos," p. 296.

54. Vasil T. Istavridis, "The Orthodox Churches in the Ecumenical Movement 1948-1968," *The Ecumenical Advance: A History of the Ecumenical Movement, Volume 2 1948-1968*, Harold E. Fey, ed., (second edition) (Geneva: WCC, 1986), p. 297, 307.

55. Theodore Stylianopoulos, "The Question of the Reception of BEM in the Orthodox Church in Light of its Ecumenical Commitment," *Orthodox Perspectives on Baptism, Eucharist, and Ministry*, Limouris and Vaporis, eds., p. 120 (emphasis original).

56. *Ibid.*, p. 121.

57. *Ibid.*, p. 126.

58. Patelos, ed., *The Orthodox Church in the Ecumenical Movement*, p. 97. John J. McDonnell, *A Comparison of the Concept of Ecumenism as Found in the Documentary Thought of the World Council of Churches and Vatican II* (Unpub. Ph. D. dissertation, New York University, 1978), p. 41, asserts: "The Modern Ecumenical Movement begun among Protestants and the World Council of Churches is wholly Protestant in origin." The Vatican-World Council discussion is predominantly a Catholic-Protestant discussion; he recognizes minimal Orthodox contribution to the WCC.

59. Vischer, ed., *A Documentary History of the Faith and Order Movement*, p. 170.

60. Stylianopoulos, "The Question of the Reception of BEM," p. 123 (emphasis added).

61. For Orthodox concerns about the historical relativity implied in the ecumenical movement, see "Christian Unity and Ecumenism," *Documents of the Orthodox Church in America* (New York: Holy Synod of the Orthodox Church in America, 1973). Archbishop Iakovos Koukoujis noted: " For us, tradition does not come under the heading of Church History. Tradition is a stream which flows through the Church from the very beginning," in Patelos, ed., *The Orthodox Church in the Ecumenical Movement*, p. 217.

62. This Christological agreement provided the basis for the WCC in 1948, amended in 1961 through the addition of a Trinitarian doxology. Simonson traces the basis to the YMCA movement, and notes that allegiance to Jesus Christ constituted "the one clear common denominator that legitimated [the delegates at Lausanne] being together." Conrad Simonson, *The Christology of the Faith and Order Movement* (Leiden: E. J. Brill, 1972), p. 23.

63. Oliver S. Tomkins, ed., *The Third World Conference on Faith and Order Held at Lund August 15th to 28th, 1952* (London: SCM Press, 1953), p. 15 (emphasis original).

64. Norman Goodall, *Ecumenical Progress: A Decade of Change in the*

Ecumenical Movement 1961-1971 (London: Oxford University Press, 1972), p. 67.

65. Vischer, *A Documentary History of the Faith and Order Movement*, p. 94.

66. *Ibid.*, p. 96.

67. "The Report of the Theological Commission on Traditions and Tradition," *Faith and Order Findings: The Final Report of the Theological Commissions to the Fourth World Conference on Faith and Order, Montreal 1963* (London: SCM Press, 1963), p. 4f.

68. *Ibid.*, p. 10.

69. *Ibid.*, p. 13.

70. *Ibid.*, p. 9.

71. *Ibid.*, p. 15.

72. *Ibid.*, p. 19.

73. *Ibid.*, p. 18.

74. *Ibid.*, p. 22.

75. *Ibid.*, p. 46.

76. *Ibid.*, p. 49.

77. The phrase is used by Patrick W. Fuerth to describe the discussion at the Uppsala Assembly, 1968, concerning catholicity. See Fuerth, *The Concept of Catholicity in the Documents of the World Council of Churches 1948-1968: A Historical Study with Systematic-Theological Reflections* (Rome: Editrice Anselmiana, 1973), p. 128.

78. W. A. Visser't Hooft, ed., *New Delhi Report: The Third Assembly of the World Council of Churches, 1961* (New York: Association Press, 1962), p. 131.

79.   See Link, *Apostolic Faith Today*; World Council of Churches Commission on Faith and Order, *Confessing One Faith: Towards an Ecumenical Explication of the Apostolic Faith as Expressed in the Nicene-Constantinopolitan Creed (381)* (Geneva: WCC, 1981); Hans-Georg Link, *One God, One Lord, One Spirit: On the Explication of the Apostolic Faith Today* (Geneva: WCC, 1988);   And Best, ed. *Faith and Order 1985-1989*, pp. 104-133.

80. Best, ed., *Faith and Order 1985-1989*, p. 129; see also the Faith and Order study conference on the *filioque* in the creed, Lukas Vischer, ed., *Spirit of God, Spirit of Christ* (Geneva: WCC, 1981).

81. Best, ed., *Faith and Order 1985-1989*, p. 138.

82. Faith and Order Commission, *New Directions in Faith and Order Bristol 1967: Reports -- Minutes -- Documents* (Geneva: WCC, 1968), p. 52.

83. *Ibid.* (emphasis mine).

84. Charles C. West, "Ecumenics, Church and Society: The Tradition of Life and Work," *Ecumenical Review* 39/4 (1987), p. 464.

85. *Ibid.*, pp. 464-465.

86. "Faith and Order: Our Oneness in Christ and our Disunity as Churches," para. 2, states: "The New Testament conceives of the unity of the Church, not as sociological, but as having its essential reality in Christ Himself and in His indissoluble unity with His people...." Vischer, ed., *A Documentary History of the Faith and Order Movement*, p. 132.

87. *Koinonia* emerged as a major theme from the Seventh Assembly of the WCC, held in Canberra, Australia, 1991. see Michael Kinnamon, ed., *Signs of the Spirit: Official Report Seventh Assembly* (Geneva: WCC / Grand Rapids: Wm. B. Eerdmans, 1991), esp. "Report of Section III," pp. 96-99, and the Faith and Order statement, "The Unity of the Church as Koinonia: Gift and Calling," pp. 172-174. On the concept of 'conciliar fellowship' see Aram Keshishian, *Conciliar Fellowship: A Common Goal* (Geneva: WCC, 1992).

88. For the text of the document, see *Ecumenical Trends* 21/7 (July/August, 1992).

89. Irmgard Kindt-Siegwalt, "Has the Emperor no Clothes?" *The Ecumenical Review* 41/2 (April, 1989), pp. 213, n1. On the critique of the political character of creeds in the European free church traditions, see James A. Nash, "Political Conditions for an Ecumenical Confession: A Protestant Contribution to the Emerging Dialogue," *Journal of Ecumenical Studies* 25/2 (Spring, 1988), pp. 241-261.

90. See for example Hogg, *Ecumenical Foundations*, p. 396, n91, regarding non-European delegates to early ecumenical mission conferences, and Kuncheria Pathil, *Models in Ecumenical Dialogue: A Study in the Methodological Development in the Commission on "Faith and Order" of the World Council of Churches* (Bangalore: Dharmaram Publications, 1981), p. 288, n. 125, concerning non-European delegates at early Faith and Order gatherings.

91. See Melanie A. May, *Bonds of Unity: Women, Theology, and the Worldwide Church* (Atlanta: Scholars Press, 1989), pp.5-6.

92. Visser't Hooft, *New Delhi Report*, p. 116.

93. H.N. Bate, ed., *Faith and Order: Proceedings of the World Conference, Lausanne, Aug. 3-21, 1927* (New York: George H. Doran Co.), p. 372. See also the discussion by May, *Bonds of Unity*, pp. 59-60.

94. Bate, *Lausanne*, p. 421.

95. *Ibid.*, p. 493.

96. *Ibid.*, p. 499.

97. *Ibid.*, p. 498.

98. *Ibid.*, p. 461.

99. Tomkins, *The Third World Conference, Lund, 1952* , p. 33

100. *Ibid.*, p. 85.

101. *Ibid.*, p. 86.

102. *New Directions in Faith and Order*, p. 25.

103. *Ibid.* (emphasis mine).

104. Margaret Nash, *Ecumenical Movement in the 1960s* (Johannesburg:

Ravan Press, 1975), esp. pp. 309-359 discusses the impact of anti-colonialism and the struggle for liberation within the ecumenical movement in general, and specifically at the Uppsala Assembly in 1968.

105. *New Directions in Faith and Order*, p. 139

106. *Ibid.*

107. Geiko Müller-Fahrenholz, *Unity in Today's World, The Faith and Order Studies on "Unity of the Church - Unity of Humankind"* (Geneva: WCC, 1978); Grennadios Limouris, ed., *Church, Kingdom, World: The Church as Mystery and Prophetic Sign* (Geneva: WCC, 1986); and Best, ed. *Faith and Order 1985-1989*, pp. 134-164.

108. Limouris, *Church, Kingdom, World*, p. 12.

109. See Müller-Fahrenholz, *Unity in Today's World*, p. 67f.

110. See Pathil, *Models in Ecumenical Dialogue*, pp. 346-388.

111. Limouris, *Church, Kingdom, World*, p. 92.

112. *Sexism in the 1970s: Discrimination Against Women, A Report of a World Council of Churches Consultation West Berlin 1974* (Geneva: WCC, 1975).

113. Constance F. Parvey, ed., *Community of Women and Men in the Church: The Sheffield Report* (Geneva: WCC, 1983). See also Melanie A. May, *Bonds of Unity*, esp. chapter IV.

114. See in particular the critical challenge set forth by Bentley G. Hicks, "The End of Confessions or a New Confession? The Ecumenical Tradition in Faith and Order," *Ecumenical Review* 41/2 (April 1989), pp. 266-275.

115. Limouris, *Church, Kingdom, World*, p. 181.

116. Melanie A. May, "Response to Wolfhart Pannenberg's 'The Future Role of Faith and Order'" in Best, ed. *Faith and Order 1985-1989*, p. 231.

117. Aloysius Pieris, *An Asian Theology of Liberation* (Maryknoll: Orbis Books, 1988).

118. Nelle Morton, "Towards a Whole Theology," *Sexism Against Women in the 1970s*, p. 64.

119. See Hicks, "The End of Confessions or a New Confession?" and Melanie A. May, "The Ordination of Women: The Churches' Responses to *Baptism, Eucharist, and Ministry*," *Journal of Ecumenical Studies* 26/2 (Spring 1989), pp. 251-269, for two critical explorations of the meaning, necessity, and lack of dialogue between Faith and Order and the churches.

Chapter 3:

Ecumenical *Praxis* in a World of Difference

Jack: If We're to begin thinking dialogically, we must first be suspicious of discourse that universalizes, idealizes, or prematurely identifies with the Other.
    -- R. Lane Kauffmann

Whole reminds us not to repeat another's speech, given to us to speak as if it were our speech, leaving our speech unspoken, and leaving the Church poorer without us.   -- Nelle Morton

Respondeo etsi mutabor.   --Eugen Rosenstock-Huessy[1]

1. The Search for Ecumenical Coherence

The Sixth Assembly of the World Council of Churches, meeting in Vancouver, Canada in 1983 foresaw the period laying before it as one impelled by the imperatives of growing together into unity, justice and peace. Central to that task, according to the Programme Guidelines Committee of the Assembly, would be "vital and coherent theology." Over its four decades of existence, the diversity of WCC programs and activities and the range of ecumenical accountabilities to which the Council responds have raised the question of whether or not it is possible to discern an ecumenical center or theological core to the WCC. How have the diverse theological perspectives and programs of the World Council interrelated? It what way does the Council continue to hold together the various and sometimes distinctive understandings of the meaning and purpose of the ecumenical movement? What

happens when conflict irrupts between programs or between churches
in the WCC? These were questions that led to the search for "a vital
and coherent" ecumenical theology through the 1980s.[2]

At first glance it would appear that the call for coherence in the
Council, and perhaps in the ecumenical movement in general, is a call
for convergences along the lines pursued by Faith and Order in its
section on unity. As I have noted above for many ecumenists the Faith
and Order movement, especially in its work toward the visible unity of
the Church, is perceived to be the heart of the ecumenical movement.
Some might even argue that the search for visible unity constitutes the
full meaning and purpose of the ecumenical movement. Accordingly
then the diversity of programs and activities pursued by the World
Council or even by other ecumenical organizations could only be
viewed as being secondary at best and disruptive of the central
ecumenical task at worst. Programs such as the Sub-Unit on Women,
the Programme to Combat Racism, or Dialogue with People of Other
Faiths which are informed by contextual theologies seem to some at
least to be responsible for fostering the contradictions and incoherence
perceived in the World Council.[3]

It is important to recall here that the Faith and Order movement itself
has not been isolated from the conflicts and contentions of historical and
cultural diversity. We have seen that in the search for the unity of the
church voices from the margins have been heard continuously, that
during a period in which Faith and Order has realized its most
important accomplishments, the contextual challenges generated by the
search for unity and renewal in the world have not been absent. These
latter voices and challenges continuously disrupt the 'center-periphery'
alignments in ecumenism, whether they be of 'North-South,' or of
'Tradition-traditions.'   The diversity of ecumenical voices have
continually opened Faith and Order to the divergence of ecclesial
communities and experiences in the world. The search for visible unity
is indeed one of the central tasks of the Faith and Order movement, but
it has not been carried out in isolation from other tasks and pursuits that
are informed by a different imperative. There has been a dialogical
relationship even in Faith and Order between the search for visible unity
and the renewal of the churches in their diversity.

Faith and Order has not been unaffected by the contextual theological
issues that have affected the whole World Council, nor is it a 'center,'
that can relegate to the ecumenical 'periphery' concerns for liberation
and justice.   The same dialogical imperatives that have been

experienced within Faith and Order impinge upon the relationship between Faith and Order and other ecumenical programs, within the WCC itself, and beyond it in the larger ecumenical movement. The need for a clearer understanding of these imperatives has compelled the Council to seek a vital and coherent theological framework that is capable of embracing the diversity of ecumenical purposes without subsuming them under a singular, dominant theme. Implicitly avoiding a 'center-periphery' model of ecumenism that would reproduce the domination that gives rise to incoherence, injustice and death, the Council has resisted defining a theological center beyond that given in the "Basis" of the WCC. It has sought instead to find a framework in which differences and diversity can 'cohere' and 'co-inhere' in ways that are mutually accountable. As Bonino has pointed out,

> Such coherence does not exclude vitality and diversity. On the contrary, it presupposes them. The mandate of the Assembly and the Central Committee excludes "a normative ecumenical theology" where differences and divergences would be reconciled or eliminated. This would be undesirable and anti-ecumenical.[4]

Bonino goes on to note that divergences, differences, and even conflicts within the World Council are not produced, but are reproduced there. The place of their production, of their creation, is in the social, cultural and confessional conflicts among Christians and the churches. "The WCC *reflects* them"; it is a mirror held to ecclesial and ecclesiastical diversity in the world today. The danger, Bonino argues, is to think that covering the mirror eliminates the diversity of the churches in the world. A similar warning is raised by Melanie May concerning the ecumenical quest for a common history and theology that would overcome pluralism and differences. Too often such an ecumenical vision "is set on reconciliation secured as differences deemed divisive are transcended." May continues,

> To take context seriously is to take difference seriously. This is also the challenge. The challenge is to conceive unity not in terms of conformity or constraint, but with regard to difference. The challenge is to cultivate bonds of unity that celebrate rather than condemn difference, to be ready to recognize and receive difference as integral to the fullness of life together.[5]

The search for a vital and coherent theology is thus a search not for an ecumenical center which reconciles difference by transcending them, either in the sense of finding a singular spiritual truth beyond them, or in the Hegelian dialectical sense of overcoming them historically (*Aufhebung*). It is a search for a framework that cultivates diversity-in-community, fostering distinctness without domination, and recognizing the irreducible character of difference over identity. M.M. Thomas calls this "a theological framework which allows many operative theological approaches to coexist and interact with each other, thus maintaining a dialogic community of theologies."[6] It continues the theological search for the *koinonia* of churches first called for in the 1919 encyclical of the Ecumenical Patriarch, raised again in the Toronto Statement of 1952, and set before the churches by the Fifth World Conference on Faith and Order in Santiago de Compostela, 1993.

If truly ecumenical, this framework would be one in which differences cohere and co-inhere in mutuality and *koinonia*. It would be an open framework, open to a future that will be different from the pasts we bring to the ecumenical encounter. This is the sense in which an ecumenical framework for theology needs to be vital, for vitality is the living quality of being open to change and the future. In this sense even a truly ecumenical council which succeeded in articulating a form of doctrinal consensus among the existing churches of the world would still not be able to lay claim to having provided the framework for a vital ecumenical theology, for such a council could not foresee the issues that will confront the churches in the future to adequately address them. The search for vitality in ecumenical theology is not only a search for a framework which embraces the irreducible diversity and difference among churches. It is one open to the new of God's time.

To engage in vital and coherent theology the WCC not only must seek a framework that enables diversity and difference in community and remains open to the future. It must do so on behalf of, and at times even in opposition to the churches that are represented within it. The WCC does not exist apart from its member churches, and without their representation it literally has no life. It does not speak for any of the churches, and it can only act on behalf of the churches as the churches collectively empower it. Nevertheless the Council does also speak *to* the churches, at times in a prophet voice and in a manner intended to move them toward one another in unity and community but also toward justice in their diverse contexts. In doing so the World Council is not only serving as a forum for critical dialogue among the churches, but it is engaging dialogically with the churches, responding to them and seeking responses. It serves the churches in this manner (its task of *diakonia*), which is nevertheless a critical service. The critical dialogue or dialogical criticism of the World Council of Churches is not a speaking for the churches, nor to them as their superior Other. It is a speaking with and among them, as communities of Christian believers grow together or apart through time.

In this sense the World Council of Churches is a site for ongoing ecumenical conversations. The pronouncements, studies, and actions which it issues carry on the dialogue or conversation that are experienced more intensely in the assemblies, conferences, and meetings of the Council and its units. The manner in which texts such as *BEM* undergo redaction through various stages, in response to previous responses of churches and movements themselves responding to various contextual situations and traditions, suggests a complex, on-going dialogue crossing time and geographical locations. This dialogical *praxis* is characteristic of every aspect of ecumenical work. Every unit and program in the WCC, its assemblies and its conferences, and especially its texts, manifest their dialogical mode of being.

The search for a vital and coherent theology is a search for a more critical framework that would sustain dialogical relationships among diverse projects which are often in tension and even at odds with one another. The search to articulate the theological basis of ecumenics is a familiar concern within the ecumenical movement, as ubiquitous as *crisis* seems to be. The search for a vital and coherent theology is perhaps the most recent manifestation in the WCC of a recurring reflection that emerges from the crisis-character of ecumenics. Ongoing self-reflection is a *praxis* that is called forth by the very nature of the ecumenical movement as both expression and agent of change. It is also a *praxis* in response to the changing character of the world. The need for a vital and coherent ecumenical theology has been perceived in reflecting upon the diversity of *praxes* in the World Council and the ecumenical movement, and the theological framework when found will presumably contribute to guiding the Council as well as churches in their *praxis* in the world. It is here ultimately that the deciding factors for vitality and coherence are to be found: in the living relationships of churches amidst the world.

To see the work of Faith and Order as a critical *praxis* in this manner raises for consideration its relationship to the living communities of faith which exist in the world. Considering the work of Faith and Order as a *praxis* asks about theological discourse in its ecclesiastical settings or contexts (which is to say its social, political, economic, cultural, and linguistic location). The *praxis* of theology is encountered in the living reality of the churches' worship (liturgy), as well as in the service in the world that churches carry on. The issues that have occupied Faith and Order have primarily concerned the unity of churches in worship, and secondarily the process through which churches forge their identities and reproduce themselves. Faith and Order has been minimally concerned with the *praxis* of the churches beyond their own doors, engaging in struggles for justice and confronting the demands for cultural transformation. In the ecumenical movement the theological *praxis* of the churches in the world has most often been associated with the movement known prior to 1948 as Life and Work, and since then in various contexts as Church and Society.

The movement for Life and Work emerged during the first quarter of the twentieth century from the search in churches of the West for a vital and coherent response to the new realities confronting modern European civilization. It was a task that continued to occupy the WCC through its study unit, Church and Society. The World Council did not carry out its search for vitality and coherence in the post-War world of Europe and North America only through study and deliberations, however, but engaged in direct ecumenical programs of service and relief with and on behalf of member churches as well. The witness and service of the Council embodied ecumenical *praxis* in areas of social relief, international political affairs, and health programs. By the end of the World Council's second decade, however, the coherence of its *praxis* in the world had begun to come apart as the Council sought to respond to the demands of a post-colonial world on the one hand and its own internal development on the other.

Since the 1960s the tensions and contradictions within the Council have increased, reflecting the tensions and contradictions among the churches and in the world. It is here, in ecumenical *praxis* amidst the multiplicity of communities and critical situations of the world today, that incoherence is most often encountered. It is here that the Council's search for vitality is most pressing. So it is here, to the *praxis* of ecumenical witness and service in the world, that I turn in search of the framework for a vital and coherent dialogical community.

2. The Search for Coherence through Reconstruction of Christendom

During the month of August, 1925 more than six hundred delegates representing Protestant and Orthodox churches from around the world gathered in Stockholm, Sweden for a Universal Christian Conference on Life and Work. Five years in the planning, the Conference represented the desire of churches and leaders from several continents to address with a unified voice the situation that confronted Christianity in the modern world. No church leader felt the demands for such a witness more strongly than the Archbishop of Uppsala, Nathan Söderblom, who was the single most important driving force behind the organization of Stockholm and the movement for Life and Work.

At the opening session of the 1925 Conference the King of Sweden welcomed the delegates from thirty-seven nations by pointing out to them the importance of their work.

Sixteen hundred years ago, the trusted men of the Church of that time met in Nicea to give expression to their faith in our Saviour and in the being and revelation of God. The meeting now held here, more than one and a half thousand years later, has a not less important aim.[7]

His vaunted comparison with Nicea was echoed in the reply to the King by Photius, Patriarch of Alexandria on behalf of the Orthodox delegates:

[As you spoke] I saw, as in a trance, the great Emperor Constantine opening with a speech inspired from above the first Ecumenical Synod....[8]

The invocation of the memory of Nicea and the unity it represented was heard again at the close of the Conference in the concluding service held in the Uppsala Cathedral. After the sermon preached by Archbishop Söderblom, Photius of Alexandria ascended the high alter and recited the Nicene Creed in Greek.

These echoes of Nicea heard in Stockholm 1600 after that original ecumenical council provide an important clue for understanding both the vision and the reality of the ecumenical movement for Life and Work. Stockholm's purpose was to explore the basis for uniting the divided churches of Protestant and Orthodox Christianity in areas of common

practical work in the modern age. Sometimes referred to as the "Nicea
of social ethics," Stockholm 1925 reflected more than any other
ecumenical conference this century the memory of the Council of Nicea
in 325, symbol of the ancient church united under Constantine.

The 'world' that the Stockholm conference addressed was the
modern, industrial world of European civilization. Rapid social changes
were taking place during the first quarter of the twentieth century.
Industry and technology had continued to expand at a rapid pace,
creating new forms of social dislocation and conflict. The world-wide
expansion of capitalism had given rise to a new era of global
imperialism on the part of European, and now U.S., colonial powers.
Developments in transportation and communication had brought
communities and nations closer together than previous generations had
imagined possible. At the same time rapid social changes had resulted
in what many perceived to be growing moral problems in the Western
world, moral issues the churches were proving ineffective in addressing.
But above all else, the devastating memory of modern warfare
witnessed by the European nations on a massive scale between 1914
and 1917 created an unprecedented challenge for Stockholm 1925.

The call to the Conference that had been sent out in 1924 listed
problems of industry, property, class conflict, nationalism, and
international peace among the chief topics for consideration at
Stockholm. The Conference was to provide an opportunity for churches
in the world to devise more effective means of addressing these issues
by acting together. The weaknesses of divided Christendom had
become apparent to those who were concerned for the witness of the
churches in the modern Western world. Stockholm was to provide an
opportunity for these churches to begin to speak and act together again
concerning the social and moral issues of the day.

Lurking in the background in the planning for Stockholm, in the
1925 Conference itself, and through the ensuing movement for Life and
Work, was a memory of the role the churches (or the one Church) had
once played in the construction of the Western world of European
civilization. The memory of Christendom, of a united church
effectively shaping society and the culture and providing direction for
social and moral life, created a painful contrast with the divided and
ineffective witness of the many churches of a modern European
civilization dominated by secular ideologies and becoming progressively
de-Christianized in its deepest ethos. At the beginning of the twentieth

century Ernst Troeltsch, in *The Social Teaching of the Christian Churches*, had perceived the collapse of the cultural synthesis of Western European Christendom that had begun several centuries earlier in the European Enlightenment and had become apparent during the course of the nineteenth century. Whatever illusions had remained concerning the 'Christian' nature of the Western nations and 'Christian influence' upon European civilization had been shattered by the War.

By the second decade of the twentieth century a significant number of church leaders had begun to realize Troeltsch's point, that all is indeed tottering as the cultural synthesis in which the dominant churches participated had came apart. As Arthur J. Brown said in his opening reply to the King, "The whole structure of civilization is menaced."[9] But if the domain with which the Stockholm conference was concerned was what Troeltsch had called "the concept of modern civilization as developed in Europe and America," it nevertheless was perceived by the planners and the delegates of the conference as presenting the most critical challenge to modern Christianity.[10] Despite the fact that even Söderblom had come to realize "that the days of European hegemony were numbered," Stockholm gave no hint of pretending to be other than a Conference concerned with the social reconstruction of European Christendom.[11] As Bengt Sundkler pointed out in his biography of Nathan Söderblom, "Europe was the horizon" of Stockholm, 1925. Sundkler quotes, uneasily, the prayer of Emanuel Linderholm with which Söderblom ended his book on the Stockholm Conference:

> Particularly we praise Thee for that Thou has entrusted Thy Gospel to our continent and its daughter-nations beyond the seas. Bestow now, O God, upon all these peoples who rule over most of the globe, to remember the greatness and responsibility of thy calling.[12]

The 1925 Stockholm Conference, and the Universal Christian Council for Life and Work to which it gave rise, were not the first international and interconfessional attempts to organize a united church response to the pressing social issues the day. Earlier organizations such as the Associated Councils of Churches in the British and German Empires for Fostering Friendly Relations between the Two Peoples, and the World Alliance for Promoting International Friendship through the Churches had paved the way for developing better understanding among the national churches of Europe and North America during the first decades of the century. Plans for a comprehensive Christian conference dealing with issues of inter-European peace had already been proposed prior to the war of 1914, and the war itself gave particular urgency to Archbishop Nathan Söderblom's efforts toward what would eventually become the Universal Conference on Life and Work.[13]

It was clear to Söderblom that the need for a united Christian response to international problems was too great to await the day when the various Christian churches would be united in confession. It was equally clear that it was necessary for the churches, and not individual Christians acting on their own behalf, to work together toward a unified response to social problems. The path to unity that Söderblom envisioned was that of practical Christianity carried out collectively by the churches. As the motto for the Stockholm conference, Söderblom proclaimed, "dogma divides, service unites."[14] While not necessarily minimizing the significant matters of dogma and confession that separated the churches, Life and Work sought to achieve cooperation among diverse national Christian traditions in their social *praxis*. At Stockholm Metropolitan Germanos distinguished between "the narrower notion of unity" in which full faith was shared, and "the wider unity" of all who accept the revelation of God in Jesus Christ. Within this wider unity, friendship and cooperation were expected to begin breaking down barriers that separated churches.[15]

The issues of nationalism and warfare that occupied the Life and Work movement were particularly relevant to those Protestant churches which were established, or national churches. Industrialization and capitalism on the other hand were of concern to virtually all of the Protestant churches in Life and Work, for these churches as a whole had historically supported and benefitted from the economic developments of global capitalism. The massive economic expansion of capitalism among the nations of the North Atlantic, and the accompanying political and cultural revolutions carried out by the European bourgeoisie, had in most cases won the silent concurrence if not the outright support of the Protestant churches in these lands. Such silent and vocal support for the economics of capitalism continues to be characteristic of many sectors within the Protestant churches still today. As Bonino has pointed out, "The Protestant churches - according to their different types and not without conflict - accompany, correct, strengthen and give expression to this historical project [of capitalism]."[16]

By the beginning of the twentieth century the magnitude of the problem had become apparent to many in the churches of the North

Atlantic. The manner in which Western commerce and businesses were penetrating all the lands of the earth and every dimension of life had become a topic of concern and debate within many sectors of the Christian communities. In response to the effects of industrialization in North America the Social Gospel movement emerged, for instance. European Christians began to explore distinctive forms of Christian Socialism. Organizations as the YMCA and the YWCA responded to industrial capitalism on a global scale by developing new forms of ministry to those within it, at the same time developing structurally in ways that reflected it. In many ways modern capitalism (along with its concomitant technological developments) had provided the prompting, but also the glue, for the new modes of ecclesiastical unity sought by the churches. By the beginning of the twentieth century capitalism had already begun to achieve an economic and social unity on a global scale, and it was this as much as anything else that had called forth from the churches a corresponding desire for unity in responsive service. As Duff noted, the practical theological work of the Life and Work movement, and later of the World Council, sought a common ethos and a common body of Christian criteria by which the churches could meet the challenge of the modern age.[17]

At first glance it might seem that the unity effected by capitalism would contradict the political disunity which was the result of the modern European nationalism that was evident in the war of 1914-1918. Anglican Bishop J. A. Kempthorne at Stockholm in 1925 had in fact pointed to these seemingly divergent trends. He criticized the divisive character of nationalism, evident in the weak support for the League of Nations; and then spoke of modern commerce which had externally unified the world so that "We are crushed into one."[18] The answer he proposed for both the disunity and crushing unity was a deeper, inward, spiritual unity set forth in the Kingdom of God.

By the next Universal Conference on Life and Work, at Oxford in 1937, however, it had become apparent that certain forms of modern nationalism were also capable of a totalizing unity. By the late 1930s nationalist and internationalist political ideologies had demonstrated a capacity to achieve unity through conquest as thoroughly as the economic domination demonstrated by capitalism. Within the Life and Work movement, totalitarianism was recognized to be another form of the unifying political spirit of modern European society.[19] The absence of German delegates from Oxford, prevented from attending by the Nazi government, underscored the demonic aspects of these modern unifying political forces. Although Life and Work did not adequately come to grips with the full character of the modern state during these years (the issue still occupies the World Council in certain respects today) the disturbing reality of modern political life had begun to confront the illusion of the so-called 'Christian nation' that was so deeply embedded in the memory of Western Christendom.[20]

Theological concerns about the character of the modern state and national European powers was not confined to the movement for Life and Work during the first decades of the twentieth century. Other sectors of the emerging ecumenical movement were also coming to grips with questions concerning the modern nation, as they were dealing with issues of Western commerce and industrial development. The most explicit discussions were taking place within the ecumenical arenas concerned with missions, however, for it was here that the points of conflict between European colonial power and non-European anti-imperialism were most directly affecting the work of the churches. Commission VII of the 1910 World Missionary Conference in Edinburgh, entitled "Missions and Government," had been assigned the task of surveying the relationship between missions and Western governments. Locating the issue within the theological tradition of Church and State in the West, it drew the conclusion that in their separate spheres missions and governments should nevertheless cooperate. German delegates tended to maintain a greater distance between the spheres, while American delegates raised more criticisms of government activities. Both German and American delegates felt comfortable with the phrase, "Christian nations," however.

Bishop Brent, participant in the 1910 Edinburgh Conference and future organizer of the Faith and Order Conference, articulated a political theology that was characteristic of the Edinburgh Conference as a whole, if not for the churches of the North Atlantic at that time:

> I would assert that it is as much the responsibility of Christian Colonial Governments to protect and promote public morals as it is the responsibility of the Christian Church itself. Christian government is a part of the Kingdom of God, at least it is an instrument through which the Kingdom of God works.[21]

The missionary attitude toward Western governments was not entirely devoid of any critical aspect. At the same session noted above that Brent addressed other delegates spoke of problems with European colonial governments who, in the missionary's view, actively as well as passively hindered the task of evangelism. The British colonial government in Northern Nigeria, for instance, was accused of actually favoring Islam, giving contracts to Muslim firms or jobs to Muslim workers over Christians and traditional African religionists ("pagans").[22] Yet despite the examples of European governments failing to demonstrate active support for missions, conference delegates maintained the terminology of "Christian nation."

The political theology which informed the delegates at Edinburgh in 1910, as it would those at Stockholm in 1925, remained within the circle of the European synthesis of church and state. Formal distinction between the two was indeed often voiced, but that was not necessarily to say that church and state were to be separated. A large number of participants in the ecumenical movement -- primarily Anglicans and Germans -- represented official state churches. But among the vast majority of delegates, Protestant as well as Orthodox, the problem of the relationship of church to state had most often been resolved in favor of the church acting as a moral soul on behalf of the state. The ecumenical task of bringing Christian principles to bear upon the political life of a Western civilization now divided into particular nation-states often began by assuming the validity of previous European political theological thought.

The role the early ecumenical movement tended to embrace was that of being a lobbyist for Christian spiritual values, acting on an international level on behalf of the values upon which secularized Western governments were supposedly founded. After the War of 1914-1917, J. H. Oldham, who had played a central role in organizing the World Missionary Conference in 1910 and was to become Chairman of the Universal Council for Life and Work in the 1930s, acted on behalf of the Continuation Committee of the Edinburgh Conference (soon to become the International Missionary Conference) as a lobbyist among the European powers at the Paris Peace Conference.[23] Oldham's principle concern was to secure the interests of foreign missions in the new power alignments after the war, which meant securing such rights as protection of mission properties. The single most significant right secured by those representing missionary interests before the European powers in Paris was that of "free exercise of religion," which provided the spiritual cornerstone for the fuller Western dogma of "individual rights," and later, of "human rights," articulated within political arenas.[24]

In the search for a new international order after the war years of

1930-1945 John Mackay recognized a deeper theological search for a new political center which could unify the world. This theological center, he proposed, would be the contribution of the ecumenical movement. "The problem which national governments have to solve, consists in finding a principle, or center of unity, for collective understanding and action," he wrote in *Theology Today*.[25]   The international community was without a center, and was seeking unity amidst its diversity. The ecumenical church, on the other hand, starts with its center of unity in Jesus Christ and moves from "the center to the circumference." A common Christian approach to the secular order was emerging within the ecumenical movement, he suggested.

The term ecumenical stood alongside "another word, no less representative" of the modern world's search for unity, according to Mackay. That other word was "totalitarianism," a movement which unifies by obliterating the distinction between society and state. The challenge of totalitarianism was behind Mackay's discussion of the 1937 Oxford Life and Work conference theme, "let the Church be the Church."[26]   The Oxford conference had been confronted with the challenge of the church's witness in a hostile state, even as it was conscious of the church as a world- wide movement. The "Message from the Conference" had summed up concisely the ecclesiastical discovery it had made: "The first duty of the church, and its greatest service to the world, is that it be in very deed the church."[27]

The reports and studies that preceded the 1937 Conference, as well as the discussions that occurred at Oxford, reflect some of the most incisive and coherent work in social ethics and theology heard by the churches of that day from the ecumenical movement. Oxford's agenda was quite full, covering issues such as race relations, economic life, class struggles, warfare, and the rise of the modern ideologies. The overall intention of the Conference was to address "the life-and-death struggle between Christian faith and the secular and pagan tendencies of our time."[28]   And at a number of places the Conference indeed realized a prophetic vision which was far ahead of the majority in the churches of its day. Concerning economic life in the modern West, for instance, Oxford called for Christian efforts in industrial society to "be turned from charitable paternalism to the realization of more equal justice in the distribution of wealth."[29]   In one of the passages which continues to resound through ecumenical discourse of the present, Oxford issued a call in 1937:

To all Christians, to a more passionate and costly concern for the outcast, the underprivileged, the persecuted and the despised in the community and beyond the community.... The church has been called into existence by God not for itself but for the world. Only by going out of itself in the work of Christ can it find unity in itself.[30]

The clarity of prophetic vision articulated at the Oxford Conference remains challenging to the ecumenical movement today. Nevertheless the horizon of the world within which Oxford spoke remained the (even for its time) limited and limiting horizon of the North Atlantic political-economic community. Several times the Other of the dominant European Self was referred to at Oxford, on one occasion as the "primitive peoples, especially those of Africa, on whom the impact of the West has fallen with shattering force...."[31] On several occasions Oxford referred to concerns of youth, and more rarely to those of women, within the modern Western world. The most consistent issue in this regard that Oxford addressed was that of racial relations in the industrial world, especially in the United States. The moments in which the horizon of Oxford opened up to the Other of the dominant European Self did not unsettle the dominant concern of the Conference, however, which was with the modern secular civilization that had come to life on the soil of European Christendom.[32]

Oxford marked a new phase in the life of the ecumenical movement. In one sense it marked the end of the distinctive movement of Life and Work, when it confirmed the decision to merge with the Faith and Order movement and together constitute a new entity, called the World Council of Churches. As a conference taking place in the shadows of war it also became a harbinger of the search for reconciliation which would characterize the ecumenical movement after 1945. Oxford also marked out clearly the fuller ecclesiological affirmations which would become more characteristic of the ecumenical movement during the second half of the century. In its search for the church as church, rid of subjugation to prevailing cultures and political orders, it offered a vision for a new ecumenical *koinonia* in mission.

Oxford demonstrated clearly that "the great new fact of our time," which Archbishop Temple had called the ecumenical movement, was as much concerned with the movement of Christian churches toward a visible expression of their unity through witness and service to the modern world as it was with confessional or dogmatic identity. Separated Western Protestant and Orthodox churches were entering into a concrete form of relationship that was to eventuate in the formation of a World Council of Churches. The Conference's ecclesiocentric view of unity was indeed a political challenge to the modern Western world. On this account both Duff and Karlström quote J. H. Nichols who claimed: "the authority of the Oxford Reports was unprecedented, at least in Protestant social ethics, and their competence enabled them to rank with the best of secular thought, a phenomenon scarcely seen since the seventeenth century."[33]   A unified theological ethos had not been heard in the West since before the Enlightenment and the emergence of the modern Western secular states. The promise of such a single vision and voice proved quite compelling for many who would follow in the ecumenical stream. The heritage of Oxford lived on in the coherent vision the ecumenical movement offered to the modern (and increasingly post-Christian) North Atlantic world.

In the period during which the World Council underwent formation European civilization was again plunged into a massive war of global proportions. The theological vision for social life that Oxford had articulated came to ecumenical life in part during these years as the incipient Council found itself already engaged in ecclesiastical affairs among warring nations. The Council was already engaged in ecumenical *praxis* by the time of its inaugural Assembly in Amsterdam, 1948. A 1942 memo from Visser't Hooft, "Reconstruction of Christian Institutions in Europe," provided the groundwork for what would become a critical ecumenical project in Europe after the war through the Division of Inter-Church Aid and Service to Refugees.[34]   The Commission of the Churches on International Affairs, formed jointly by the WCC and the IMC in 1946, would provide an ecumenical presence within international structures such as the United Nations.[35] Following the Amsterdam Assembly and in response to growing ecumenical concerns regarding the role of women in church and society the Council established a Commission on Life and Work of Women in the Church.

Within the structure of the new World Council the Universal Christian Council for Life and Work was to be continued as a study division called Church and Society. The themes it would continue to pursue during the 1950s would be reflected in the Assembly sections and throughout the various program sectors of the overall Council. The ecumenical search for a responsible society became one of its central tasks called for at Amsterdam, as the churches continued their search for a united voice in society.

Heated discussion at Amsterdam had occurred over the relationship of the WCC to the antagonists in the Cold War. The decision of the Assembly was that the ecumenical movement was to become a Third Way in the modern world, a spiritual alternative to totalitarian communism and exhausted *laissez faire* capitalism. While both Duff and Bock point out that during the 1950s the WCC often supported Western liberal democracy and its accompanying economic system of free enterprise, the debate Amsterdam over communism and liberal democracy nevertheless indicated that the ecumenical movement remained open to both options.[36] The deeper issue reflected in the debate at Amsterdam concerned the true inheritance of Western civilization.[37] The spiritual values of the Third Way of the ecumenical movement all too often shared with liberal democracy *and* communism the historical social and political memory of European Christendom.

By the end of the 1950s it was clear that the social world of the ecumenical movement could not be confined to the horizon of European Christendom. That world was increasingly being challenged by churches living through revolutionary situations and engaged in anti-colonialist struggles. The social forces within Faith and Order that opened up its horizon beyond the North Atlantic center would appear in the WCC's work concerning Church and Society as well to challenge the churches to move beyond reconstructing Christendom. In the late 1950s the formation of Asian and African regional councils, and the growing strength of non-European churches within the WCC began to show in the discussions of social life and witness. Beginning in 1955 Church and Society undertook a study on "Churches Facing Rapid Social Change," directed primarily toward situations of developing nations. The resulting International Ecumenical Study Conference on Social Change, held in 1959 in Thessalonica, Greece, marked a significant change in the social discourse of the WCC, and served as an indicator of the ecumenical irruption and disruption that lay ahead.

3. Toward a *Praxis* of Solidarity

The 1960's witnessed an irruption within Church and Society that was to affect the whole World Council. It was an irruption of the colonized, oppressed, subjugated peoples and communities of the world experienced on every level of ecumenical life. As an irruption of ecumenical 'others' from outside the dominant North Atlantic political community's circles of power, it brought about a sharper awareness of the social and political imperatives lodged within the historical memory of colonized and subjugated peoples. The result was a visible shift in the ecumenical axis of the World Council of Churches. Where the dominant axis around which the ecumenical movement revolved had been one whose poles were formed by the twin imperatives of unity and mission, a new axis, that of solidarity across historical boundaries of oppression, emerged for the ecumenical movement in a significant way. Alongside ecumenical concerns for reconstructing the basis for Christian social values in the post-Christian West emerged the revolutionary imperatives of a post-colonial global community.

The Second Assembly of the World Council of Churches, held in Evanston, Illinois, in 1954, had called for a study of Asian, African and Latin American realities in light of the decolonialization of the world. The development of Asian and African regional ecumenical associations during the 1950s further strengthened the collective voices from outside the North Atlantic political community in the ecumenical movement. At the same time the issues of racial and sexual discrimination within the North Atlantic communities were kept before Council as well during the decade.. The Church and Society study of the phenomenon of rapid social change and of Third World nationalism, the work of the Council on race relations (resulting in the establishment of a Secretariat for Racial and Ethnic Relations in 1959), and the continuing work of the Department on Co-operation of Men and Women mark the presence of these various concerns within the World Council during this period.

By the time the Third Assembly of the World Council of Churches gathered in 1961 in New Delhi, India (significantly, the first Assembly held outside the North Atlantic world), issues of Third World liberation and the struggles for justice within the First World had become critical within the movement as a whole. Recognizing the need to address the irrupting social issues in a more comprehensive manner, New Delhi authorized the calling of a World Conference on Church and Society, what was to be the third such ecumenical conference in the tradition of Stockholm 1925. The resulting World Conference on Church and Society, held in Geneva, 1966, proved to be the first study conference in the tradition of Life and Work or Church and Society in which the shift in theological axis would be so apparent.

According to most observers, the 1966 Geneva Conference had significantly "enlarged the ecumenical dialogue."

The strong representations from the Churches of Africa, Asia, Latin America, and the Middle East meant that those from the Western Churches were introduced to a new ecumenical dialogue which challenged their customary views about the way in which the Gospel is related to our world.[38]

That dialogue had been initiated by those struggling against racial and colonial oppressions of the 'Christian' nations of the North Atlantic. For Western participants at Geneva, the 'non-Western' world (which had been ideologically constructed by colonialism in a number of ways, and reproduced in the missionary view of the world) became the concrete world of poverty, exploitation, and uncontrolled technological development -- in short, the oppressed.

This is not to say that the axial shift was complete at Geneva. Western theologians still maintained their dominant voices, speaking for a theology of revolution on behalf of others, for instance. The modern Western nation-state was assumed in the discussions of nationalism. The "center of power" was still located in the technologically dominant ("developed") nations of the West, and the dialogue between First and Third Worlds often assumed implicitly a Western theological agenda on behalf of the larger ecumenical movement. This agenda remained intact following the 1966 Geneva Conference, and continued to be reproduced in World Council pronouncements or actions under a variety of theological guises. Despite the continuing presence of the dominant Western theological agenda even after 1966, however, Geneva marked a significant moment in the emergence of a new ecumenical discourse from outside the Eurocentric framework of Church and Society.

Much of the discussion at Geneva in 1966 was couched in the language of a "theology of history" that embraced secularization and revolution.[39]   Within many sectors of the churches, and within ecumenical discourse in general the categories of history and historical consciousness had emerged in the 1960s as a powerful force shaping the discourse of faith. But while the language and consciousness of historical change were sharper in the discussions at Geneva, they were not necessarily new to ecumenical discourse on social ethics. The relation of God's activity to human history had been one of the areas for study already at the Oxford Conference in 1937. It was an issue closely related in fact to the very heart of the Life and Work movement which sought to formulate a common understanding among the various churches concerning the churches' social ethic in the modern world.

The demand for such a social ethic was raised fundamentally by what was a historical problem.

J. H. Oldham, in the introduction to the Oxford study book, *The Kingdom of God and History*, had noted:

> What is at stake is the future of Christianity. The Christian foundations of western civilization have in some places been swept away and are everywhere being undermined. The struggle today concerns those common assumptions regarding the meaning of life without which, in some form, no society can cohere.[40]

H. D. Wendland's contribution to this study volume raised the problem explicitly as being that of the relationship between "sacred history" and "secular history." Sacred history, according to Wendland, was first the historical event of the incarnation, including the life, death and resurrection of Jesus Christ. This Christ is Lord over all history, and is therefore the center of history. A qualitatively new historical epoch was inaugurated by Christ, "the special mark of which is the fact of the church, and the history of the church, in the midst of and interwoven with secular history."[41] Wendland was careful to distinguish between sacred history and church history; the former is a theological reality, the latter a social-historical reality. They are two dimensions of one particular historical human community.

> Thus although sacred history and church history can never coincide, the church, in spite of her own worldliness, remains the bearer of sacred history within secular history....Hence sacred history can be sought and found only in the church; for she [sic] alone possesses the Word of God, and the sacraments as means of grace.[42]

This is the basis upon which one can speak of Christian ages, or a Christian world, the author asserted. Institutions, political and social developments, and even forms of power have been permeated with Christian values, and have taken into themselves elements of the Christian message. At the same time, they can forget their sacred source, referring only to themselves. This is the origin of secularism, which is post-Christian.[43] Wendland concluded his discussion of history by noting Tillich's suggestion that each people has a special historical vocation given by God, serving the growth of the whole of Christianity. Concretely this referred to the contribution of the European peoples to Christianity. But conversely, it was only through the Christian gospel that the peoples of Europe came to see themselves as unities and as a civilization. So the sacred history of Christianity in the West was also the ideology binding Western civilization into a cohesive fabric.[44]

Tillich had indeed spoken of national vocations in his essay included in the Oxford study volume, but he had not confined the vocation to European nations. Instead, Tillich had argued that "Every human group may become a 'bearer' of history" insofar as they are a group, that they have the power to maintain their own existence with their own set of values.[45] The ultimate meaning of all human history is realized in the Kingdom of God, Tillich continued, and that Kingdom is born by the church. "But the church is more than the Christian churches and their precursors. The church is the community of those partly visible and partly invisible, who live in the light of the ultimate meaning of existence, whether in expectation or in reception."[46]

The task of Christian missions, Tillich concluded, was to gather those invisible members living in expectation and lead them to the visible church living in reception, "and in so doing to transform potential world history into actual world history to give humanity a unified historical consciousness."[47] History, the totality of remembered events, belongs to concrete communities; a unified historical consciousness could only belong to a unified humanity. Such a unified humanity is ultimately the meaning of the Kingdom of God, and the church in which the Kingdom is visible and received in turn is sociologically identified with the Christian West.[48] Thus even Tillich identified sacred history, or the Kingdom of God, with the historical memory of Western nations.

The discussion of 'salvation history' continued in European biblical and theological circles through the middle decades of the twentieth century.[49] At Geneva the question of the relationship between God's history of salvation and human history was raised again, this time in the context of the failure of the totalizing ideologies of the twentieth century (capitalism and communism), accompanied by a turn away from the search for "meaning in history." The overthrow of world systems was discussed as a real possibility in a world of accelerated technological change. Among the factors posing the new questions of history most acutely was the fact that: "The cultures of the world have been caught up into the universal history of this change at the same time as former colonial nations have been receiving their political independence and asking about their self-identity in the midst of it."[50]

The relationship between God's judgement and redemption, and human history was posed anew at Geneva, but this time from the context of the histories of non-Western nationalism. Speaking from an Asian context, T. B. Simatupang told the conference delegates during one of the plenary sessions that Asian Christians participated in two separate fellowships; one was the ecumenical fellowship of Christians, and the other was the national community in which Christians were a minority. "This fact made the dialogue with majority Christian groups in the West difficult."[51] Theological discourse shaped in the context of two fellowships continued to be informed by Christian history, Section II concluded. But clearly along with the theological sources of Scripture and Christian history or tradition (which was at the same time European history or tradition), non-Western participants at Geneva were drawing upon national histories and nationalist revolutionary struggles as theological sources.

Alongside a revolutionary theology from the non-Western world, the Geneva conference articulated a theological understanding of technology which had emerged in European ecumenical/missionary discussions at the beginning of the decade.[52] The de-sacralization of nature, supposedly located in the Jewish and Christian theology of creation, was taken as the starting point for science and technology. Sweeping away all "animistic-pantheistic identification of nature with God,"[53] social categories of human history were privileged in the technology discussion. Biblical existence (and therefore biblical revelation) was said to have been "historical," displacing timeless structures and categories of thought. Relative meaning could be found in history, conference participants agreed; highly ambiguous, however, was what precise meaning adhered to their concept of "history."

The de-sacralization thesis which informed much of the ecumenical discussion of history and technology of that period was one articulated by the Dutch theologian, Arend Th. Van Leeuwen, in his book, *Christianity and World History.* Van Leeuwen's thesis, evident in much of the discussion of technology at Geneva, was that the revolutionary history of the West and modern technocratic civilization are direct descendants of Christianity.[54] According to Van Leeuwen, technocracy "is an historical phenomenon thrown up by Christian civilization itself -- a recent phase in the continuous process of structural modification which Christianity has undergone in the course of its history, particularly in the West."[55] This most recent phase of Christian history linked modern European culture with pre-modern European history (which was for Van Leeuwen identified closely with Church history) so that in the encounter with the "full power of Western civilization," as interpreted by the Church, the voice of Jesus Christ is heard.[56] The modern civilization of Europe and North America was no less Christian that the *Corpus Christianum* of medieval Europe, according to Van Leeuwen; it was only a new phase.

At Geneva in 1966 the discussion of technology often remained closely related to that of history and historical consciousness. Both were understood as manifestations of modern, European civilization, and for many participants both were accepted as legitimate descendants of biblical and Christian thinking. Consciousness of social and cultural relativity, and of the manner in which human subjects create their own world (historical consciousness) was closely related to consciousness of human mastery over material existence or the forces of nature (technology).[57] Both, furthermore, bore universal significance. The history of the world could be said to be one, and this brought about by the modern age (technology, capitalism, colonial expansion), many participants at Geneva agreed.[58]

On the other hand, the fact that the relative structures of human history remain closed to total investigation and are constantly being reshaped by God's actions through human subjects was also affirmed at the 1966 World Conference on Church and Society.[59] At this point there appears to be some confusion in the Conference's understanding of "the meaning of history," confusion regarding how the history of European colonialism and missions, or the history of Third World anti-colonialist revolutions are to be understood theologically. Closely related to this confusion regarding the meaning of history at Geneva was considerable ambiguity regarding technological developments. In both of these cases the privileged position of the history of the West for Christian faith, and the universalization of the modern European experience of technocracy, both of which had previously dominated ecumenical social discourse, began to be challenged.

In the decade that followed the 1966 Geneva Conference the challenge to the dominant Western ecumenical agenda regarding church and society was to become institutionalized within the WCC, but not necessarily within the Department on Church and Society. The Department on Church and Society (after 1971 to be the Sub-Unit on Church and Society within Programme Unit I: Faith and Witness) played a role in developing several of these new programs and studies after the 1960s, but Church and Society primarily continued to pursue issues of technological development, usually within the First World context.

Standing in succession to the discussion in the late 1940s and 1950s on the search for a "Responsible Society," the work of Church and Society broadened somewhat in the 1970s to include consideration of ecological issues, a theme introduced into World Council discussions as early as 1961 by Joseph Sittler in a paper presented before the New Delhi Assembly.[60] The Fifth Assembly in Nairobi directed the Council to continue to explore issues of technology and ecology under the heading of "The Contribution of Faith, Science and Technology in the Struggle for a Just and Sustainable Society."[61] The result was the WCC Conference on Faith, Science and the Future, held in Cambridge, Massachusetts in July of 1979.[62]

In line with its primary focus on science and technology have been the studies and concerns of the Sub-Unit on Church and Society on energy and nuclear power; and on bio-ethical issues such as genetic engineering.[63] That these issues have constituted the primary focus for Church and Society has not meant that other issues of justice and liberation for women, people of color, or Third World nations have not been considered. Furthermore the Sub-Unit on Church and Society has carried out its studies under mandates from successive Assemblies of the World Council. The manner in which the World Council has distributed its various studies and programs across several Programme Units, and has relegated Church and Society to studying issues of science and technology within what is primarily a First World context, is indicative of the enduring dichotomy in ecumenical *praxis* however.

A better picture of the World Council's ecumenical *praxis*, and the theological reflection which has been generated regarding issues of church and society, can be seen by looking at the spectrum of Units and Sub-Units of the full Council. After 1971 the Council operated under three Programme Units: Faith and Witness, Justice and Service, and Education and Renewal. The social plate of the Council has certainly been full, including work on racism, the struggle for women's rights, economics, justice for youth, disarmament, medical concerns, refugees, dialogue with other faiths, and education. Much of these other concerns and activities have represented forms of ecumenical *praxis* which assume a Third World setting, and they have developed out of liberation perspectives that are not of dominant Western origin. Two examples of ecumenical programs concerning racism and sexism demonstrate the tensions at work within this larger arena of ecumenical *praxis*.

At the beginning of its history the Life and Work movement had identified race relations as a matter of critical importance to the churches of the Western world. As early as 1926 J. H. Oldham had undertaken a study on this social problem. Setting the issue within the context of the emerging anti-colonialism of that day, Oldham nevertheless argued for an enlightened form of imperialism and for maintaining the separation of races in to a certain degree.[64] The Oxford Conference in 1937 represented a significant advance in both its analysis of racial discrimination and its call for an end to all forms of racial exploitation. Amsterdam continued the ecumenical call for an end to racism in churches and in society, focussing its attention in particular on anti-Judaism in Western society.

The Second Assembly meeting in Evanston had received preparatory materials dealing with race relations across the globe, including in the U. S. and South Africa. Following a plenary address by Benjamin Mays, President of Morehouse College, the Evanston Assembly took a stronger stand than had previous Life and Work Conferences or World Council Assemblies, denouncing racial discrimination as sin against God, calling upon churches to repent, supporting civil rights, and defending interracial marriage.[65] One of the resolutions adopted by Evanston was for a Secretariat on Racial and Ethnic Relations, a resolution which was finally implemented in 1960 when Daisuke Kitagawa was appointed to the new post within the Department on Church and Society.[66] The Sharpeville killings in South Africa in March of 1960 led to a World Council delegation visit and the Cottesloe Consultation of December, 1960. Although the resulting statements from the Consultation were extremely mild given the reign of terror and oppression in South Africa under Apartheid, the event served to heighten ecumenical attention on racial oppression.[67]

The period between 1966 (the World Conference on Church and Society in Geneva) and 1968 (the Fourth Assembly of the World Council in Uppsala) witnessed a rapid shift to a more radical direction in the World Council's responses to racism. The 1966 Conference in Geneva dealt with racism specifically in Section IV, "Man and Community in Changing Societies." The Final Report from that Section noted that the growing strength of African Nationalism and the appearance of "Black Power" in the U.S.A. were setting the agenda for the struggle against racism. The fact that South African Anglican

Bishop Alpheus Zulu had been denied a passport to attend the Conference, and that Dr. Martin Luther King, Jr., had to cancel his Sunday appearance at the Conference on account of events in Chicago drove home the dimensions of power those in the struggle were confronting. The Report linked racism in the United States with the Vietnam War, and drew further the interconnections between racism and other forms of social, economic, and political oppression in the contemporary world.[68] The recommendations that went out from the Conference called upon churches to engage in corporate action to eradicate racism from both church and society.[69]

The intensification of the struggle against racism continued at the Uppsala Assembly in 1968, where the African American writer, James Baldwin, addressed the Assembly concerning racism in the Christian churches. The Uppsala Assembly voted to recommend the creation of a new effort directed toward the elimination of racism, urging the Council to "undertake a crash programme" that would not only study racism but would organize in coalition projects and provide resources to those engaged in the anti-racism struggle.[70] A Department on Church and Society Consultation held at Notting Hill, London, in May of 1969 went even further in recommending economic sanctions against corporations that "practise blatant racism," reparations to exploited peoples, the establishment of a separate WCC unit on racism, and, "that all else failing, the Church and churches support resistance movements, including revolutions, which are aimed at the elimination of political or economic tyranny which makes racism possible."[71] The result was the creation by the Central Committee of the WCC in August of 1969 of what was perhaps the single most controversial program in the history of the WCC, the Programme to Combat Racism (PCR).[72]

The PCR was empowered to provide grants to organizations combatting racism from a Special Fund set up for this purpose. The grants, made without control over the manner in which they are spent, were intended to be a concrete sign of the World Council's solidarity with those struggling on the front lines for justice and freedom.[73] Significant grants have been made to organizations such as SWAPO and the ANC, but also to groups in other parts of Africa, as well as to groups in Asia, Latin America, and North America.[74] Despite widespread criticism from sectors of the churches of the First World, the PCR has maintained its work of addressing racism on a global scale and supporting those engaged in direct struggles as a sign of solidarity on behalf of the entire World Council.[75]

The WCC's involvement in the struggle against racism through the PCR and especially through grants made from the Special Fund have revealed the issue of racism to be a fundamental cause of division among churches. The PCR would not have survived if it, and the struggle against racism it represents, did not have significant support from churches in the Council and from other sectors of the ecumenical community. The controversy over PCR, usually concerning its support for organizations that espouse violence as a legitimate strategy for change, has generally come from sectors of the First World where support for the racist regime in South Africa is strongest. The silence of PCR's detractors concerning other forms of overt and structurally covert sanctioned violence carried out by governments, corporations, and individuals, suggests that the divisive issue is not necessarily violence *per se* but the legitimacy of racism in political and social life.

The issue of racism is perhaps more divisive than denominationalism and confessionalism in the Council today, leading some to note that today it is dogma that unites while service divides. It would be too simplistic, however, to regard the issue of racism as one which is non-theological, or as a matter which is not of concern for the doctrinal unity of the churches. Racism is a central theological concern, as the World Council has recognized, and the divisions among churches concerning the WCC's actions against racism are as much matters of dogma as the confessional differences among churches are social and historical.[76] The difference is that until recently racism has not been addressed in the confessional documents of the dominant white churches of the North Atlantic community. Being relegated to the non-theological domain outside the confessions of faith racism has received silent theological approval.[77] Racism has marked the confessional statements of the dominant white churches of the world through its absence. It has been present however in the confessions of those who have suffered its oppression.[78]

In regard to questions of church unity, racism is as divisive of the churches as baptism, eucharist or ministry. Between the churches which are historically related to the dominant white North Atlantic world (the churches of Northern Europe, the U.S.A., Canada, Australia and New Zealand, and the white-dominated churches in South Africa) and the churches among communities which have suffered from the racism of the North Atlantic the absence of a common confession on racism in their background and in their history presents significant obstacles to

koinonia in the future. Unlike the common historical memory of a
unified confessional church in the West which can serve as the basis for
unity among the confessional differences of churches, on the matter of
racism there is no common confessional memory. There is instead a
five-hundred year history of oppression through colonization,
enslavement, and genocide. Here commonality will only be found in
the commitment to a different future, one in which racism will finally
be eliminated. And the path to the community of this common future
is the way of solidarity. To the degree that the PCR embodies this
praxis of solidarity it embodies an ecumenical confession of reconciled
community without oppression across the historical boundaries
constructed through injustice.

Racism has divided the churches of the world historically as well as
today; there has of also been considerable racism *within* the churches
and communities of the West over the course of the last five hundred
years, creating within connected churches walls of separation dividing
people from each other.   By its very nature racism constructs
social-cultural boundaries defining a particular group or community of
people as 'other.' Where the oppression of racism has been structurally
between communities, however, the oppression of sexism has most
often been structurally between men and women within community.
This is not to say that sexism is any less a concern for collective action
on the part of the churches. As Jacquelyn Grant argued at the WCC
1981 Sheffield Conference on "The Community of Women and Men in
the Church," the issue of sexism cannot be confined to being personal
and private.   It has been publicly operative in ecclesiastical
communities, in most of them, for the greater part of the history of the
Christian churches. Nor can sexism and racism be separated in such a
way that one subsumes the other. Racism and sexism, together with
classism, are "ingrained and inextricably linked."[79] At the same time
they are historically distinct as modes of oppression, and require
distinctive modes of analysis. An examination of the World Council's
response to sexism and gender oppression in both church and society
reveals similar themes regarding unity through solidarity of *praxis*.

By the end of the nineteenth century the role of women in
industrialized societies had begun to change rapidly. In sectors of the
churches of the West women were becoming more active in public
forms of ministry as preachers and missionaries. In both church and
society challenges to the dominant forms of patriarchal organization had

begun to be heard. Within the ecumenical movement, the question of the role of women in the church had been raised at the First World Conference on Faith and Order, at Lausanne, in 1927 (as we saw above). Surprisingly, however, issues of women in church and society were not addressed in any significant manner within either the International Missionary Council or the Life and Work movement prior to 1948. The Life and Work Conferences at Stockholm in 1925, and again at Oxford in 1937, were virtually silent on the issue of women in society, even though at Oxford approximately two dozen of the four hundred twenty-five delegates were women. No significant discussion took place on the issue of women in church and society until the Amsterdam Assembly of the World Council in 1948.

Amsterdam identified the "Life and Work of Women in the Church" as a topic for study. It wasn't until after the 1948 Assembly that the Commission on Life and Work of Women in the Church was formed, however. One of the factors contributing to the establishment of the Commission (renamed "Co-operation of Men and Women" in the 1950s) was the interest shown by churches in response to an earlier questionnaire sent out by the WCC regarding women in the church. The information gathered from the questionnaires, together with further research, became the basis for a book in 1952 written by Kathleen Bliss, entitled *The Service and Status of Women in the Churches.*

Bliss examined the ecumenical work that was already being done through women's voluntary organizations in churches, and the current status of women in professional and ordained leadership in the churches. She found much in the way of organized work from many different parts of the world, performed by groups of women or of women and men cooperatively, that was ecumenically important. (For the most part these efforts were taking place outside the main streams of the ecumenical movement that had fed into the World Council of Churches, however.) Her conclusion was that despite the work being done, and the demands still before the churches that women were being called to meet, the churches remained "deeply divided in what they think about the place of women in the modern world and in the Church."[80] She appealed for the churches to turn away from theoretical arguments about the role of women in the church and at the same time, (borrowing a phrase from Karl Barth) "for women to 'show what they can do.'"[81] The opportunities for women to minister in the world as well as in the church would then be opened up.

The World Council continued during the 1950s to address causes of women in the churches, through the Commission and through various pronouncements on women, family, and community made by WCC Assemblies. But overall relatively little attention was paid to the issues and concerns affecting women in ministry or the churches. Discussion concerning the role of women was usually considered to fall under the ministry of the laity. When the Faith and Order Commission did undertake study of women in ordained ministry, published in 1964 as *Concerning the Ordination of Women*, it did so from a perspective that assumed the ordination of women to be an obstacle to church union.[82]

In the published histories and interpretations of the World Council even in the 1960s virtual silence reigned concerning the Commission on Co-operation of Women and Men, or the issue of women in church and society in general.[83] Where mention was made regarding women it was often merely in passing. The only mention Madeleine Barot received in H. Krüger's essay on "The Life and Activities of the World Council of Churches" in the second volume of the WCC's official history, for instance, was a passing nod to one who "untiringly reminded the W.C.C. of the concerns of women in the Churches."[84] The significant contributions of Barot, and the concerns she spoke for, remained absent from official interpretations of the ecumenical movement.[85]

The absence of women, of both the First and Third Worlds, again marked the 1966 World Conference on Church and Society in Geneva. The presence at the Conference of the "strong representations" of men from the Third World is evident in the final reports from Geneva, 1966.[86] The presence of the African American voice of Dr. Martin Luther King, Jr., who was prevented from speaking at the Conference in person on account of the situation in Chicago during the summer of 1966, was recognized precisely because it was absent in person from the Conference. But the absence of women is hardly noticed by the Reports from Geneva. Only a footnote at the beginning of Part III, on "Men and Women in Changing Communities," in the Report from Section IV of the Conference notes this missing voice.

> The sub-section that dealt with this subject noted that two of its members were women and that the proportion of women to men in the Conference as a whole was even lower, in spite of the fact that the membership and activity of women in the churches is far greater than that of men.[87]

The Report from Section IV did go on to resist attempting to define the roles of women, and the relationships between women and men, noting the divergence of views on these issues but reminding the churches that structures and roles were changing. While the Report at one point noted, "It is a serious issue affecting cooperation of men and women in churches when women hear a call to the ordained ministry and their vocation is denied on sexual grounds," there was no mention of women in the church in the Section Report's "Conclusions and Recommendations," only a series of recommendations concerning resources for women, responsible parenthood, and contraception.[88] The "far greater" membership and activity of women in the churches was not to have a significant impact on ecumenical discourse even at the 1968 Uppsala Assembly, despite the radical turn of the movement in other areas during the 1960s. The watershed in the World Council concerning women's oppression was not to take place until 1974, at Berlin in the consultation on "Sexism in Church and Society."

The 1974 Berlin Consultation, organized by the Sub-Unit on Women in Church and Society (which was by then under Programme Unit III: Education and Renewal) brought together women and men from First and Third World contexts to address the multifaceted character of sexual oppression in church and society. The papers and reports from Berlin, published in 1975, suggest the consultation not only succeeded in engaging in theoretical analysis and proposing practical steps for churches to take, although it accomplished both of these. More importantly, the consultation enabled women of different social and cultural contexts, together with men, to begin to reflect together around their common and divergent experiences of gender oppression, and its interrelation with other forms of oppression. The result was a new experience of ecumenical community. As one participant, quoted at the beginning of the published report of the consultation, said, "None of us returns home the woman she was when she came."[89]

Among the initiatives from Berlin was a recommendation to the churches and to the WCC to continue to study issues of women in the church in light of the consultation's conclusions. At Accra the following year the Faith and Order Commission responded to the initiative, and a working paper for a study on women and men in community was presented to the Nairobi Assembly in 1975.[90] The recommendation that came from Nairobi set in motion the ecumenical study program on "The Community of Women and Men in the Church."[91] Because the program was to explore issues relating to ministry and community, as well as church and society, it was lodged primarily within the Commission on Faith and Order but conducted together with the Sub-Unit on Women in Church and Society. Described as having "the most extensive grass-roots participation of any such project in the history of the World Council of Churches," the Community study took place over several years and involved numerous local studies; regional consultations in Africa, Asia, Latin America, the Middle East, Europe and North America; and several special consultations on Scripture, anthropology, and the ordained ministry.[92]

The culmination of these local and regional studies was the international consultation which took place in Sheffield, England, in 1981. The process of the study itself enabled what WCC General Secretary Philip Potter called "the tremendous insights and wisdom" to emerge "from below," enriching the churches and challenging them toward a deeper theological understanding.[93] Not only were issues of sexual oppression and exclusion identified and debated, but issues separating First World women from Third World women (including African American women) were explored, as were the interconnections between sexism, racism and classism which form a web of oppression. It was important that the purpose of the consultation was not to formulate a critical feminist theology, nor to provide a critique of sexism in the church, but to begin to live toward a new community of women and men. More than an occasion for delivery of papers, consideration of reports, and formulations of recommendations to the churches and the WCC, the Sheffield consultation embodied a concrete *praxis* of women and men engaging in dialogue in community together.

It was this aspect of the Community of Women and Men project that Mercy Amba Oduyoye emphasized in her report to the Central Committee of the WCC in 1981:

> A new quality and freedom of spiritual/human life happened [at Sheffield] as we worked out our tensions, expectations, and real differences. In our confrontation, we found that we were not struggling against each other, but that we were committed to becoming a people, in search of a common goal; in that pursuit we discovered community.[94]

Echoing others' observations about the significance of the process that led to Sheffield, and the manner in which a new experience of community between women and men in the church occurred there, Oduyoye continued:

With the three years preparation we are just beginning to experience what this study is all about -- not an ideology of equality -- but a new life in Christ, a life of partnership, solidarity, unity, and renewal.[95]

Whether Sheffield did indeed mark the beginning of a new ecumenical experience within the WCC, however, and whether the process of partnership and solidarity has continued to be pursued in relation to unity and renewal within Faith and Order, remains disputed. Melanie May has argued that the "Community of Women and Men in the Church" program represented an insurrection "against the effects of the theological discourse on unity formulated by the Commission on Faith and Order."[96] The fact that the conclusion of the Community study process at the Commission on Faith and Order meeting at Lima, Peru, in 1982, coincided with the culmination of the *BEM* project is indicative, says May, of the manner in which Faith and Order has considered difference divisive, has in fact turned away from diversity, and instead has opted for one mode of unity.[97]

Officially the Commission on Faith and Order took up the Community study into the on-going work on "The Unity of the Church and the Renewal of Human Community." A 1985 Prague consultation within the Renewal program sought to continue the process "post-Sheffield."[98] It did so, however, under the banner of "Beyond Unity-in-Tension," giving credence to May's assertion. At the same time the Renewal program has not continued the process of study and engagement in community which both preceded and occurred at Sheffield, a living *praxis* which enabled those who participated in the Sheffield program to experience a taste of a new ecclesial reality.[99] Apart from the experiences of partnership and solidarity which were intentional in the initial Community project, the attempt to articulate partnership and community remain unconnected, and even incoherent.

Within the WCC overall the Sheffield experience, and the ecumenical commitment to solidarity with women, have not been forgotten, despite whatever conclusions we might draw concerning the fate of the Community study within Faith and Order. In 1987 the Central Committee of the World Council declared an Ecumenical Decade of Churches in Solidarity with Women, challenging the churches of the world to continue to seek to realize the vision for a fuller community. Regional and local ecumenical responses to the Ecumenical Decade have continued the dialogue.[100] Even in ecumenical arenas where the issues remain highly charged, in discussions among

Orthodox and Protestant churches concerning ordination of women for instance, "the bridges were never burnt," the dialogue has not gone silent.[101] The interior process of dialogue and renewal has continued.

One of the conclusions the Sheffield consultation reached was that renewal in community is not possible apart from the experience of solidarity across gendered, racial, class and cultural lines of division. The experience of community across these lines enabled the Consultation to move beyond the framework for ecumenical reflection which is possible within existing ecclesiastical structures and environments, dominated by masculinist thought and rituals of power. The new ecclesial reality which began to be experienced among those involved in the three-year process that led to Sheffield pointed the way toward an new authority, a new "authoring," of community among women and men. In this sense the *praxis* of solidarity generated in the process leading to Sheffield became a source and resource for the new community called for from Sheffield.[102]

The experience of solidarity which became central to the reflection process that led to Sheffield enabled the Consultation to move significantly beyond the 'Tradition *vs.* traditions' debates which have often hindered ecumenical discussions. Solidarity allowed participants to recognize existing differences and even contradictions without attempting to move beyond them to a homogeneous theology or ecclesiology. The project demonstrated the manner in which solidarity opens up ecumenical discourse and practice to the essentially heterogeneous and even heterological experiences of Christian communities in the world today. The result, reflected in the Section Report on "Tradition and Traditions -- A Chance for Renewal?" was an affirmation of local traditions and the community they generate apart from the dominant traditions of Western church history.[103] The renewal of local traditions, those of the Third World as well as of the First world, those of women as well as of men, becomes possible in a new community of solidarity and partnership. As Constance Parvey noted in her reflections on the Consultation:

> The closer we as churches come to one another, the more we are motivated to study, preserve, and cherish our own distinct identity, our special languages and stories. In the search for reasons why the church can and cannot become one, the churches are challenged to their very roots and to their diversity. In terms of theology the experience of the community study has shown that the closer the issues compel the

churches to come to their sources, the more likely they are to discover commonalities in theology, yet wide divergences in history and tradition.[104]

The centrality of solidarity in the experience of renewed community amidst the webs of oppression has been realized in other programs and sections of the World Council. Through most of the 1980s the Programme to Combat Racism has pursued "Women Under Racism" as one of the areas of priority in its work. More recently the Commission on Inter-Church Aid, Refugee and World Service, under the impact of a major WCC consultation on *diakonia* held in 1986 in Larnacam, Cyprus, has moved toward the creation of regional groups for setting priorities and developing strategies so that decision making would take place where needs arise.[105] One of the program initiatives launched after the Vancouver Assembly, "Justice, Peace and the Integrity of Creation," sought to relate local struggles for justice with environmental concerns, moving churches toward solidarity and mutual commitment (or covenant) for creation, uncovering the essential interconnectedness among issues that are too often separated. The 1990 Seoul World Convocation issued a series of commitments for churches of the world to affirm as part of their covenanting for peace, justice, and the integrity of creation.[106] Finally, as noted above, since 1987 the WCC has been in Ecumenical Decade of Churches in Solidarity with Women.

Yet the experiences of solidarity remain partial and fragmentary within the ecumenical movement, even today. The *praxis* of solidarity and partnership, where it has taken place, has pointed toward coherence and vitality. The consensus that has emerged over the last two decades regarding racism, for instance, and the manner in which the heresy of Apartheid has come to be regarded as *status confessionis* for many churches, indicates a greater degree of coherence in the ecumenical movement than one might expect to find given the current global political situation.[107] The failure of the churches to reach a similar degree of consensus around issues of sexism in the churches and in society indicates how far the ecumenical movement yet remains from achieving coherence in and through its *praxis*.

Both the Programme to Combat Racism and the Community of Women and Men study have shown that the avenue to vitality and coherence in the ecumenical movement is that of solidarity and mutual commitment across racial, gendered, class and cultural boundaries. Such ecumenical *koinonia* is not built upon a common past among the churches, but reflects a commitment to a common future. It is not the coherence of a unified Christendom in the past to which this *praxis* is pointing. Rather, it points toward God's new ecumenical future.

In other words the experience of *koinonia* in diversity is eschatological, and the road to it is through solidarity and mutual commitment. The *praxis* of solidarity in the churches is the only avenue to overcoming the apparently insurmountable ecumenical divides which confront us today -- the divisions between women and men, between First and Third worlds, among races, confessions, peoples, and nations. At the same time it is the *praxis* of solidarity that will enable the churches to begin to live amidst the contradictions of radical difference experienced in the contemporary ecumenical situation. Solidarity transforms those who participate not by eliminating difference but by enabling community through *koinonia*.

The theological model for *koinonia* and solidarity, emerging from the Community study but being experienced throughout the World Council in its various programs, is that of the Trinitarian experience empowered by the Spirit.[108]   Being rediscovered in the contemporary ecumenical movement is the dialogical community of God, of Jesus and his "Abba" to whom he prayed, and of the Spirit who descended upon Jesus and who is now sent among Christ's people. The trinitarian mode of living encompasses distinction without separation, a life of coherent coinhering. Trinitarian life offers a model for the dialogical experience of *koinonia* through solidarity, for the *praxis* of solidarity embodies pluralism without eliminating difference.[109]   The result of this vital dialogical living which is being experienced in churches on local levels across the world is renewed community, renewed tradition, renewed appreciation for the Trinitarian *oikonomia*, and a renewed commitment to mutual traditioning. It is a new vision for the mission of the churches as well, the subject of the next chapter.

Notes

1. R. Lane Kauffmann, "The Other in Question: Dialogical Experiment in Montaigne, Kafka, and Cortazar," *The Interpretation of Dialogue*, Tullio Maranhao, ed. (Chicago: University of Chicago Press, 1990), p. 159; Nelle Morton, "Towards a Whole Theology," *The Journey Is Home* (Boston: Beacon Press, 1985), p. 67; and Eugen Rosenstock-Huessy, *I Am an Impure Thinker* (Norwich, Vt: Argo Books, 1970), p. 2.

2. Jose Miguez Bonino, "The Concern for a Vital and Coherent Theology," *The Ecumenical Review* 41/2 (April, 1989), pp. 160-176.

3. Paulos Mar Gregorios, "Towards a Basic Document," *Ecumenical Review* 41/2 (April, 1989), pp. 184-193.

4. Bonino, "The Concern for a Vital and Coherent Theology," p. 164.

5. Melanie A. May, "Response" to Jeffrey Gros, "Interpretation, History and the Ecumenical Movement," *Ecumenical Trends* 16/7 (1987), p. 131.

6. M.M. Thomas, "Will Koinonia Emerge as a Vital Theological Theme?" *Ecumenical Review* 41/2 (April 1989), p. 177.

7. G. K. A. Bell, ed., *The Stockholm Conference 1925: The Official Report of the Universal Christian Conference on Life and Work* (London: Oxford University Press, 1926),   p. 46.

8. *Ibid.*, p. 48.

9. *Ibid.*, p. 50. Metropolitan Germanos explained later in the conference that the call for a League of Churches by the Ecumenical Patriarch in the 1920 encyclical was "in response to grave dangers threatening the whole Christian edifice," and to "the festering sores which the world war revealed in the Christian body," p. 628.

10. Ernst Troeltsch, *Protestantism and Progress: The Significance of Protestantism for the Rise of the Modern World* (Philadelphia: Fortress Press, 1986), p. 20. Troeltsch argues that while early Protestantism contributed to the formation of modern culture, it did so indirectly and unwillingly. He saw the vast strength of the modern state and the impact of modern science as both rendering impossible the active, formative role played by the medieval church in re-creating culture. On the other hand, modern Protestantism has reconciled itself with the modern age.   James H. Nichols,*History of Christianity, 1650-1950: Secularization of the West* (New York: Ronald Press, 1956), p. 11, points out that Protestantism achieved a synthesis of religion and reason through evangelical faith, and Protestant countries actually took leadership in shaping modern Western culture as well as taking that culture to non-Western peoples through missions.

11. Bengt Sundkler, *Nathan Söderblom: His Life and Work* (Lund: Gleerups, 1968), p. 385.

12. *Ibid.*, p. 331. See especially chapter 9, entitled "Great European," pp.

383ff.

13. See Nils Karlström, "Movements for International Friendship and Life and Work, 1910-1925," *A History of the Ecumenical Movement*, Rouse and Neill, eds., pp. 521-530. See also Darril Hudson, *The World Council of Churches in International Affairs* (Leighton: Faith Press Ltd., 1977), pp. 24-25.

14. See Darril Hudson, *The Ecumenical Movement in World Affairs* (London: Weidenfeld & Nicolson, 1969), p. 82. Sundkler notes that the motto originated with Rev. Kapler of Prussia, but Söderblom adopted it for the Life and Work conference; see Sundkler, *Nathan Soderblom*, p. 340.

15. Bell, *The Stockholm Conference 1925*, p. 629.

16. Jose Miguez-Bonino, "A 'Third World' Perspective on the Ecumenical Movement," *Ecumenical Review* 34/2 (1982), p. 117. His paper was presented at the Faith and Order Commission, in Lima, in reference to the "unity of humankind" discussion.

17. Edward Duff, *The Social Thought of the World Council of Churches* (London: Longmans, Green and Co., 1956), p. 295.

18. Bell, *The Stockholm Conference 1925*, p. 417.

19. See Paul Bock, *In Search of a Responsible World Society: The Social Teachings of the World Council of Churches* (Philadelphia: Westminster Press, 1974), p. 124f.

20. J. H. Oldham, ed., *The Oxford Conference (Official Report)* (Chicago: Willett, Clark and Co., 1937), p. 68f.

21. World Missionary Conference, 1910, *Report of Commission VII: Missions and Governments* (Edinburgh: Oliphant, Anderson & Ferrier/NY: Fleming H. Revell Co., 1910), p. 164.

22. *Ibid.*, p. 157.

23. Hudson, *The Ecumenical Movement in World Affairs*,   p. 44.

24. *Ibid.*, p. 47. Ans J. van der Bent, *Christian Response in a World of Crisis: A Brief History of the WCC's Commission of the Churches on International Affairs* (Geneva: WCC, 1986), makes the connection between the missionary concerns for religious freedom and the development of human rights discourse in international affairs of the twentieth century: "There were several reasons why the WCC in its early years was eager to act as a champion of human rights. Behind it was the long missionary tradition struggling to secure freedom to propagate the gospel. Thus the freedom to 'hold and change one's faith, to express it in worship and practice, to teach and to persuade others, and to decide on the religious education of one's children' was of vital ecumenical importance. Religious liberty in fact was considered to be the cornerstone of the entire edifice of human rights." (27) Warren Lee Holleman, *The Human Rights Movement: Western Values and Theological Perspectives* (New York: Praeger, 1987), explores in more detail the Western cultural bias in contemporary discourse regarding human rights. Holleman points out that the concept of 'human rights' in Western political discourse is characterized by "a

positive view of the human being as individual," and "a negative view of the human being as community, particularly in terms of political community."(27) In the case of religious freedom this meant a positive view of the individual missionary's right to propagate beliefs, and a negative view of the non-Western community's political right to maintain its own religious/social/political life.

25. John A. Mackay, "Ecumenical: The Word and the Concept," *Theology Today*, 9/1 (1952), p. 3.

26. John A. Mackay, *Ecumenics: The Science of the Church Universal* (Englewood Cliffs, NJ: Prentice-Hall, 1964), p. 4.

27. Joseph H. Oldham, ed., *The Oxford Conference (Official Report)* (Chicago: Willett, Clark and Co., 1937), p. 45.

28. *Ibid.*, p. 2.

29. *Ibid.*, p. 87.

30. *Ibid.*, p. 62.

31. *Ibid.*, p. 175. See also p. 173.

32. *Ibid.*, pp. 180-184.

33. The memo, along with reflection on its importance by W. A. Visser't Hooft, can be found in Kenneth Slack, ed., *Hope in the Desert: The Churches' United Response to Human Need, 1944-1984* (Geneva: WCC, 1986), pp. 1ff.

34. See Hudson, *The World Council of Churches in International Affairs.*

35. J. H. Nichols, *Democracy and the Churches*, p. 235, quoted by Duff, *Social Thought of the World Council of Churches*, p. 36; and by Karlström, "Movements for International Friendship and Life and Work," p. 591.

36. Duff, *Social Thought of the World Council of Churches*, pp. 202-220, and especially 288f.

37. See the John Foster Dulles/Joseph Hromadka debate, in Section IV of the Amsterdam Assembly Report, "Christian Responsibility in Our Divided World," W. A. Visser't Hooft, ed., *Man's Disorder and God's Design: The Amsterdam Assembly Series* (New York: Harper and Brothers, 1948).

38. World Council of Churches, *Christians in the Technical and Social Revolutions of our Time: The World Conference on Church and Society, July 1966* (Geneva: WCC, 1966), pp. 41- 42.

39. *Christians in the Technical and Social Revolutions of Our Time*, p. 98.

40. H. G. Wood et al, *The Kingdom of God in History* (Chicago: Willett, Clark & Co., 1938), p. vii.

41. *Ibid.*, p. 149.

42. *Ibid.*, p. 153.

43. *Ibid.*, p. 155.

44. *Ibid.*, p. 179.

45. *Ibid.*, p. 111.

46. *Ibid.*, p. 122.

47. *Ibid.*

48. *Ibid.*, p. 141.

49. See Geiko Müller-Fahrenholz, *Heilsgeschichte zwischen Ideologie und Prophetie: Profile und Kritik Heilsgeschichtlicher Theorien in der Ökumenischen Bewegung zwischen 1948 und 1968* (Freiburg: Herder, 1974).

50. *Christians in the Technical and Social Revolutions of our Time*, p. 199.

51. *Ibid.*, p. 33.

52. See Arend Th. van Leeuwen, *Christianity in World History* (New York: Charles Scribners, 1964).

53. *Christians in the Technical and Social Revolutions of our Time*, p. 197.

54. See van Leeuwen, *Christianity in World History*, p. 403; Richard Shaull cited Van Leeuwen in his (Shaull's) preparatory essay for Geneva, "Revolutionary Change in Theological Perspective," *Christian Social Ethics in a Changing World: An Ecumenical Inquiry*, John C. Bennett, ed. (New York: Association Press, 1966), p. 23.

55. Van Leeuwen, *Christianity in World History*, p. 408.

56. *Ibid.*, p. 409.

57. See the Faith and Order study, "God in Nature and History," *New Directions in Faith and Order, Bristol 1967: Reports - Minutes - Documents* (Geneva: WCC, 1968), p. 7-32.

58. At the fourth plenary session at Geneva, Richard Shaull criticized the "a-historical way of thinking" which he claimed has dominated theology and ethics, preventing Christian involvement in history; in response Roger Shinn warned against the tendency to deify history. The earlier plenary session three had already heard M.M. Thomas suggest that the movement from nature to history paralleled a movement from the sacred to the secular for theology. Shinn's warning should have been heard in several sections of the conference, and by the ecumenical movement in general. See *Christians in the Technical and Social Revolutions*, p. 25; 27; 21-22.

59. *Ibid.*, p. 200.

60. See Joseph Sittler, "Called to Unity," *Ecumenical Review* 14/1 (1962), p. 185f. Sittler's paper was also reflected in the Faith and Order Commission's study "Unity of the Church - Unity of Humanity."

61. David M. Paton, ed., *Breaking Barriers: Nairobi 1975* (Grand Rapids: Wm. B. Eerdmans, 1976), p. 303.

62. See Paul Abrecht, ed., *Faith, Science and the Future* (Philadelphia: Fortress Press, 1979); Roger L. Shin, ed., *Faith and Science in an Unjust World: Report of the WCC Conference on Faith, Science and the Future*, Vol. 1: *Plenary Presentations* (Geneva: WCC, 1980); and Paul Abrecht, ed., *Faith and Science in an Unjust World: Report of the WCC Conference on Faith, Science and the Future*, Vol. 2: *Reports and Recommendations* (Geneva: WCC, 1980).

63. See John Francis and Paul Abrecht, eds., *Facing Up to Nuclear Power: A Contribution to the Debate on the Risks and Potentialities of the Large-Scale Use of Nuclear Energy* (Edinburgh: St. Andrew's Press, 1976); and

Manipulating Life: Ethical Issues in Genetic Engineering (Geneva: WCC, 1982).

64. Joseph H. Oldham, *Christianity and the Race Problem* (Chautauqua, NY: The Chautauqua Press, 1926). Oldham wrote on p. 3, "Since the beginning of the present century we have become increasingly aware that the tide [of European colonial expansion] has been met by one flowing in the opposite direction." On p. 94 however he defended the rule of "backward people" by "more advanced" people on humanitarian grounds, and again on pp. 108ff. advocated for a relationship of "cooperation" between England and India analogous to that between capital and labor. On p. 153 he made one of his most startling assertions concerning the "conservation of racial integrity" in arguing against racial inter-marriage, an assertion that is by no means peripheral to his understanding of the relationship between the races and reveals Oldham's work to be far less progressive than it is usually credited for being: "In view of what the white race has actually accomplished in history it is evident that certain qualities that make for human progress are present in that race. The lack of historical achievement up to the present among the black peoples suggests that while they may possess other desirable qualities, those which have made white civilization possible may not be distributed among them in the same degree. We cannot be certain that this is so, but it is possible, or, as many would say, probable." This meant, Oldham continued, that racial intermingling risks the loss to humankind of "qualities which have largely contributed to human progress. The risk is far too great to be run." The statements from the Oxford Conference and the Evanston Assembly reveal the ecumenical movement as a whole to have advanced far beyond Oldham's racism however.

65. W. A. Visser't Hooft, ed., *The Evanston Report: The Second Assembly of the World Council of Churches, 1954* (New York: Harper and Row, 1955), pp. 153-155, 158. The narrative account of Dr. Benjamin Mays speech before the Assembly is found on pp. 42-44. The Rev. Peter Dagadu of the Gold Coast spoke several days earlier on the effects of white racism upon all Africans, pp. 37-38.

66. Paul Abrecht, "The Development of Ecumenical Social Thought and Action," in *The Ecumenical Advance: A History of the Ecumenical Movement, Vol. 2, 1948-1968*, Harold E. Fey, ed., p. 245.

67. See the WCC delegation report, *Mission in South Africa: April-December 1960* (Geneva: WCC, 1961).

68. *Christians in the Technical and Social Revolutions of our Time*, p. 160-161.

69. *Ibid.*, p. 175.

70. Norman Goodall, ed., *The Uppsala Report 1968: Official Report of the Fourth Assembly of the World Council of Churches* (Geneva: WCC, 1968), p. 241.

71. Ans J. van der Bent, ed., *World Council of Churches' Statements and*

Actions on Racism 1948-1979 (Geneva: WCC), pp. 26-27.

72. *Ibid*; see also the section in Hudson, *The World Council of Churches in International Affairs*, pp. 106-111.

73. Barbara Rogers, *Race: No Peace Without Justice* (Geneva: WCC, 1980), p. 97. The criteria for grants from the Special Fund were adopted by the WCC Executive Committee in 1970. See van der Bent, *World Council of Churches' Statements and Actions on Racism*, p. 31.

74. Hudson, *The World Council of Churches in International Affairs*, lists the PCR grants for 1970 to 1976 (excluding 1972). While the PCR states that grants are made for humanitarian purposes, it is careful not to attempt to dictate or control their use, as such control breaks the relationship of solidarity the grants are intended to forge.

75. Marlin VanElderen, *Introducing the World Council of Churches* (Geneva: WCC, 1990), pp. 34 and 62 notes the controversy generated by the PCR over the course of its life. Hudson, *The World Council of Churches in International Affairs*, in chapter 2, entitled "White Devils," examines the controversy within the WCC and the North Atlantic churches that greeted the creation of the PCR. Rogers, *Race: No Peace Without Justice*, examines the issues surrounding the PCR through the lens of a PCR Consultation held in 1980. Perhaps the best example of a sustained attack on PCR is to be found in the work of Ernest W. Lefever; see, for instance, his *Amsterdam to Nairobi: The World Council of Churches and the Third World* (Washington: Ethics and Public Policy Center, 1979), and *Nairobi to Vancouver: The World Council of Churches and the World, 1975-87* (Washington: Ethics and Public Policy Center, 1987).

76. The theological basis for the WCC's struggle against racism is articulated well in Rogers, *Race: No Peace Without Justice*, pp. 1-21. The final Statement from the 1980 Consultation that her book reports states in its opening paragraph: "Every human being, created in the image of God, is a person for whom Christ has died. Racism, which is the use of a person's racial origins to determine the person's value, is an assault on *Christ's* values and a rejection of *His* sacrifice. Wherever it appears, whether in the individual or in the collective, it is sin. It must be openly fought by all those who are on Christ's side, and by the Church as the designated vehicle and instrument of Christ's purpose in the world." (emphasis original) The paragraph succinctly sums up the Christological, anthropological, and ecclesiological doctrinal issues at stake in the struggle against racism. See also *Racism in Theology and Theology Against Racism* (Geneva: WCC, 1975).

77. Michael Kinnamon, *Truth and Community: Diversity and its Limits in the Ecumenical Movement* (Grand Rapids: Wm. B. Eerdmans, 1988), esp. pp. 59ff., examines the developments within the ecumenical movement which have led to the racism of South African Apartheid being declared a heresy, and a matter of *status confessionis* within the ecumenical community.

78. James M. Washington, *Frustrated Fellowship: The Black Baptist Quest for Social Power* (Macon, Ga: Mercer University Press, 1986), examines the theological and confessional role anti-racism played in the formation of Black Baptist associations and in the struggle for Black Baptist national denominational identity in the U.S. The prominence of the term "African" in the names of two of the major streams of Black Methodism in the USA, the African Methodist Episcopal Church and the African Methodist Episcopal Zion Church, indicates a similar awareness of the theological and ecclesiological importance of racial identity and of the quest for historical liberation.

79. Constance F. Parvey, ed., *The Community of Women and Men in the Church: A Report of the World Council of Churches' Conference, Sheffield, England, 1981* (Philadelphia: Fortress Press, 1983), p. 5.

80. Kathleen Bliss, *The Service and Status of Women in the Churches* (London: SCM Press, 1952), p. 185.

81. *Ibid.*, p. 199.

82. Department on Faith and Order, *Concerning the Ordination of Women* (Geneva: WCC, 1964). Proceedings of a 1970 consultation on the ordination of women, sponsored by the Commission on Women in Church and Society, were published in Brigalia Bam, ed., *What is Ordination Coming To?* (Geneva: WCC, 1971).

83. Especially surprising is the silence concerning women in church and society in the studies on the World Council and "social issues." Duff, *The Social Thought of the World Council of Churches*, Bock, *In Search of a Responsible World Society*, and Hudson, *The World Council of Churches in International Affairs* all ignore the subject for instance.

84. Hanfried Krüger, "The Life and Activities of the World Council of Churches," in *The Ecumenical Advance*, H. Fey, ed., p. 50.

85. Melanie A. May, *Bonds of Unity: Women, Theology, and the Worldwide Church* (Atlanta: Scholars Press, 1989), is the most comprehensive study to date on the WCC and issues of women and sexism.

86. *Christians in the Technical and Social Revolutions of our Time*, p. 41.

87. *Ibid.*, p. 162.

88. *Ibid.*, p. 165. See also p.p. 177-178.

89. *Sexism in the 1970's: Discrimination Against Women: A Report of the WCC Consultation West Berlin 1974* (Geneva: 1975), p. 5.

90. Commission on Faith and Order, *Uniting in Hope: Reports and Documents from the Meeting of the Faith and Order Commission* (Geneva: WCC, 1975); see also Parvey, *Community of Women and Men*, pp. 11-13.

91. Paton, *Breaking Barriers: Nairobi 1975*, pp. 113-115.

92. Parvey, *Community of Women and Men*, p. ix; see May, *Bonds of Unity*, for a thorough exploration of the process leading up to and beyond Sheffield 1981.

93. Parvey, *Community of Women and Men*, pp. 24-25.

94. *Ibid.*, p. 81.

95. *Ibid.*

96. May, *Bonds of Unity*, p. 6.

97. *Ibid.*, p. 129.

98. Thomas F. Best, ed., *Beyond Unity-in-Tension: Unity, Renewal and the Community of Women and Men* (Geneva: WCC, 1988).

99. See the contribution by Constance F. Parvey to the 1985 Prague Consultation, "The Continuing Significance of the Community of Women and Men in the Church Study: its Mixed Meanings for the Churches," in Best, *Beyond Unity-in-Tension*, p. 40.

100. See Melanie A. May, ed., *Women and Church: The Challenge of Ecumenical Solidarity in an Age of Alienation* (Grand Rapids: Wm. B. Eerdmans / New York: Friendship Press, 1991).

101. Milia Khodr, "Woman's Challenge to Orthodox Christianity," *WSCF Journal: A Quarterly* (Sept. 1990), p. 21. For a contrasting voice from an Orthodox woman, see Stephanie Yova Yazge's essay in *Women and Church*, May, ed., "From One Orthodox Woman's Perspective," pp. 65-69. The ecumenical dialogue concerning women in the Orthodox church dates back to at least the late 1970s; see for instance the reports from the 1976 Consultation of Orthodox Women held in Agapia, Romania, in Constance J. Tarasar and Irina Kivillova, eds., *Orthodox Women: Their Role and Participation in the Orthodox Church* (Geneva: WCC, 1977).

102. Parvey, *Community of Women and Men*, pp. 135-138.

103. *Ibid.*, pp. 138-144. See also Lorine M. Getz and Ruy O. Costa, eds., *Struggles for Solidarity: Liberation Theologies in Tension* (Minneapolis: Fortress Press, 1992); and T. Richard Snyder, *Divided We Fall: Moving from Suspicion to Solidarity* (Louisville: Westminster/John Knox Press, 1992).

104. *Ibid.*, p. 164

105. See Thomas F. Best, ed., *Vancouver to Canberra 1983- 1990: Report of the Central Committee of the World Council of Churches to the Seventh Assembly* (Geneva: WCC, 1990), pp. 176-177.

106. *Ibid.*, pp. 147-151. See also Preman Niles, *Resisting the Threats to Life: Covenanting for Justice, Peace and the Integrity of Creation* (Geneva: WCC, 1989); and D. Preman Niles, ed., *Between the Flood and the Rainbow: Interpreting the Conciliar Process of Mutual Commitment (Covenant) to Justice, Peace and the Integrity of Creation* (Geneva: WCC, 1992).

107. See Kinnamon, *Truth and Community*.

108. The rediscovery of the theological importance of the doctrine of the Trinity is too great to document in an endnote, but relevant to the issues of unity amidst diversity and community, I would note the statement from the Nairobi Assembly that unity grounded in the tri-unity of God insures the diversity of the church, in Paton, *Breaking Barriers: Nairobi 1975*, p. 61; concerning Sheffield, see Janet Crawford, "The Continuing Significance of the

Community Study: Sheffield and Beyond," in Best, *Beyond Unity-in-Tension,* pp. 52-53. See also Konrad Raiser, *Ecumenism in Transition: A Paradigm Shift in the Ecumenical Movement?* (Geneva: WCC, 1991),pp. 91-96.

109. On the Trinity and the *oikonomia* of God see Catherine Mowry LaCugna, *God for Us: The Trinity and Christian Life* (San Francisco: HarperCollins, 1991), and Leonardo Boff, *Trinity and Society* (Maryknoll: Orbis Books, 1988).

Chapter 4:

Renewing Mission

That the New and Renewal are peaks of human life, that one can define the human by the desire for the new and by the capacity for renewal -- is perhaps a basic truth, but a truth. --Emmanuel Levinas[1]

1. Missions and Ecumenics

During the closing weeks of 1938 four hundred and seventy delegates from almost seventy nations gathered on the campus of the Madras Christian College in Tambaram, India for a World Meeting of the International Missionary Council (IMC). Amidst the reports and deliberation of the conference the decision the previous year by Faith and Order and Life and Work to merge was considered in light of its consequences for the IMC. At one point the delegates noted in a Section Report on "Co-operation and Unity" their interest in the proposed World Council, but added cautiously:

> We look forward with confidence to the part which the younger churches will play in the future work of the Council. We trust that in the application of the constitution care will be taken to ensure that the membership of the Council is genuinely representative of indigenous leadership.[2]

Stressing the importance and integrity of the IMC, Tambaram reaffirmed the independence of the Missionary Council while endorsing cooperation with the WCC (shortly to be concretized through the formation of a Joint Committee). Despite the close relationship which emerged, and a great deal of overlap in programs and personnel, the two bodies maintained their separate identities during the period of formation and first years of the World Council.

Both organizations were concerned with the ecumenical quest for unity and mission. Both had taken up consideration of issues concerning confessional or denominational differences, the relationship of the churches to social life, and the relationship between Western and non-Western churches. Together with other world ecumenical bodies such as the YMCA, the YWCA, the World's Student Christian Federation, and the World Alliance for International Friendship, the IMC and now the WCC were both expressions of and contributors to world Christianity's increasing consciousness of being one community, noted William Paton in his address on "The Church and the World Community" at Tambaram. Through personal friendships and mutual responsibility universal Christian fellowship was becoming a reality. Paton pointed out the importance of the WCC in this regard:

> The proposals for the formation of a World Council of Churches are in some ways the most significant attempt yet made to gather together these movements toward a world Christian fellowship and to give to this widely distributed spirit and aspiration an adequate outward embodiment.[3]

Despite these factors, however, there were reasons for maintaining the separation of the IMC from the emerging WCC. Paton explained that the Faith and Order movement had had an ecclesiastical focus regarding unity, while Life and Work had been concerned with the relationship of Christian faith to modern society. As we have seen above, the questions of confessional and denominational unity with which Faith and Order primarily dealt were issues that emerged historically from the context of the Western European churches. Likewise the modern social reality addressed by Life and Work was specifically that of the post-Christian Western civilization. The distinct task of the IMC, however, was to be "a constant reminder of the Christian obligation to the evangelization of the world."[4] The "world" in its case was the human community which lay outside the domain of Western Christian faith. As a "constant reminder" the IMC served to define the boundaries of the Christian community, even as it sought to extend those boundaries and eradicate the difference between Christian and non-Christian. Its primary focus on world mission mandated the

IMC's separate organizational identity according to Paton.

At the time of the Tambaram meeting the world in which missions operated was still defined as those lands beyond Christendom, and the IMC was still concerned primarily with the development of churches outside European civilization. While the identification of missions with non-Western contexts would come to be challenged and eventually overturned in ecumenical discourse over the next several decades, the continuing independence of the IMC was in part due to the fact that non-European churches were better represented in its deliberations. IMC membership included representation from national councils and mission boards, whereas membership in the WCC was restricted to churches recognized by the WCC as being autonomous. Because Western churches continued to exercise control over significant numbers of non-European churches historically related to Western missions, non-Europeans were more likely to be participants in the IMC.[5] Furthermore, the common Western Protestant conceptualization of the world outside the domain of European civilization as constituting "mission lands" relegated the emergent national and regional associations of churches in Africa, Asia, and even Latin America to being those of the "mission" churches (usually called the "younger" churches after 1928) and thus outside Western Christendom. The result was to give African, Asian, and Latin Americans greater presence and visibility within the IMC than they initially had in the WCC.

That the IMC survived as an independent organization through the 1950s had as much to do with it being an important vehicle for non-European ecumenical interests (in spite of its Western domination) as it had to do with the division between unity and mission. Within the IMC non-European church leaders exercised more power than they could have initially within the WCC. At the same time, as we shall see, the manner in which the IMC institutionalized missionary relationships between Western and non-Western churches virtually guaranteed its eventual demise as an independent institution. That came in 1961 when the IMC merged into the WCC to become the Commission on World Mission and Evangelism. Thus in 1961 the WCC came to hold together three separate streams of the ecumenical movement in one institutional framework. Two of them, Faith and Order and Life and Work (Church and Society), were identified primarily with the ecumenical search for unity; the third, the IMC, was identified primarily with missions. As the third stream, missions did not come belatedly to the ecumenical movement however. Indeed, as Norman Goodall wrote in 1972, "The oldest strand in the modern ecumenical movement is that which is concerned with the world mission of the Church."[6]

The WCC, and the ecumenical movement in general, have often been depicted as descendants of the modern missionary expansion of the Western churches.[7] The extension of Protestant and Catholic churches in non-Western societies is commonly portrayed as the first phase of a process though which both a global Christian community emerged and the theological meaning of universality and unity of Christian faith will eventually be achieved. Through the missionary movement and the subsequent ecumenical movement for church unity Christianity is said to have realized in history its inner ideal as a world religion. For this reason Henry P. Van Dusen, President of Union Theological Seminary, New York, argued in 1959 for according missions priority among the two developments (missions and unity) that together "constitute the most significant feature of Christianity in the modern era...."[8]

> While each of these historic developments had its origin at about the same time, the dawn of the nineteenth century, and while they advanced side-by-side through the past hundred and fifty years in close contact and mutual influence, they have *not* been merely parallel. The relationship has been intimate and interdependent; it has *not* been strictly reciprocal. On the contrary, causative influences have moved preponderantly from the first to the second. The *Christian World Mission* has been the principal parent of the effort after *Christian Unity*.[9]

Another significant proponent of causative relationship between missions and unity was William Richey Hogg whose *Ecumenical Foundations: A History of the International Missionary Council And Its Nineteenth-Century Background* has exerted considerable influence within ecumenical studies. According to Hogg, as Protestant individuals and churches began organizing missionary operations, they found themselves drawn across confessional boundaries for strategic purposes in mission societies. The scandal of a divided Christendom was seen as a hindrance to propagation of the Gospel, for if Christians differed among themselves concerning their interpretations of the Gospel, that same Gospel could not easily be presented as absolute truth. European and North American missionaries stationed in non-Western situations also found themselves cooperating across confessional boundaries in strategic matters; but more importantly they discovered "Christian fellowship" among themselves. Thus, said Hogg, Western mission supporters and Western missionaries initiated the conferences which "became a main current flowing into Edinburgh, 1910."[10]

The causative historical relationship that has often been attributed to the history of modern Western missions in the ecumenical movement has not only served as a structuring principle controlling the meaning of the ecumenical movement. It has served to connect the modern ecumenical movement almost exclusively to the history of churches in Western Europe (Protestant as well as Catholic) in a master narrative of global Christianity. The history of the expansion of Western missions has been given privileged theological status, serving hermeneutically to link the majority of non-Western churches with the Apostolic era and the Gospels by way of Western church history. The same missionary expansion, and the history of the North Atlantic political, industrial, and cultural expansion of which it was a part, are credited with having re-opened contact between the Latin European and Eastern Orthodox churches, and even with stimulating renewal in inter-Orthodox relations.

Such is the relationship, for instance, that the former President of Princeton Theological Seminary, John A. Mackay described in his important "textbook" on *Ecumenics: The Science of the Church Universal*. The missionary movement, he argued, "is rightly regarded as the greatest and most significant spiritual movement in the history of Christianity."[11] It has inspired and made possible the field of ecumenics as a theological discipline. Ecumenics, according to Mackay, is the field of study of the missionary effort of the church in the present, the extending of the ministry of the church both geographically and socially, in its dimensions of breadth and depth.

The rediscovery of the church as church (Oxford, 1937) was facilitated by the discovery of the mission of the church. For this reason missions could no longer be treated in isolation from the role that the whole church had as a world missionary community. "The inescapable perspective that the Missionary Movement created is: *the mission of the whole Church in the total world situation*."[12] Grounding his perspective christologically, Mackay fixed his theological gaze first upon Jesus, the historical man who gave human history a fresh start through his resurrection from the dead. It was Jesus who established the church in history, and gave to it the historical mandate (linked with Peter) to disciple all nations. The ecumenical task was to realize God's eternal purpose in creating a new community, the church, which God designed to fulfill Christ's purpose in history. Thus the missionary movement is the "chief expression in history of God's redemptive action."[13] Missions, understood christologically as the whole work of the church, had given rise to the field of ecumenics.

This theological transformation of missions into ecumenics found its institutional counterpart ultimately in the integration of the International Missionary Council into the World Council of Churches at the New Delhi Assembly in 1961. Three years prior the 1961 Assembly, at the 1958 IMC Assembly in Ghana, Walter Freytag had raised the fact that Western missions were experiencing limitations, "lost directness," and even an "endangered image" in the changing global realities of the post-War world.[14] The earlier stage, in which missions took the Gospel into nations where there was no church, had been superseded by a situation in which churches were in all countries, bound together in ecumenical fellowship now in the WCC. The initiative practiced by Western missionaries in non-Western churches was being restricted in the new situation of growing independence (political and ecclesiastical).[15]

In response the Ghana Assembly recalled the final statement from the 1952 IMC Willingen Meeting and reaffirmed missions as an expression of God's mission.[16] The exact contours of this *missio Dei* could still not be discerned by the IMC delegates at Ghana, but the fact that the missionary movement itself was in a time of crisis seemed evident. A new vocabulary for missions had emerged from the IMC during the late 1940s and through the 1950s. For instance, a new form of "partnership" between formerly sending and receiving churches became a critical concern at the Whitby IMC Meeting in 1947.[17] Affirmation of the missionary imperative of the churches to be in solidarity with the world in which they live was articulated first at Whitby in 1947 and expanded on at Willingen in 1952.[18] But most important, a critique of the vocabulary of "younger" and "older" churches, terms which had continued to structure relationships between Western churches and a great number of non-Western churches in the ecumenical movement, was heard at Ghana in 1958.   James K. Matthews, in a background paper prepared for Ghana on the subject of "partnership," pointed explicitly to the verbal trouble:

> Almost before they became commonly used about 1928 the inadequacy of the terms, 'younger' and 'older' churches was sensed. Their use at all seemed almost a denial of the universality of the Church; and their continued use, a mark of unrealized partnership.[19]

The Statement received by the Ghana Assembly confirmed this judgment rejecting the validity of 'younger/older' church distinctions. Erik W. Nielsen, in his reflections on the tasks confronting the IMC, argued that "the churches in Asia and Africa must be taken much more seriously...."[20] The 1958 Ghana Assembly, in approving a plan of integration into the WCC, confirmed not only that the context of the ecumenical movement was changing but that basic questions regarding the very nature of missions could no longer be regarded apart from the emerging global relationships among churches in a post-colonial world. It was not merely coincidental that the same year Mackay's study on ecumenics was published another book was published entitled, *Missionary Go Home!* In that other text James Scherer wrote: "The times of political, cultural and ecclesiastical mission are nearly past, and they will never return."[21]

2. Missions, Christendom, and the non-European Other

To the delegates at the Edinburgh World Missionary Conference in 1910 it would hardly have seemed possible that the word "crisis" could be used to describe the movement in which they were engaged. While there were in Edinburgh's deliberations hints of the controversies that lay ahead, the conference as a whole presented the picture of a self-confident, triumphant Western Christendom.[22] The consensus of the conference concerning the close relationship between European- North American civilization and Christianity blinded it to the inner contradictions of this civilization -- contradictions that would become more apparent in the succeeding decades. Kenneth Scott Latourette, describing the conference from the stand-point of the late 1940s, said:

> In the Conference addresses one searches in vain for any hint of the wars which were so soon to convulse mankind [sic]. Some recognition was given to the rising tide of nationalism in the East and to the problems which this presented to the Christian forces. But there was no prophetic sense of what was coming upon the world.[23]

On one of the final days of deliberations, the delegates voted unanimously to create a Continuation Committee that would carry on the conference work of study and counsel. "This was Edinburgh's climatic moment," wrote W. Richey Hogg.[24] The conference came to its feet and spontaneously broke into the Doxology in praise. The Continuation Committee was formed on the last day of the conference, with John R. Mott as chairperson and J.H. Oldham the salaried secretary, positions similar to those they would hold a decade later when the IMC was organized as successor to the work of the Continuation Committee.[25]

Between the organization of the IMC in 1921 and the first Assembly of the WCC in 1948, two IMC conferences defined the shape of mission discussions within the Council. In 1928 delegates to the IMC met in Jerusalem, and confronted a number of critical issues, including racism and the question of Christianity's relationship to other religions and to secularism in the modern age.[26] A decade later, in Tambaram, delegates again discussed fundamental questions about the relationship between Christian faith and other religions, and between Christian faith and the modern world.[27] In 1938 however, even though the number of non-European participants had increased to nearly half of the delegates, the position articulated by Hendrik Kraemer in his book written for the conference, *The Christian Message in a Non-Christian World*,[28] dominated the discussions.

The Jerusalem and Tambaram conferences together reveal a great deal of ecumenical confusion concerning the relationship between Christian communities and their socio-cultural matrices. At the heart of the confusion is the question of the relationship between Christianity and the history of Western civilization. At the same time this confusion is overlaid with issues concerning the relationship between the Christian and 'non-Christian' religions, obscuring important historical and cultural dimensions of the matter. In the IMC's struggle to articulate a mission theology adequate to the changes which were taking place across the globe during the first half of the twentieth century one can discern a fundamental ambiguity concerning the relationship between Christian faith and the history of Europe, an ambiguity that often surfaced in discussions concerning the relationship of religion and culture.

The social and cultural contexts of non-European peoples were rendered Other in the dominant mission theology of the Western churches by being named "non-Christian."[29] While primarily articulated in religious terms, such theology served ideologically to exclude social, political, and cultural forms of non-European life as well. The goal of missions was not only the extension of Christian faith or founding of Christian communities in new locations; conversion was explicitly defined as the eradication of religio-cultural beliefs, practices, and institutions among non-European peoples. Christian mission by definition appeared to many to require the practice of religiocide or ethnocide, both being variants of genocide. Conversion meant erasure of social and cultural memory of the non-Christian religious Other, and its replacement by a Christian memory which was essentially European or Eurocentric. Such mission theology identified the Christian religion with European political, social and cultural history. The converse of this identification, that the non-Western world was until recently non-Christian, rendered non-European Christian communities anomalous and even invisible.[30]

This theology of mission was built upon the premise that European history was synonymous with Church history. Since Christianity historically was primarily a European religion, Christian missions would by definition mean the advance of European historical cultural identity. While the Christian faith had spread from Palestine into several continents during its early centuries, eventually it became the dominant religion in the Greco-Roman world of the Mediterranean basin and then in what would become Western Europe. There in Europe it played a major formative role in social, political, and cultural life unparalleled in any other civilization. In a Latin form, and under the hierarchical rule of the church of Rome, Christianity would be the principal religion of European civilization up through the modern era. For Roman Catholic theologies of mission the historical primacy of the See of St. Peter in Rome secured what for Protestants was a more general cultural primacy expressed in liturgy, theology and practice. For both Protestants and Roman Catholics, European civilization was predominantly Christian and European cultural forms alone were legitimate modes for expressing Christian faith. Non-European forms of Christianity were viewed as inferior or degenerate, and non-European cultural forms rejected because of their association with 'pagan' (non-Christian) religious practices.[31]

The assumption that European cultural history and Christian faith were synonymous required another, equally tenuous assumption that European Christianity at least in its historical form was a homogeneous social-political-cultural-religious synthesis. The memory of a unified Western Church, and of the totalizing cultural synthesis of the Western medieval *Corpus Christianum* has functioned as a powerful myth within the ecumenical movement over the past century.[32] It has obscured the actual historical diversity of European Christianity, accepted the dominant historical appraisal of so-called 'heresies,' and minimized the histories of European communities of dissent. It has also eclipsed the historical significance of non-Christian religions to European history, contributing to anti-Jewish and anti-Islamic currents in European Christian practice and to the suppression of women's spirituality.[33]

The myth of the unified social-cultural synthesis of *Corpus Christianum* (and it is a myth, for European civilization was never so unified as it has looked in hindsight) has tended to structure the European encounter with non-Europeans in terms of an encounter between Christian and non-Christian religions. The roots of the myth lie deep in the historical encounter between Latin European Christianity and Islam a millennium ago when the armies of *dar-al Islam* first threatened Christian Europe and further isolated the Latin churches. Its militaristic expression as a 'Crusade' emerged in the twelfth century of the common era, when Islam was portrayed in Western European Christian theology as constituting the single greatest threat to Christendom and to the very existence of Christian faith and Christians took up a 'Holy War' against infidels.[34] During the period of European colonial and missionary expansion into Latin America, Asia and Africa, it was often the aggressive convictions against Islam that were extended to apply to the other religions Europeans encountered.[35] At the dawn of the modern period European Christianity knew the powerful symbolism of a unified *Corpus Christianum* confronting a world of heretics, unbelievers, pagans and heathens.

Within Europe, the period following the Enlightenment of the seventeenth and eighteenth centuries was marked by a significant "de-Christianization" of the dominant institutions and intellectual life of the society. The rise of modern science and the nation-state were joined with philosophical and even theological movements which severed the synthesis of church and civilization.[36] The resulting religious liberalism in Europe and North America in the nineteenth century allowed the comparative study of religion to gain acceptance at least within certain intellectual sectors of Western society.[37] Christianity continued to be granted a privileged position within cultural discourse of the West, but as the 'heritage' of the modern West, now called the "Judeo-Christian tradition."[38] Significantly many in the churches of the West came to accept this new conception of their heritage which allowed European-American civilization to become post-Christian, while rendering the rest of the world non-Christian.

It was in this nineteenth century atmosphere, but holding to a memory of the medieval synthesis of Christendom, that the 1910 Edinburgh conference was called to consider problems encountered by missions in the non-Christian world.[39] Commission IV of the 1910 conference specifically examined other religions, attempting to locate points of contact as well as themes for missionary apologetics. The Commission's preparatory question concerning the possible problem of the "Western form" of Christianity proved to be unintelligible to those missionaries who submitted responses for the conference.[40] On the other hand, the problem of the "alternative" West was proving to be a perplexing dilemma. Several of the respondents in the Commission report perceived the modern, secular West, associated with materialistic values and the critical intellectual practice of science, as competing with mission for the heart of the non-Christian world.[41]

At the Jerusalem Meeting of the IMC in 1928, the two challenges addressed by the preparatory documents of Section I were again the non-Christian religions and modern secularism. The theme of Christ being the fulfillment of non-Christian religions, critically bringing other religious faiths to their own inner perfection, was articulated in several preparatory papers as well as in the conference sessions at Jerusalem. Christian exclusivism and the concomitant missiological practice of eradication of non-Christian beliefs were expressed at the 1928 Meeting. But the fulfillment thesis was also articulated, most notably in contributions by Asian delegates such as T.C. Chao, Francis C. Wei, and Justice P. Chenchiah.[42] Alongside the debate concerning the missiological relationship between Christian and non-Christian religions was another, focused on the preparatory paper by Rufus Jones, "The Secular Civilization and the Christian Task."[43]

In his paper, Jones argued that the breakup of the unity of the church in Europe, coupled with rising nationalism and the development of humanism, resulted in a large fraction of those living in "Christian lands" no longer turning their attention to the ministrations of the church. The task which confronted the church demanded renewal of discipleship in order to evangelize the modern secular world, both Western ("at home") and non- Western ("foreign fields").[44] Secularism had raised the challenge that the churches in the post-Christian world stood in a fundamentally equal position to the churches in the non-Christian world insofar as the missionary task was concerned. Jones' conclusions warrant extended quotation:

> We go to Jerusalem, then, not as members of a Christian nation to
> convert other nations which are not Christian, but as Christians within a
> nation far too largely non-Christian, who face within their own borders
> the competition of a rival movement as powerful, as dangerous, as
> insidious as any of the great historic religions. We meet our fellow
> Christians in these other countries, therefore, on terms of equality, as
> fellow workers engaged in a common task. More than this, we go as
> those who find in the other religions which secularism attacks, as it
> attacks Christianity, witnesses of mankind's [sic] need of God and allies
> in our quest of perfection.[45]

Rufus Jones' paper not only challenged the churches of the West to
their own renewal of faith. By posing the modern, secular West as a
non-Christian situation it disrupted the connection between the churches
of Europe and European civilization, and thus severed these churches
from the history of Christendom. The churches of the West were in a
missionary context parallel to that of churches outside Europe and North
America. In this new situation of equality, all churches lived in a non-
Christian world. Furthermore, the "great historic religions" of the world
were no longer the Other to be eliminated. As other religions, they
remained rivals. But in facing the modern, secular Western culture they
were allies. Christians engaged concretely with missions could not fail
to see the implications of Jones' characterization of other religions in
a more positive light as allies and co-workers.

The criticisms of Jerusalem were heard throughout the ecumenical
movement, beginning at the conference itself.[46] The danger of
syncretism was raised by many. Others not at Jerusalem, most notably
Karl Barth, seriously challenged the missionary interest in secularism.[47]
Barth perceived the confrontation with secularism to be misguided, for
the real threat in the modern era was posed by new religions:
Communism, Fascism, and Americanism. These "secular" religions fell
under his more general critique of religion. He leveled his 1932 attack
upon the Jerusalem meeting from this critical perspective, for Jerusalem
had in his view taken a positive approach to human religiosity.

It was Hendrik Kraemer who brought the Barthian perspective to the
missionary movement most forcefully in his 1938 publication of *The
Christian Message in a Non-Christian World*. Debate continues in
ecumenical circles concerning Kraemer and his theology of Christian
exclusivism.[48] But read in light of Rufus Jones' conclusions at
Jerusalem, that the new historical situations of churches in a modern,

non-Christian world called for a new relationship between Christian and non-Christian religions, *The Christian Message* can be seen to be an attempt to give the "Christian world/non-Christian world" historical dichotomy, and the underlying historical concept of Christendom, a powerful new articulation.

The Christian Message in a Non-Christian World opened with an analysis of the crisis of relativism and secularism in Western civilization, and the crisis the West had brought about in the civilizations of the East. In the West relativism was perceived particularly as a problem for theology because Christianity, as a religion of revelation, stood for absolute truth and could not treat skepticism as comparatively innocent. The struggle was between the relative and the absolute, the church's "abiding tension between its essential nature and its empirical condition."[49]

The church, claimed Kraemer, is a divine-human society, living between two histories as an empirical institution. Within an empirical and sinful order, the church is nevertheless founded upon a new divine order brought to light by Jesus Christ. The tension, or "crisis" of the present was that the *Corpus Christianum* had collapsed, exposing the manner in which the divine vision had been blurred by the attempt to create a Christian civilization.[50] The reorientation of the church regarding its relationship toward the world was now possible on account of the crisis. This was true as well for missions, since the bondage of Christendom had been broken on the one hand, and the prestige of the colonial West was so low on the other. A theology of missions was called for in this time of crisis, one which could perceive the transcendent dimension of missions through the eyes of faith, revealed by divine grace.[51]

In this new situation, the movement from missions (colonial model) to indigenous churches (interdependent model) was now possible. Up to this point Kraemer was following a path similar to the one taken by Rufus Jones in 1928. But then Kraemer diverged from the possibility of meeting the non-Western churches on an equal footing. The church of the twentieth century was said to be in a situation analogous to that of the church of the Roman empire. However:

> The comparison must not be stressed too hard, because one of the most marked differences is the important fact that in all sorts of ways, perceptible and imperceptible, Christian influences for centuries have molded the life and outlook of the "Christian world."[52]

This established crucial historical priority for Kraemer.

> The older Churches by their missionary initiatives and activity are the
> parents of these Churches and the cause that Christianity in the
> non-Christian continents has established itself and attained there to a
> position of new and great responsibility.[53]

Theologically, Jesus Christ was the foundation, the cause, of the
churches. Missiologically and historically, the Western churches were
the foundation, the cause, the parent, of non-European churches. While
Kraemer looked forward to interdependence among adult churches, the
non-Europeans would remain adult children.

This meant that the movement of faith was marked by translation of
Western forms into non-Western ones. The concepts, experiences, and
ideas engendered in the course of history by revelation do not
adequately encompass revelation, Kraemer argued. They are the
historical effect of it, however, and so revelation is grasped through
them. But the irreducible origin of Christian faith is found in the
historical revelation, the event, witnessed to in the Bible. Kraemer
termed this "Biblical realism": a narrative of divine activities which
escapes religious or philosophical reductions to a coherent system. It
is presented as a Word which must be accepted on its own merit,
without human collaboration. It can only be presented as
incommensurable with all other religiosities. Biblical realism presents
Christian faith as the ongoing crisis of all religions -- including the
Christian religion.[54]

The kingdom of God is supra-historical, so that there can properly
be no Christian culture. But there is tension, a dialectical relationship
between the divine and human history. There is movement, history, and
an empirical society shaped in this tension, and this history continues
the history inaugurated in the Bible, according to Kraemer. Study of
this history requires eyes of faith with which to perceive the absolute
that has been in relationship with the empirical history of the institution
called the church. Hence for Kraemer there are non-Christian religions
and a Christian religion. Those Christians living in the "non-Christian
world" are forced into a critical stance toward "the whole cultural,
social and political structure and heritage of the people whom they
physically and spiritually are a living part" in a way that Christians
living in the West are not.[55] Other religions are approached only
through difference and antithesis, with no affirmation.

Here it becomes clear that it was not God who was the subject of Kraemer's missiological discourse, but the history of the Western churches. The empirical history of these churches, in their doctrinal and experiential development, was revelatory. The only difference between Christian history and non-Christian history is that "Empirical Christianity has stood and stands under continuous and direct influence and judgement of the revelation in Christ."[56] This revelation is only encountered historically, in one place, and that is the history of the Western churches. Thus in christological language Kraemer described the missionary vocation as "the point of contact" between God's grace and non-Europeans.[57] No other point of contact was possible. "The Christian revelation places itself over against the many efforts to apprehend the totality of existence."[58]

Those essential dogmas which have been articulated in the course of the empirical history of the Western church are not merely historical products, but are expressions of the essential structure of revelation. "They belong either explicitly or implicitly to the core of Biblical realism and are the heritage of the Christian Church."[59] Kraemer's conclusion closes the possibility of a new, and therefore of a different theology, for a non-European faith.

Apart from this fundamental argument and many more that could be suggested, the arising Younger churches can never live and develop as if the Christian Church had no history and had not coined a rich treasure of universally-used and respected religious terminology.[60]

Kraemer's next sentence indicated the attitude toward the cultural and social histories of non-European Christians inherent in this missiological concern for the history of the European churches:

Why be so deeply concerned about the religious heritage of the civilizations in which the Younger churches grow up, but wholly unconcerned about the religious heritage of their own Christian religion and of that body, the Church, which rightly claims their prime loyalty?[61]

At this point the central issue confronting the churches for Kraemer is revealed to be not so much the transcendent meaning of the Gospel of Jesus Christ as it is the churches' "prime loyalty" concerning their social and cultural histories. It was the place of the cultural and religious heritage of Western civilization that Kraemer sought to preserve, and that Tambaram struggled with (for even though Kraemer's position dominated the discussion in 1938, it did not go unchallenged[62]). One of the more forceful challenges came in a volume of essays entitled *Rethinking Christianity in India*, published in Madras prior to the Tambaram meeting and in response to Kraemer's book. In an essay included in *Rethinking Christianity in India* as an Appendix, Judge P. Chenchiah confronted Kraemer's underlying text regarding the religious heritage of Christian Western cultural memory with an alternative judgement regarding Christendom: "The solidarity of Christendom in the West and the prestige of Western culture in the East are both passing away."[63]   According to Chenchiah, Kraemer failed to comprehend the full meaning of the collapse of the Western *Corpus Christianum* which had resulted in its moral disintegration.

Eastern Christians were no longer going to become traitors to their own cultural heritage as Kraemer's position implied, Judge Chenchiah went on. Neither traditions nor theology, from the West or from the past, were considered binding on the church of India's future. "Let it be clearly understood that we accept nothing as obligatory save Christ."[64] In a similar vein, G.V. Job in the initial essay in the volume, asserted that "The Indian Church will be a city without foundation whose maker and builder is God."[65] The church in India is not to be built upon the historical and cultural foundations of Western Christendom, and its prime loyalty would therefore not be to the Western past. This was not to say that the Indian churches which had been founded by Western missions could deny their past or pretend to have been born in a vacuum, Job acknowledged. It was to say instead that as Indian Christians they "would take not only the [Western] Christian heritage, but also the Hindu heritage into [their] purview," accepting the principle, "the more the merrier."[66]

For Chenchiah, Job, and the other contributors to this volume, the cultural and religious heritage of India were a critical principle whereby the traditions, dogmas, and doctrines of the West would be evaluated, in light of their importance to the Indian church. In the discussion surrounding Tambaram new theological positions were being explored, but more important, a new relationship of churches to the diverse political and cultural communities of the world began to emerge. Tambaram was not the first place where non-Eurocentric understandings of church history and of theology and culture were heard in the ecumenical movement; it was a place where the lines were drawn most clearly in the debate however.[67] Tambaram met on the eve of a second cataclysmic European war that became global. It became a witness to the demands of the age for de-colonization of Christian theology, beginning with a new understanding of the relationship of Christian faith to the heritage of the Western *Corpus Christianum.* Noted D. Preman Niles in 1982: "From the time of Azariah and then of Chenchiah, it had become apparent that it will be difficult to discharge our theological as well as missiological tasks as long as we feel constrained to justify ourselves at the court of western theological and missiological thought."[68]

This is not to say that Kraemer's vision of the Western cultural heritage did not remain operative within the ecumenical movement, even in non-European contexts, after the war. To a degree it did. His concept of "biblical realism" was not generally embraced, and his exclusivist doctrine of revelation was increasingly criticized in the decades following 1945. But the doctrinal character and the fundamental historical identities of Asian, African, and even Latin American Christians and churches in the ecumenical movement remained partially captive within a realm of theological discourse, a "New Christendom," whose content was not God but the Western theological heritage.

3. Defining the Boundaries of Christendom

Following the War of 1939-1945, new political movements for de-colonization in Africa, Asia, and Latin America brought the cultural heritage of Christian churches into sharp focus. At stake, as Freytag understood in 1958 at Ghana, was the very concept of foreign missions from "Christian nations." Willingen's theological affirmation of missions as belonging to God (*missio Dei*), while seeking to transcend the historical and cultural conditions underlying the expansion of Western church missions tended to obscure the fact that the missionary-actors through whom the dynamic factor of historical change (conversion) was supposedly effected remained predominantly North American or European.[69] Further complicating the matter was the ambiguous relationship between the North Atlantic churches on the one hand, and the political system of liberal democracy and economic system of liberal capitalism on the other. The result was a tension between two fundamental understandings of mission that would became characteristic of the ecumenical movement after the 1950s. A "New Christendom" was called for on the one hand, and a commitment to the growing nationalist and liberationist movements in Asia, Africa, and Latin America on the other. These two projects presented divergent understandings of the manner in which Christian communities relate to and participate in social and political reality.

The post-War world of the West witnessed the process of secularization continuing to challenge the churches' self-perceptions regarding their place in Western culture. Despite numerical gains on the part of churches in some instances, over-all awareness of the decline of traditional Christian influences upon the social and cultural life of the nations of Western Europe and North America increased in the decades following 1945. One significant response to the phenomenon of a "de-Christianized" West was to assert the "Christian" character of this modern civilization by way of parentage, and thus to provide the basis for a new understanding of Christendom.

So it was that Hans Herman Walz argued in the *Ecumenical Review* in 1958 that modern civilization, including "the historical perspective" and "secularization," have grown from the soil of the Christian West.[70] In an allusion to Kant and Bonhoffer, Walz concluded that the world has now come of age, and that the church therefore should relinquish its role as tutor.[71] This was not to say that the mission of the church was unrelated to social reality. Rather, secularization (which Walz distinguished from the ideology, "secularism") is the way in which the church solves the problems of the world. It is the fruit now removed from the tree. His argument was to be made during the following decade in a number of ways as North Atlantic theologians sought to come to grips with what appeared to be a post-Christian world.[72] Christendom had been the symbol of a world in which faith and social reality had been integrated, the world of historical existence, or as Walz said, "the social incarnation of the Christian faith in place and time."[73] A New Christendom would stand as a similar symbol, integrating secularization and faith over against the threat of "secularism."[74]

The symbol of a New Christendom of "the total body of Christians in their life in the world" not bound by national and cultural identity was adapted by Ronald Orchard in his reflection upon missions in a post-Colonial era. This New Christendom was the world-wide Christian community, overlapping the institutional lives of the churches but not necessarily coterminous with them. Orchard felt that the concept of a New Christendom would continue the distinction between the Christian and the non-Christian in the modern world. From the Christian base missions would continue to be sent out into the non-Christian world. The concept of a New Christendom, however, "provides a 'base' for missions which is world-wide, and in principle delivers a particular mission from identification with a particular nation and culture."[75]

Orchard was aware of the difficulties involved in making the conceptual change necessary for this New Christendom to become an effective basis for missions. The inherited conceptions of missions as crossing geographical and cultural frontiers, from Christendom to non-Christendom, tended to obscure the current situation and hamper the emergence of a new understanding of mission.[76] For most Western Christians mission still meant sending individual representatives from the "home" base into non-Christian cultural situations. So Orchard wrote in 1959:

> It may be that our slowness in recognizing in thought and action the existence of such a world-wide base, and the continuing influence of the idea of Christendom, conceived in terms of a Western geographical-cultural entity, as the base of the Christian mission partly accounts for the slow emergence of missions in the so-called younger churches.[77]

Despite Orchard's hopes for a re-conceptualization of missions from a world-wide base, in practice missions continued to be sent out from the West. For all practical concerns, the economic and institutional basis for missions remained under the control of churches that were located historically in the shadows of the old European Christendom. The concept of New Christendom partially obscured the reality of the particular cultural or national identities of the mission 'sent out' and thus served partially to mask their Western identity. The proposal for a New Christendom held a hidden North Atlantic subject, one who was obscured by its reference to the global Christian community.[78]

The new nationalism of Asian and African churches was challenging this hidden subject of missions and theology in the 1950s, exposing the rifts between Western and non-Western churches. The question asked by Asian Christians, from the perspective of the non-Western church, was not what God is doing through Western missions, but "What is God doing in and through the national movements in Asia?"[79] From this perspective the relationship to the Western nations and churches was not one of a common Christendom, but one of Western "political domination and technical and cultural penetration."[80] Asian, African, and Latin American churches also faced the questions raised by secularization in the modern period, especially in regard to the rapid social change brought about through urban industrial development throughout the non-Western world. But the crisis of modernism, and the breakdown of Christendom had a fundamentally different meaning for those who had been under colonial rule. Most significantly, the relationship between ecumenical Christianity and liberal democracy was challenged by the new nationalism. As M. M. Thomas stated in 1947, "it is only a truth if I say that the presence of the Soviet power in the United Nations Organization is the one hope of these nations to preserve their right to resist and sustain their opposition."[81]

A similar stance was articulated at the Willingen IMC meeting in 1952 in an address by J. Russell Chandran of India, entitled "The Christian Mission and the Judgment of History." Recognizing that revolutionary situations of the day had brought about a crisis in missions, Chandran drew a distinction between the plural missions of the churches and the one Mission, which is Christ's commission to preach the Gospel in every culture. The plural missions of the churches "may undergo many radical changes in structural organizations, strategies and the like," in light of the changing environment or situations in which the Gospel is proclaimed.[82] The churches' task is to communicate the one Mission which is from God, however, a task they may in fact hinder as well as help.[83] Chandran provided several examples of the betrayal of Christianity by the West, noting that he had often been asked "whether a religion which has not given the western powers a sensitive conscience about war was worth while preaching to Indians."[84] The task before missions in this situation was to respond to the revolutionary situations of the contemporary world in light of the judgement upon the Western churches in order to carry out the one Mission of God in the world.

Chandran then sounded a prophetic note concerning what seemed to him at that time to be the "greatest revolutionary change" with which the churches had to reckon: the Communist revolution.[85] He cautioned against confusing the witness to the incarnate Lord with a stance for or against Communism, pointing out the dangers specifically of presenting Christian programs as being anti-Communist. In terms that prefigured themes to be developed more fully in the liberation theologies of the 1960s and 1970s, Chandran argued in 1952:

Communism cannot merely be understood as a demonic force in the world. On the contrary, it represents an inevitable phase in the growth of society. It represents the legitimate claim of all people to full participation in economic and political life. We can never forget that the justice for which Communism stands is rooted in Biblical insights. *We should also recognize that Communism is a judgment on the Church's failure to preach liberation to the socially and economically dispossessed peoples. It is a judgment on the Church's failure to witness to the incarnate Lord by accepting solidarity with the world.*[86]

Chandran went on in his address to discuss religious and cultural aspects of the revolutionary environment of Christians living in situations outside Western countries, and to pose specific suggestions for missions in response to these new imperatives. In hearing and responding to these imperatives he was not alone in the IMC, for by the 1950s other Asian, African and Latin American Christians involved in the anti-colonialist struggles in their countries and churches found themselves equally engaged in processes of religious and cultural reconstruction. A central aspect of cultural reconstruction in Asia and Africa in particular entailed the revival of non-Christian religions, drawing Asian and African Christians into mutual interaction in various degrees with religious histories that were also deemed 'non-Christian.' As Paul Devanandan stated, "[Asians] realize that a good deal of their national culture is closely related to their religious ideas, and that a cultural reintegration necessarily involves a religious reconstruction."[87]

Resurgent religions may have differed in their contributions to nationalist movements, or in their doctrinal affirmations. "But they are all agreed in their opposition to the missionary expansion of Christianity, for obvious reasons."[88] Devanandan's plea was that Christians not strengthen the anti-Christian drive of the renascent religions of Asia by furthering exclusivism or proselytism, and seek instead inter-religious dialogue and co-operation. His own engagement in interfaith dialogue entailed a common search for human community, moving toward a common understanding among the world religions.[89]

The two-fold critique of Western Christian missions, socio-political and religio-cultural, made by Thomas, Chandran, Devanandan, and others from non-Western churches, was addressing the fundamental identification of Western missions with Western colonialism and imperialism in the modern era. The socio-political context in which Western churches began to encounter cultures and religions beyond the boundaries of Christendom in the modern era (after 1500) was one of European colonialism and imperialism. As Kaj Baago noted in 1966, the missionary movement "was filled to the brim with western colonialism and imperialism."[90] Too often Western missions served as the religious ideology of the military and economic expansion of Western colonialism.[91]

This is not to say that all missionaries engaged directly in the political and economic penetration by the North Atlantic nations into the non-European world. Such active economic or political participation did happen in the nineteenth century, less so in the twentieth. More characteristic has been the indirect (and often unconscious) support provided by missions, in the area of ideological penetration and structural support for colonialism. Arthur Schlesinger has argued that missionaries were agents "of the Western assault on non-Western societies," not in the area of economic or political imperialism, but in their "cultural imperialism."

> Cultural imperialism means purposeful aggression by one culture against the ideas and values of another. The mere communication of ideas and values across national borders is not in itself imperialism....Such communication becomes aggression only when accompanied by political, economic, or military pressure.[92]

William R. Hutchison has noted that the ideology "Christian civilization" characteristic of North Atlantic churches during the nineteenth and early twentieth centuries conferred on these churches what he calls "the right to define" regarding culture and civilization.[93] The "fine spiritual imperialism" of missions reflected a more general attitude of cultural supremacy in Western colonialism which was often also racist.[94] Missionary vocabulary was replete with militaristic terminology, describing the expansion of Christianity as "occupying a field," or even as the "conquest of the world for Christ." And while European or U.S. colonial governments did not always support missionary activities within their regions of control, mission theorists from the turn of the century saw the capitalist and colonialist enterprises as an act of divine providence, the earthen vessels in which the Gospel was being carried to the ends of the earth.[95] Even a respected ecumenical leader as Max Warren of England as late as 1967 affirmed approvingly the missionary movement's contribution "to a particular social revolution -- the emergence of a bourgeoisie in those lands to which the expansion of Europe has taken the ideas of western man [sic]."[96]

Of course the missionary enterprise cannot be entirely characterized so negatively, nor did missions always serve unambiguously the ideology of Western imperialism. Dejung noted that at the Edinburgh Conference of 1910 the interests of the colonized over those of the colonial governments emerged as a critical point in the discussion concerning the relationship between church and state.[97] Lamin Sanneh has more recently argued that Christian missions, in their vernacular work in Scripture translations, have supported nationalist causes and stimulated indigenous cultural renewal.[98] The work of missionaries in education alienated many Africans from their own cultural life, served to train them for Western vocations, and disrupted the socialization patterns that undergirded African society. But it also provided the training for a number of nationalist leaders in Africa.[99] Missionary efforts in health care and social reform, while likewise not always being unambiguous in their effects, have nevertheless been an important contribution from missions.

Not often considered, however, have been the concrete contributions missions made to the Western churches themselves, or the reasons why Western churches and nations supported missions so enthusiastically. A reduction of missions to Western cultural imperialism fails to explain completely the expansion of Western churches after the nineteenth century. Other modes of cultural imperialism were at work in the Western history of colonial domination, and quite often Western national interests were not easily reconciled with missionary interests. Nor did the all of the churches of the ecumenical movement engage in missionary activities with the same degree of enthusiasm as did the dominant Protestant denominations in North America and Western Europe. There were other, often hidden, aspects of missions which only begin to be understood when examined in the light of the experience of the disintegration of Western Christendom. Alongside the call of the Spirit to Mission another dynamic was operative in the missions sent from Western churches. That other dynamic was the historical process that created the modern secular West, accompanied by the disintegration of the cultural synthesis of Christendom and the further fragmentation of the churches as well.[100] A critical factor at play in the emergence and development of the modern missionary movement was the Western churches' search for the regeneration of the *Corpus Christianum*.

Gustav Warnack at the end of the nineteenth century noted that the pietistic revivals of Protestantism had generated the first and most lasting initiatives for foreign missions in the modern era. Pietism had demonstrated within European culture the continued vitality of the Christian faith over against its modern detractors. Foreign missions were likewise an expression of such vitality, and a demonstration of Christianity's ability to grow.[101]   At the same time, faced with the collapse of the Western cultural synthesis of the *Corpus Christianum* and the impending demise of Christianity in the West, some mission apologists saw in the growth of Christianity outside of the North Atlantic a hope for renewal of Christianity in the West.   So the concluding section on African religions in the Report of Commission IV at the World Missionary Conference at Edinburgh in 1910 noted:

> The best of the converts on the soil of uncivilized heathenism, according to the evidence received, represent a beautiful type of piety....And just as many a parent has re-earned religious lessons by coming into touch with the piety of childhood, so it may well happen that the Christianity of Europe is destined to be recalled, if not to forgotten truths, as least to neglected graces, by the infant churches....[102]

The sharp conclusions drawn by J.C. Hoekendijk half a century after Edinburgh 1910 still demand attention:

> To put it bluntly: the call to Evangelization is often little else than a call to restore "Christendom," the *Corpus Christianum*, as a solid, well-integrated cultural complex directed and dominated by the church.[103]

At the beginning of the century Ernst Troeltsch had already noted that missions represented a response to the decline of Christianity in the West. Troeltsch argued that the ideological role they played on the part of Western civilization in their efforts to restore and extend the *Corpus Christianum* lay in the manner in which missions were extending Western technological and scientific culture under the guise of a renewed Christendom, on behalf of a universal and unified modern world.   Within this universal culture in a unified modern world, missions continued to carry out their ideological task by recreating generational boundaries, and often unwittingly by maintaining relationships of dependency.[104]

The analysis of both Hoekendijk and Troeltsch reveals much about the several factors at play in the motives and dynamics of Western Christian missions. But it does not adequately portray the meaning of mission that has emerged from churches and ecclesial communities beyond the boundaries of Western Christendom. Despite the ideological functions missions played on the part of Western churches, those outside the consensus of Christendom (Old or New) have not rejected the mission of the church. In several instances in the ecumenical movement's dialogue concerning mission those from beyond the borders of Christendom have resisted theological reproduction of European churches and the accompanying dependency, and have instead articulated a new understanding of missions from the local perspectives. From these initiating moments we can begin to discern a new theology of mission in the ecumenical movement.

4. Re-Marking the Boundaries of Christian Mission

"Local churches working assiduously together to relate themselves to all that is human is what we call the ecumenical movement," wrote Adeolu Adegbola in an essay entitled "Ecumenism for all People," contributed to a 1984 volume in honor of Philip Potter.[105] It accurately depicts the ecumenical vision for mission which has emerged from beyond the North Atlantic circle of churches, those that hold to the memory of Christendom. The emphasis upon the local nature of mission, and the essential relation between mission and church, emerged in the IMC discussions of the 1950s alongside the discussions of Christendom and crisis in mission. Willingen, which had emphasized the manner in which mission is first of all of God, had likewise called for a deeper and more active solidarity on the part of all the churches with their local situations as the response to God's mission to all peoples. The Ghana Assembly continued to affirm the manner in which each local ecclesial community bore responsibility for mission.[106] In the early 1960s the affirmation of missions belonging to all churches of the world found expression in ecumenical phrases such as "all in each place," or "mission on six continents."[107]

The vision of local churches in each place relating their faith fully to their particular situations required modes of cooperation and interchurch relating other than those structured by the ecumenical bodies dominated by the Western churches furthermore. The need for such

structures beyond national councils became increasingly clear to many
of the non-Europeans involved in the ecumenical movement after 1945.
We have already seen above that the resistance to Western domination
of ecumenical dialogue led first to support for the independence of the
IMC, and then later contributed to the decision for its integration into
the WCC. But neither the IMC nor the WCC could prove to be
effective vehicles for regional cooperation outside Europe and North
America. In time new ecumenical structures reflecting the local and
regional *praxis* of mission in each place, on all continents, emerged.
Some have continued relatively unrelated to Western centers of
ecclesiastical power, while other such structures, the regional councils
in Asia and Africa in particular, have engaged dialogically with the
ecumenical bodies of the North Atlantic. These local and regional
movements have witnessed to a de-centering of the ecumenical vision
for mission and for unity. Not always articulated unambiguously, and
often partially obscured by the Western theological discourse in which
it was embedded, this witness has nevertheless pointed toward cultural
and historical forms of pluralism no longer centered around the memory
of Christendom. The themes and insights which emerged from the
regional ecumenical movements have been an important contribution to
the ecumenical theology of a de-centered *oikoumene*.

The Joint Committee of the IMC and WCC in 1947 voted to appoint
an Asian regional secretary. The move was not fully supported by
Asian church leaders who organized, eventually with IMC and WCC
support, an East Asian Christian Conference that met in 1949.[108] The
Joint Committee's appointment in 1950 of R. B. Manikam of India as
the Asian Regional Secretary likewise failed to meet with full approval
from a number of Asian churches, and in 1956 the Asia Council of
Ecumenical Missions was organized as a joint action of mission boards
and Asian churches. Despite meeting initial resistance from the IMC
as being contrary to the overall goals of ecumenical missions, the
concept of an Asian Council was eventually embraced by the
Missionary Council.[109] The result was the inauguration in 1959 of the
East Asia Christian Conference (EACC) (now the Christian Conference
of Asia [CCA]) as a permanent regional body with three secretaries.[110]

A similar movement among African Protestant churches in the period
following 1945 led to the formation of the All Africa Conference of
Churches (AACC) in 1958.[111] The inaugurating conference was held
under the auspices of the Christian Council of Nigeria, and as in the

case of the EACC, won the support of the IMC which held its 1958 world meeting in Accra just prior to the AACC inaugural assembly in Ibadan. Receiving reports concerning the IMC and WCC, and one on the formation of the EACC, delegates to the Ibadan conference were conscious of the unique demands and responsibilities confronting Africa as a continent, and looked toward the contribution Christian churches would make to the emerging reality of Africa.[112]

Issues of social and political life dominated both regional bodies in their first assemblies, meeting at a time when the struggles for decolonization were reshaping their continents. India's achievement of independence in 1947 stood as an important marker for the Asian churches. The 1949 Asian conference met in Bangkok just after the completion of the Chinese Revolution. In Africa, eighteen nations achieved independence in the years between 1958 and 1961 alone. Both regional conferences dealt with problems of rapid social change and disruption of traditional patterns of life.[113] Both endorsed the growing nationalism of Asia and Africa as being positive in value, in spite of concerns voiced from the North Atlantic world.[114] The Bangkok conference in 1949 had affirmed a role for the churches in the Asian revolutions, and had cautiously embraced the recent Chinese revolution as the best option for that nation.[115] By the 1963 AACC meeting in Kampala, a stronger theological critique of colonialism and a clearer affirmation of revolution could be heard.

Richard Andriamanjato and Ndabaningi Sithole raised the banner in Kampala of a de-colonized theology, and drew the revolutionary and liberative implications concerning the character of Christian faith. The compliance of Christians in colonialism raised fundamental questions for the history of the African churches, they pointed out.[116] The Kampala meeting was reminded that the churches did not yet know how to disengage themselves from the embrace of colonialism, since African church leaders especially had not been trained in ways that would foster such disengagement. But the challenge of freedom and equality could not be ignored.

> Should we not remind ourselves that the Church ought to present itself to the world as the messenger and the witness of that revolution which began in accomplishing that supreme act which reconciled man [sic] to God.[117]

Realizing the equality of all human beings was one of the results of the revolutionary message of the Christian Gospel. The political values of democracy seemed not only consistent with the Gospel, but appeared to be the historical result of God's intervention in human experience. On the other hand, since European colonialism was profoundly undemocratic and a practice of inequality, its association with Christian faith distorted the meaning of Christianity in the minds of many Africans.[118] The conclusions drawn from authentic Christian faith, undistorted by colonial ideology or European history, were undeniable: "Christ in His great desire to save the world broke through every sphere of life, including the political sphere, in order to announce liberation and liberty."[119]

At Kampala the theological meaning of social and political liberation was articulated in the context of African struggles for independence, a theme which was to be pursued and enlarged upon in successive conferences in the years that followed. In both African and Asian regional ecumenical movements the centrality of liberation to the Gospel of Jesus Christ would become a common theme by the 1970s, as it would for numerous communities across the world struggling against suffering and oppression.[120]

The theologies of liberation (Catholic and Protestant) have not been concerned with restoring the unity of Western Christendom. Where unity has emerged as a demand and an ecumenical practice, as in South India in 1947, it has been in response to national liberation rather than to the memory of Christendom. Missions, the churches and theologians in the EACC and the AACC have both argued, must likewise be liberative. In order to be so missions must be developed from within the churches in their national or regional settings, and must be under their own control.[121] Both the Asian and African conferences expressed in the early 1960s uneasiness with mission relationships, and at the Kampala conference the recommendation was made that "assisting churches should be prepared to respond to invitations from the Church in Africa in accordance with abilities and qualifications requested," a recommendation which would be articulated more forcefully a decade later in the call for a moratorium.[122] Unity and mission were being reformulated in light of de-colonization, nationalism, and liberation.

Demands for greater local control over missions sent from the North Atlantic, and calls for at least a limited moratorium on missions, had been raised sporadically in missions discussions prior to the 1970s, often without eliciting much in the way of response from the West.[123] The furor raised by Europeans and North Americans in response to John

Gatu's call in 1974 at the All Africa Church Conference in Lusaka for a moratorium on Western missions was therefore somewhat unexpected. The response from missiologists and churches of the North Atlantic was in part due to the fact that the call had been initiated from outside the domain of North Atlantic ecclesiastical control, and indicated in part at least an unwillingness by the dominant churches to address the continuing problems of ecclesiastical colonialism.[124] But the call for a moratorium was not necessarily a step toward the construction of a new theology of mission so much as it was an attempt to clear theological space among non-European churches in which they could begin to engage in their own reflective work.

It was in search of a method for theological reflection and construction outside the domain of the missions of the Eurocentric churches that led Shoki Coe in the early 1970s to articulate a new paradigm termed, "contextualization."[125] Drawing upon earlier ecumenical discussions of mission, Coe pointed out that the "text" of *missio Dei* is only found incarnationally within the "contexts" of the *oikoumene*, in all of their ambiguities.[126] The older theology of "indigenization" had conceived of the text of mission as a static affair, a planting of a text in the unchanging soil of culture. The bewildering reality of the Third World, however, was that of dynamic change, of converging socio-political and religio-cultural forces, both old and new. The context of the Third World was not that of the *Corpus Christianum*; it was that of other living faiths and cultural traditions, of economic poverty and of political oppression.[127] Contextualization meant critical participation (discernment) in this reality, not importation of inherited "texts" from Western Europe.

> Authentic theological reflection can only take place as the *theologia in loco*, discerning the contextuality within the concrete context. But it must also be aware that such authentic theological reflection is as best, but also as most, *theologia viatorium*; and therefore contextuality must be matched by the contextualization which is an ongoing process....[128]

The method of "contextualization," of doing theology from within the social, political, religious, and cultural contexts of the Third World, enabled the contours of a new ecumenical theology to begin to appear.[129] Among Third World churches distinctive emphases were being articulated, and common concerns emerging within the various regions of the *oikoumene*, due to the various historical experiences of these churches. But until these distinctive aspects could be articulated in their diversity, and points of convergence as well as divergence expressed, the ecumenical impact of contextual theology would not be fully realized. Distinctive characteristics were rooted in the diverse historical memories churches nurtured, and in the diverse historical identities of the cultures of the *oikoumene*. The opening to contextualization of theology demanded more than ever dialogue among Third World churches.

By the early 1970s it was becoming clear to a number of Third World theologians that the presence of European theologians, and the institutional structures of the WCC, were proving to be a hindrance to the dialogue called for through contextualization. Through discussions among Latin American, Asian and African theologians at Louvain, Belgium in 1974, a proposal for an Ecumenical Association of Third World Theologians (known as EATWOT) emerged. Broader support for the association was sought and received at the WCC Assembly in Nairobi in 1975, and at the Theology in the Americas Conference that same year. By the inaugural meeting of EATWOT in Dar es Salaam, 1976, Protestant and Catholic theologians representing Asia, Africa, Latin America, and Black North America were able to forge an organizational relationship for non-Eurocentric contextual ecumenical theological reflection.

EATWOT has continued over the last seventeen years through its regional conferences and associations to deepen understanding of the theological meaning of liberation in Asian, African, Latin American, and Black North American contexts.[130] Since 1981 it has also taken up reflection upon the issue of oppression of women in churches and societies of the Third World.[131] At first distinctive aspects of the critique of Eurocentric theology and missions emerged from the various regions represented in EATWOT. Latin American theologians made socio-political analysis central to their theological reflection, African theologians articulated their critical theology from a perspective which began with analysis of cultural poverty, and Asian theologians were particularly concerned about the theological meaning of the great religious traditions of Asia. Black theologians were particularly, although not exclusively, concerned about the analysis of racism, and women in EATWOT raised their concerns about the oppressive forces of sexism. Through the process of dialogue however these various critical concerns have influenced and shaped one another so that the analysis and theological construction of each region or group in EATWOT has become significantly more complex and inter-related with other perspectives and theologies.

The intensive contextual theological reflection and dialogue that has taken place in EATWOT has uncovered multiple forces and trajectories converging and diverging in the multiple histories of those who have not been at the center of Western Christendom's historical experience. EATWOT has indicated the manner in which ecumenical differences and commonalities are found outside the gates of Christendom. As Orlando Costas has noted, the death of Jesus outside the city is a sign that salvation is found among the outsiders and hence is a judgment upon the historical project of Christendom intent upon dividing "insiders" from "outsiders."[132] The attempts by the dominant churches of the North Atlantic to maintain the divide are challenged by contextual ecumenical projects such as EATWOT that have embodied new forms of pluralism in a de-centered *oikoumene*.

There are implications as well for the content of the ecumenical memory of history. Emmanuel Ayandele has argued that the history of Western missions in Africa can not provide the content for the memory of the history of the churches in Africa.

> For, rightly considered, an African Church must necessarily be the product of an organic growth on the African soil, an institution in which Christianity is incarnate within the African milieu. This was how the "historic Churches" introduced into Africa had developed in their metropolitan countries.[133]

The churches that were usually studied by history scholars were imitations of their Western "parent" churches, claimed Ayandele. Therefore instead of African church history exploring what Africans have made of Christianity, "it has tended to remain a part of the missionary presence, encouraging expansion without real growth."[134] Those churches in Africa that are truly African, he argued, are the indigenous churches. Most often they

> have been presented as unorthodox aberrations and bastards, beyond the pale of redemption and absolutely unqualified to be considered legitimate branches of the Church Universal.[135]

It has not only been the histories of churches of Africa or Asia that have been outside Christendom, and thus outside the discussion of unity and mission which has characterized the ecumenical movement's search for the *Una Sancta* that the creed speaks of. Within the geographical boundaries of Christendom itself the dangerous memories of histories of 'outsiders' have been present and remain today. These other experiences, though often ignored or suppressed, have also been present within the ecumenical movement as well. One such witness was made at the 1928 Jerusalem Meeting of the IMC, by John Hope, President of Morehouse College. Hope's preparatory paper had set before the Council an interpretation of Black experience which was at the same time a liberative interpretation of the Gospel.

There was "no doubt" in Hope's mind that the slaves' comprehension of Christ, and their "living out Christ did as much as anything else to make the abolition of slavery possible." He asserted, in a time when white Europeans were generally considered by ecumenical theologians and missiologists to be the only ones capable of making history, that in a mysterious way the African slaves in North America freed themselves "through the power of Jesus Christ as the Negro found Christ in chains."[136] The missionary imperative that Jones set before the Council was echoed in other papers in the volume concerning South Africa. Despite this, however, the final report of the Section, and the issue of racism in general, remained virtually ignored in responses within the ecumenical movement until the 1960s.[137]

This suggests that there have been within the ecumenical movement, within the missionary movement, within the larger historical project of Christendom, other histories and memories that have remained only partially, if at all, visible from the perspective of dominant Western theology. These others -- of communities of the poor, of ethnic, cultural or racial minorities, and of women -- have maintained histories and memories of resistance as well. Consciousness of their histories does not lie along the axis of unity and mission. Contextualization, on the other hand, no longer regards the hidden memories of other histories as peripheral to an ecumenical center. Along this new axis for ecumenics and mission the consciousness of these multiple histories calls for new commitment to local (contextual) theology and new relationships of solidarity among churches living on the margins and beyond the boundaries of Christendom.

The impact of these contextual theologies, and of the *praxis* of solidarity in a de-centered *oikoumene*, has been felt within the WCC, and specifically within the unit that has carried on the work of the IMC, the Commission on World Mission and Evangelism (CWME). Already in the early 1970s the development of liberation perspectives and methods of contextualization began to challenge dominant concepts of mission and evangelism, irrupting full-force in 1973 at the Bangkok Assembly of the CWME.[138] The 1970 initiation in the WCC of the program on Dialogue with People of Living Faiths and Ideologies has created something of a structural divorce between missions and inter-religious dialogue and has prevented full integration or interaction between these twin tasks of the ecumenical movement. Nevertheless the socio-political and cultural dimensions of missions have begun to be addressed more critically and contextually in the CWME since 1973.

The criticisms of this development that emerged during the 1970s from Western Europe and North America led CWME to begin a process of examining the convictions undergirding missions and evangelism in preparation for the 1980 World Conference on Mission and Evangelism at Melbourne.[139] The result was the publication in 1982 of *Mission and Evangelism: An Ecumenical Affirmation* issued by CWME.[140] Beginning from a Trinitarian theological perspective, and with the proclamation of the crucified and risen Christ, the statement outlined an incarnational theology of mission. True to its sub-title it affirmed proclamation as extending the call to conversion, noting, "Each person is entitled to hear the Good News."[141] While the call to repentance and conversion always begins with the repentance of the one doing the calling, it extends to individuals, groups, and nations as a call for justice and new relationships in all realms of life. Mission was to be done in Christ's way, *An Affirmation* claimed, bringing good news to the poor in all six continents.

In a critical section on unity and mission, *An Affirmation* joined unity to renewal and inculturation, so that unity was understood in relation to the multiplication of diverse congregations in various communities of the world. The growing cultural diversity of churches in the world was regarded as a positive result of missions and evangelism. The statement asserted that "the unity we look for is not uniformity but the multiple expression of a common faith and a common mission."[142] Mission that crosses cultural boundaries especially requires an incarnational *praxis* of solidarity through participation, it suggested.

CWME has continued to explore the implications of these insights into the relationship between mission and the diversity of churches,

advocating an incarnational understanding of mission through
participation and partnership. Yet despite the efforts CWME has
extended to realize this vision of an incarnational mode of mission
among the churches of the world, the commitment of the churches
themselves to a contextual practice of mission and to solidarity remains
elusive. Despite the vision for mission in Christ's way which was
articulated in the 1989 CWME Conference at San Antonio, Texas, an
incarnational mode of mission and *praxis* has not become a reality very
far beyond the pages of the conference papers and section reports. So
the report from Section IV of the San Antonio Conference noted:

> For more than a quarter of a century the quest for new models to express
> genuine partnership has been on the agenda of the WCC. Many
> excellent ideas have been expressed but not a great deal has happened.
> This is why there is a clear and urgent need for a renewed call to
> commitment and action.[143]

In his response to the San Antonio conference Christopher
Duraisingh reminded his hearers of an eschatological vision of mission
that is at the same time "*rooted in our 'common memory'* within the
ecumenical movement and its mission history."[144] That common
memory, however, Eugene L. Stockwell described as "our checkered
Christian history of arrogance and intolerance."[145] It is a history of
political domination, cultural sexist oppression, and destruction of life.
Stockwell's' sharp reminder of the failures of the history of the
ecumenical movement serve as a caution against allowing one
ecumenical memory to serve for the whole. For the domain of
ecumenical memories is greater than any one dominant community or
history. There is a surplus of ecumenical memories, often brought to
the common table of the movement from outside its central vision and
beyond its working boundaries. The contextual voices from outside the
major streams of ecumenism in this century represent "uncommon
ecumenical memories." And the hopes for community contained in
them for the future emerge along the pathway of solidarity. For both
the renewal of mission and the mission of renewal in the ecumenical
movement the pathway of unity amidst diversity, which is the pathway
of solidarity, leads to new ecumenical memories, and a new
understanding of what it means to be faithful amidst the multiplicity of
histories and cultures in the world today.

Notes

1. Emmanuel Levinas, *Time and the Other [and Additional Essays]*, Richard A. Cohen, trans. (Pittsburgh: Duquesne University Press, 1987), p. 121.

2. *The World Mission of the Church: Findings and Recommendations of the International Missionary Council, Tambaram, Madras, India, December 12th to 29th, 1938* (London: International Missionary Council, 1939), p 129.

3. *Addresses and Other Records: Meeting of the International Missionary Council, at Tambaram, Madras, India, December 12th to 29th, 1938*, Volume VII, *The Madras Series* (New York: IMC, 1939), p. 116. Paton's address was entitled, "The Church and the World Community."

4. *Ibid.*, pp. 116-117.

5. The *Minutes and Reports of the Meeting of the Provisional Committee of the World Council of Churches, Buck Hill Falls, Penn., April 1947* (Geneva: WCC, 1947), note on p. 69, under the Report of the Joint Committee, that "The Joint Committee recommends that the World Council of Churches consider ways by which the constituent organizations of the International Missionary Council may find a recognised place in the functioning of the World Council of Churches." The report also notes that the fifty places allocated to churches of Asia, Africa, Latin America, and the Pacific Islands for the upcoming Assembly are to be coordinated through the IMC.

6. Norman Goodall, *Ecumenical Progress: A Decade of Change in the Ecumenical Movement 1961-1971* (London: Oxford University Press, 1972), p. 21.

7. See Ruth Rouse and Stephen Charles Neill, eds., *A History of the Ecumenical Movement 1517-1948*, Third Edition (Geneva: WCC, 1986), pp. 216, 324, 345-349, and 727; William Richey Hogg, *Ecumenical Foundations: A History of the International Missionary Council and Its Nineteenth-Century Background* (New York: Harper and Row, 1952), p. 98f; Geoffrey Wainwright, *The Ecumenical Movement: Crisis and Opportunity for the Church* (Grand Rapids, Mi: Wm. B. Eerdmans, 1983), p. 1; Norman Goodall, *The Ecumenical Movement: What It Is and What It Does* (London: Oxford University Press, 1961), pp. 8-9; John A. Mackay, *Ecumenics: The Science of the Church Universal* (Englewood Cliffs, NJ: Prentice Hall, 1964), p. 108; and "Ecumenical Diary," *Ecumenical Review* 32/2 (1980), p. 193 for example.

8. Henry P. Van Dusen, "Christian Missions and Christian Unity," *Basileia: Walter Freytag zum 60. Geburtstag*, Jan Hermelink and Hans Jochen Margull, eds. (Stuttgart: Evangelische Missionsverlag, 1959), p. 490.

9. *Ibid.*, p. 491 (emphasis original)

10. Hogg, *Ecumenical Foundations*, p. 17. Van Dusen, "Christian Missions and Christian Unity," gave significant weight only to those efforts by

missionaries and subsequent non-Western churches. From the unitive efforts in the "Mission Field" sprang the "originating impulses," (p. 501).

11. John A. Mackay, *Ecumenics: The Science of the Church Universal*, p. 31.

12. *Ibid.*, p. 31 (emphasis original). Mackay's definition of "ecumenics" can be seen to bear similarities to the definition of "missiology" which is current among Conservative Evangelicals. The major difference is that the Evangelical movement maintains that the Christian church is not yet present among all cultural groups, and hence "cross-cultural evangelism" by specialists is required above the witness of each church in its own place. The depiction of cultural groups in which Christian churches have not yet been "planted" as "hidden people" continues the nineteenth century conception of mission as among "foreign" peoples, rendering them Other, as will be discussed in section 2 below. See J. D. Douglas, ed., *Let the Earth Hear His Voice: International Congress on World Evangelization. Lausanne, Switzerland, Official Reference Volume* (Minneapolis: World Wide Publications, 1975).

13. Mackay, *Ecumenics*, p. 166-167.

14. Ronald K. Orchard, ed., *The Ghana Assembly of the International Missionary Council 28th December, 1957 to 8th January, 1958: Selected Papers, with an Essay on the Role of the I.M.C.* (London: Edinburgh House Press, 1958), pp. 140-143. ·

15. Leslie Newbigin, "Mission to Six Continents," *The Ecumenical Advance: A History of the Ecumenical Movement, Volume 2, 1948-1968*, Second Edition, Harold E. Fey, ed., (Geneva: WCC, 1986), p. 185.

16. The "Statement on the Missionary Calling of the Church" had affirmed: "The missionary movement of which we are a part has its source in the Triune God Himself...." (Norman Goodall, ed., *Missions Under the Cross: Addresses Delivered at the Enlarged Meeting of the Committee of the International Missionary Council at Willingen, in Germany, 1952* [London: Edinburgh House, 1953], p. 198). The phrase *missio Dei* came to be associated with Willingen. See Georg F. Vicedom, *The Mission of God: An Introduction to a Theology of Mission* (St. Louis: Concordia Press, 1965).

17. See C. W. Ranson, ed. *Renewal and Advance: Christian Witness in a Revolutionary World* (London: Edinburgh House, 1948), Part III, "Partners in Obedience," pp. 173-198; and Kenneth Scott Latourette and William Richey Hogg, *Tomorrow is Here: The Mission and Work of the Church as Seen from the Meeting of the International Missionary Council at Whitby, Ontario, July 5-24, 1947* (New York: Friendship Press, 1948), Chapter 6, "Partners in Obedience," pp. 105- 120. The opening section of this volume acknowledges not only that "The World of Tomorrow is Here," but that more specifically revolution and de-colonization are here.

18. The call for solidarity was originally made in the one of the final statements at Whitby, but expanded upon at Willingen. Ranson, ed., *Renewal*

and Advance, p. 120: "This new and acute sensitiveness to the implications of our ambassadorship of Christ can only prove effective by deeper consciousness of that fact that belonging to Christ means at the same time responsibility for and solidarity with the world and our fellow-men [sic], along with a sense of being strangers and sojourners in the world and in our nation." See Goodall, *Missions Under the Cross*, pp. 190-191, and 193.

19. Orchard, *The Ghana Assembly*, p. 36.

20. *Ibid.*, p. 213.

21. James A. Scherer, *Missionary Go Home! A Reappraisal of the Christian World Mission* (Englewood Cliffs: Prentice-Hall, 1964), p. 39.

22. Hogg, *Ecumenical Foundations*, p. 396, lists the seventeen (out of a total of twelve hundred) Asian delegates at Edinburgh. No Africans attended, and Latin America was excluded from the conference because it was considered a Catholic -- hence a "Christian" and not technically a "mission" -- area. Bishop V. S. Azariah and Cheng Ching-yi are noted as speakers in the conference records. There were disagreements among the North Atlantic representatives at Edinburgh, most notably protests by Germans against Anglo-American domination. See Karl-Heinz Dejung, *Die Ökumenische Bewegung im Entwicklungskonflikt 1910-1968* (Stuttgart: Ernst Klett Verlag, 1973), p. 31. R. K. Orchard, *Out of Every Nation: Discussion of the Internationalizing of Missions* (London: SCM Press, 1959), notes on p. 19: "Thus already by 'Edinburgh 1910' the conception of 'Western Christendom' as the base of the Christian world mission is being questioned as a result both of the weakening of Christian influence in the structures and standards of Western civilization and of the emergence of growingly responsible churches in the once 'non-Christian world.'"

23. Kenneth Scott Latourette, "Ecumenical Bearings of the Missionary Movement and the International Missionary Council," *A History of the Ecumenical Movement*, Rouse and Neill, eds., p. 357.

24. Hogg, *Ecumenical Foundations*, p. 130.

25. The connection between Edinburgh 1910 and the Life and Work movement is made concretely in the person of Oldham. In 1934 Oldham took the position as secretary for the Universal Council on Life and Work.

26. See *The Jerusalem Meeting of the International Missionary Council March 24-April 8, 1928*, Volumes I-VII (New York: IMC, 1928), esp. *Volume I: The Christian Life and Message in Relation to Non-Christian Systems of Thought and Life*, and *Volume IV: The Christian Mission in the Light of Race conflict*. John Hope, President of Morehouse College, presented a preliminary paper in this latter volume, "The Negro in the United States of America," noted below.

27. See *The World Mission of the Church: Findings and Recommendations of the Meeting of the International Missionary Council, Tambaram, Madras, India, Dec. 12-29, 1938* (New York: IMC, 1939).

28. Hendrik Kraemer, *The Christian Message in a Non-Christian World* (Grand Rapids: Kregel Publications, 1961). (This is the fifth edition of the 1938 original.)

29. See Charles H. Long, *Significations: Signs, Symbols, and Images in the Interpretation of Religion* (Philadelphia: Fortress Press, 1986), pp. 63-75.

30 D. Preman Niles, "Christian Mission and the Peoples of Asia," *CTC Bulletin* 3/1 (1982), p. 40, asks: "Where in this scheme do we Asian Christians belong?"

31. Dale T. Irvin, "From One Story to Many: An Ecumenical Reappraisal of Church History," *Journal of Ecumenical Studies* 28/4 (Fall 1991), pp. 537-554.

32. Stephen Charles Neill, in *Colonialism and Christian Mission* (New York: McGraw-Hill Book Co., 1966), p. 39, writes: "In the Middle Ages all history was Church history. The Church was effectively present in every aspect of the lives of mankind [sic], even of those who most emphatically denied by their lives what they professed with their lips."

33. Concerning anti-Judaism, see Rosemary R. Ruether, *Faith and Fratricide: The Theological Roots of Anti-Semitism* (New York: The Seabury Press, 1974). On the existence of non-Christian indigenous religiosity in Christian Europe see Margaret A. Murray, *The Witch-Cult in Western Europe* (Oxford: Oxford University Press, 1971). At the 1910 Edinburgh Conference, J. Warneck of Germany noted the value of studying "animistic religions" not only because they are encountered in Asia and Africa, "but because we find remnants of this primitive religion also in the great religions of the East, *and even in Europe*, wherever Christ has not become the king...."(emphasis added). See *World Missionary Conference, 1910, Report of Commission IV: The Missionary Message in Relation to Non-Christian Religions* (New York: Fleming H. Revell Co., 1910), p. 299.

34. See R. W. Southern, *Western Views of Islam in the Middle Ages* (Cambridge: Harvard University Press, 1962); and E. R. Daniel, "Apocalyptic Conversion: The Joachite Alternative to the Crusades," *Traditio* 25/1 (1969), p. 127-154. Concerning Europe's indebtedness to Islam, see John R. Hayes, ed., *The Genius of Arab Civilization: Source of Renaissance* (Cambridge: MIT Press, 1983). Thomas Aquinas already defines the non-Christian as Europe's 'Other' in his *Summa Contra Gentiles* (London: Burns Oates & Washbourne, LTD, 1924), p. 4.

35. Kaj Baago, "The Post-Colonial Crisis of Missions," *International Review of Missions*, 55/3 (1966), p. 329. Concerning the European religious response to indigenous peoples in Latin American Tzvetan Todorov, in *The Conquest of America: The Question of the Other*, Richard Howard, trans. (New York: Harper and Row, Publishers,1984), writes on p. 108: "In order to describe the Indians, the conquistadors seek comparisons they find immediately either in their own pagan (Greco-Roman) past, or among others geographically

closer and already familiar, such as the Muslims. The Spaniards call each of the first temples they discover a 'mosque,' and the first city glimpsed during the expedition of Hernandez de Còrdoba will be named, Bernal Diaz tells us, Great Cairo."

36. See Franklin L. Baumer, *Modern European Thought: Continuity and Change in Ideas, 1600-1950* (New York: Macmillan, 1977); Owen Chadwick, *The Secularization of the European Mind in the Nineteenth Century* (Cambridge: Cambridge University Press, 1975); Warren Wager, ed. *The Secular Mind: Transformations of Faith in Modern Europe* (New York: Holmes & Meier, 1982); and Ernst Troeltsch, *The Social Teaching of the Christian Churches* (Chicago: University of Chicago Press, 1981).

37. Joseph M. Kitagawa, "The History of Religions in America," *The History of Religions: Essays in Methodology*, Mircea Eliade and Joseph M. Kitagawa, eds. (Chicago: University of Chicago Press, 1959), p. 5.

38. *Ibid.*, p. 9. In the same volume of essays Ernst Benz writes: "As I came to understand the essence of one non- Christian religion, it became at once increasingly clear to me to what extent and to what degree of depth our Western attitude, our intellectual, emotional, and volitional reaction to other religions, is modified by the European Christian heritage." ("On Understanding Non-Christian Religions," p. 120).

39. The Report of Commission IV of the conference was entitled, "The Missionary Message in Relation to Non-Christian Religions." Volume I of the Jerusalem Meeting of the IMC in 1928 was entitled, *The Christian Life and Message in Relation to Non-Christian Systems of Thought and Life.*

40. *The Missionary Message in Relation to Non-Christian Religions*, pp. 29 and 120, e.g.

41. *Ibid.*, pp. 112, 129, and 150 e.g.

42. *The Jerusalem Meeting of the IMC: Volume I, The Christian Life and Message*, p. 45, 292, 319 e.g. Hogg, *Ecumenical Foundations*, states that the conflict involved continental Germans opposed to Anglo-Saxon missiologists, p. 247. He virtually ignores the Asian defense of fulfillment.

43. *The Christian Life and Message*, p. 231.

44. *Ibid.*, p. 266.

45. *Ibid.*, p. 273.

46. *Ibid.*, p. 345f., records Robert Speer's account of the continental concerns over syncretism, and the common understanding which the conference seemingly achieved on these issues.

47. Karl Barth, "Questions which 'Christianity' Must Face," *Student World* 25 (1932), p. 93f. See also W. A. Visser't Hooft, "Karl Barth and the Ecumenical Movement," *Ecumenical Review* 32/2 (1980), p. 131.

48. Antonio R. Gualteri, "The Failure of Dialectic in Hendrik Kraemer's Evaluation of Non-Christian Faith," *Interreligious Dialogue: Facing the Next Frontier*, Richard W. Rousseau, ed. (Scranton, Pa.: Ridge Row Press, 1981),

p. 90: "most of the books on missiology published after 1938 are obliged to make reference to Kraemer's position and to indicate how their own resembles it or differs from it." On Kraemer, see Carl F. Hallencreutz, *Kraemer Towards Tambaram: A Study in Hendrik Kraemer's Missionary Approach* (Uppsala: Gleerup, 1966).

49. Kraemer, *The Christian Message*, p. 25.
50. *Ibid.*, p. 27.
51. *Ibid.*, p. 35.
52. *Ibid.*, p. 38.
53. *Ibid.*, p. 39.
54. *Ibid.*, p. 88.
55. *Ibid.*, p. 105.
56. *Ibid.*, p. 145.
57. *Ibid.*, p. 140.
58. *Ibid.*, p. 113.
59. *Ibid.*, p. 333.
60. *Ibid.*, p. 334.
61. *Ibid.* See Karl Barth, *Church Dogmatics, I/2: Doctrine of the Word of God* (New York: Charles Scribner's Sons, 1956), p. 343, concerning doctrines and practice of the Protestant church in particular : "As symptoms, as predicates of the subject Jesus Christ -- and we can take them seriously in retrospect -- they have acquired, and had, and do have the force of truth: the force of the confession and attestation of the truth."
62. See the articles in the *International Review of Missions* 78/307 (July 1988), esp. by Carl F. Hallencreutz, "Tambaram Revisited," pp. 347-359, and by M.M. Thomas, "An Assessment of Tambaram's Contribution to the Search of the Asian Churches for an Authentic Selfhood," pp. 390-397.
63. D.M. Devasahayam, et al, *Rethinking Christianity in India* (Madras: Hogarth Press, 1938), "Appendix," p. 5.
64. *Ibid.*, "Appendix," p. 8.
65. *Ibid.*, p. 17.
66. *Ibid.*, p. 20.
67. Important for the Asian churches in particular were the Shanghai National Christian Conference of 1922 and the Java Conference of the WSCF in 1933. See F. Rawlinson, ed., *The Chinese Church as Revealed in the National Christian Conference held in Shanghai, Tuesday, May 2, to Thursday, May 11, 1922* (Shanghai: The Oriental Press, 1922); and *Christ and Students of the East: The Report of the Java Conference of the World's Student Christian Federation, Tjiteureup, Java September 6-14, 1933* [n.p.].
68. Niles, "Christian Mission and the Peoples of Asia," p. 37.
69. Vicedom, *The Mission of God*, p. 46-47, argued: "The church and its mission cannot be conceived apart from God and can therefore be understood only from the viewpoint of the existence of God and His [sic] mission." He

admits no social or cultural factors impinging upon missions. But his strictly theological definition obscures the distortions of *missio Dei*.

70. Hans Herman Walz, "Christendom in a Secularized World," *Ecumenical Review* 10/3 (1958), p. 280.

71. See Immanuel Kant, "What is Enlightenment?" in *On History*, Lewis White Beck, ed. (Indianapolis: Bobbs-Merrill, 1967); and Dietrich Bonhoffer, *Letters and Papers from Prison* (New York: The Macmillan Co., 1953), p. 341f.

72. See Paul van Buren, *The Secular Meaning of the Gospel* (New York: The Macmillan Co., 1963); and Harvey Cox, *The Secular City* (New York: The Macmillan Co., 1965). For the discussion of secularism at Jerusalem, 1928, see Rufus M. Jones, "Secular Civilization and the Christian Task," *The Jerusalem Meeting of the IMC, Volume 1*, pp. 230-276. See A. Th. van Leeuwen's thesis concerning technocracy above, Chapter III.

73. Walz, "Christendom in a Secularized World," p. 283.

74. For a positive assessment of Secularism as the common faith of the modern age developing the catholicity of *unum in pluribus*, see Horace M. Kallen, *Secularism is the Will of God: An Essay in the Social Philosophy of Democracy and Religion* (New York: Twayne Publishers, Inc., 1954).

75. Ronald K. Orchard, "The Concept of Christendom and the Christian World Mission: A Question," *Basileia*, Hermelink and Margull, eds., p. 481.

76. R.K. Orchard, *Missions in a Time of Testing: Thought and Practice in Contemporary Missions* (London: Lutterworth Press, 1964), p. 98.

77. R.K. Orchard, *Out of Every Nation: A Discussion of the Internationalizing of Missions* (London: SCM Press, 1959), p. 47.

78. Orchard in fact stated in "The Concept of Christendom and the Christian World Mission," p. 475, that he did not mean "to minimize the very considerable importance of the continuing influence of standards owing much to the influence of the Gospel in the corporate life of many Western communities. They are of real importance and must be taken with real seriousness by the Christian world mission in those countries. It is, however, to say that in those countries the community in general no longer acknowledges a corporate obedience to the Christian faith."

79. M. M. Thomas, *Towards a Theology of Contemporary Ecumenism: A Collection of Addresses to Ecumenical Gatherings (1947-1975)* (Madras: Christian Literature Society, 1978), p. 45.

80. *Ibid.*, p. 46.

81. *Ibid.*, p. 15. See also Rajah B. Manikam, *Christianity and the Asian Revolution* (New York: Friendship Press, 1954); and Dejung, *Die Okumenische Bewegung im Entwicklungskonflikt*, p. 90.

82. Goodall, *Missions Under the Cross*, p. 95.

83. For a fuller discussion of the change from "missions" to "mission" in the ecumenical movement see Philip Potter, "From Missions to Mission:

Reflection on Seventy-Five Years of the IRM," *International Review of Mission* 76/302 (April 1987), pp. 155-172.

84. Goodall, *Missions Under the Cross*, p. 96.

85. *Ibid.*

86. *Ibid.*, p. 98 (emphasis mine).

87. Paul David Devanandan, "The Shock of the Discovery of World Religions," *Student World* 53 (1960), p. 217.   See also Devanandan, *Preparation for Dialogue* (Madras: CISRS, 1964).

88. *Ibid.*, p. 218.

89. M. M. Thomas, *Risking Christ for Christ's Sake: Toward an Ecumenical Theology of Pluralism* (Geneva: WCC, 1987), pp. 90-94.

90. Kaj Baago, "The Post-Colonial Crisis of Missions," p. 324.

91. See Stuart Creighton Miller, "Ends and Means: Missionary Justification of Force in Nineteenth Century China," *The Missionary Enterprise in China and America*, John K. Fairbank, ed. (Cambridge: Harvard University Press, 1974). Ernst Troeltsch, "Die Mission in der modernen Welt," *Gesammelte Schriften II* (Tubingen: J. C. B. Mohr [Paul Siebeck], 1913), p. 796: "Contemporary mission is the expansion of the religious ideology of Europe and America in close connection with the extension of the European sphere of influence."

92. Arthur Schlesinger, Jr., "The Missionary Enterprise and Theories of Imperialism," *The Missionary Enterprise in China and America*, Fairbank, ed., pp. 363-4.

93. William R. Hutchison, "A Moral Equivalent for Imperialism: Americans and the Promotion of 'Christian Civilization, 1880-1910," *Missionary Ideologies in the Imperialist Era: 1880-1920*, Torben Christensen and William R. Hutchison, ed. (Denmark: Aros, 1982), p. 168. See also Kavalam M. Panikkar, *Asia and Western Dominance*, (New York: Collier, 1954), p. 279-284; and Enrique Dussel, *A History of the Church in Latin America: Colonialism to Liberation (1492-1979)* (Grand Rapids: Wm. B. Eerdmans, 1981).

94. Hutchison, "A Moral Equivalent for Imperialism," p. 176. For further illustrations from missionary theologies of the time see Josiah Strong, *The New Era or the Coming Kingdom* (New York: Revell, 1893); Gustav Warneck, *Modern Missions and Culture: Their Mutual Relations* (Edinburgh: R. W. Hunter, [1882]); and esp. D. L. Leonard, "The Anglo-Saxon and the World's Redemption," *Missionary Review of the World* 7 (1894), pp. 748ff. Lest the racial superiority thesis be dismissed too easily as confined to the foreign missionary enterprise, see Reinhold Niebuhr, "Anglo-Saxon Destiny and Responsibility," in *Christianity and Crisis* 3/16 (Oct. 4, 1943), pp. 2-4, where the "destiny" of the Anglo-Saxon people (a "racial" group that is Niebuhr's "us") on behalf of world peace is explicitly defined in "religious terms."

95. Gustav Warneck, *Outline of a History of Protestant Missions from the Reformation to the Present Times* (New York: Revell, 1906), p. 172.

96. Max Warren, *Social History and Christian Mission* (London: SCM Press, 1967), p. 118. Warren further explains, "It was this social force, which under the guise of commerce, imperialism and the missionary movement, impinged upon the ancient cultures of Asia and the hitherto undiscovered cultures of Africa."

97. Dejung, *Die Okumenische Bewegung im Entwicklungskonflikt, p. 25.*

98. Lamin Sanneh, "Pluralism and Christian Commitment," *Theology Today* 45/1 (1988), p. 27-28.

99. Emmanuel A. Ayandele, *African Historical Studies* (London: Frank Cass & Co., Ltd., 1979), p. 77.

100. Ernst Troeltsch, *The Social Teaching of the Christian Churches* (Chicago: University of Chicago Press, 1981), Vol 1, esp. pp. 280-327.

101. See Warneck, *Outline of a History of Protestant Missions*; and Gustav Warneck, *Modern Missions and Culture: Their Mutual Relations* (Edinburgh: R.W. Hunter, 1882). A similar conception of the vitality and growth of Christianity being exhibited through Western missions is found in Kenneth Scott Latourette, *The Emergence of a World Christian Community* (New Haven: Yale University Press, 1949);

102. *The Missionary Message in Relation to Non-Christian Religions,* p. 36-37.

103. Johannes Christiaan Hoekendijk, *The Church Inside Out* (Philadelphia: Westminster Press, 1964), p. 15. See further, pp. 16-24.

104. Ernst Troeltsch, "Die Mission in der modernen Welt," *Gesammelte Schriften II* (Tubingen: J.C.B. Mohr [Paul Siebeck], 1913), p. 779.

105. Pauline Webb, ed., *Faith and Faithfulness: Essays on Contemporary Ecumenical Themes, A Tribute to Philip A. Potter* (Geneva: WCC, 1984), p. 55.

106. Orchard, *The Ghana Assembly,* p. 181.

107. The New Delhi Assembly in 1961 had referred to "all in each place," *The New Delhi Report: Third Assembly of the World Council of Churches in New Delhi, 1961* (London: SCM Press, 1962), p. 116. "Mission in six continents," though often associated with the 1963 CWME conference in Mexico City, is remembered by Lesslie Newbigin as having originated also at New Delhi; see his reflections on "A Mission to Modern Western Culture," in *The San Antonio Report: Your Will be Done: Mission in Christ's Way,* Frederick R. Wilson, ed. (Geneva: WCC, 1990), p. 162.

108. Hans-Ruedi Weber, "Out of All Continents and Nations: A Review of Regional Developments in the Ecumenical Movement," *The Ecumenical Advance: A History of the Ecumenical Movement: Volume II, 1948-1968,* Harold E. Fey, ed., (second ed., Geneva: WCC, 1986), pp. 67-73; see also U Kyaw Than, ed., *Toward Kuala Lumpur: Workbook for the Inaugural Assemby of the East Asian Christian Conference* (Rangoon: Rangoon Gazette, 1959), p. 6.

109. See in particular Alan A. Brash, "Regional Responsibility: Its Joy and Pain," in *Hope in the Desert: The Churches' United Response to Human Need, 1944-1984*, Kenneth Slack, ed. (Geneva: WCC, 1986), p. 46.

110. U Kyaw Than, ed., *Witnesses Together, being the Official Report of the Inaugural Assembly of the East Asian Christian Conference, held at Kuala Lumpur, Malaya, May 14- 24, 1959* (Rangoon: Rangoon Gazette, 1959).

111. Weber, "Out of All Continents," pp. 73-79.

112. See *The Church in Changing Africa: Report of the All Africa Council of Churches, held at Ibadan, Nigeria, January 10-19, 1958* (New York: Friendship Press, 1958).

113. See Paul Abrecht, *The Churches and Rapid Social Change* (New York: Doubleday Book Co., 1961). The WCC statement, *The Common Christian Responsibility toward Areas of Rapid Social Change* (Geneva: WCC, 1956), addressed disruptions of life in Africa and Asia.

114. See *The Christian Prospect in Eastern Asia: Papers and Minutes of the East Asian Christian Conference Bangkok, December 3-11 1949* (New York: Friendship Press, 1950); *The Church in Changing Africa*, pp. 47-57; and especially All Africa Churches Conference, *Africa in Transition: The Challenge and the Christian Response*, (Geneva: WCC, 1963), pp. 11-32; *ibid.*, p. 66: "The two dominant motifs of African nationalism -- liberation and consolidation -- are the exact opposite of those of Western nationalism -- colonialism and divisiveness."

115. See East Asian Christian Conference, *The Witness of the Churches in the Midst of Social Change: A Survey of Ecumenical Social Thought* (Rangoon: Rangoon Gazette, 1959), pp. 20ff; see also the EACC report, *Christian Service in the Revolution: Report of the Consultation held November 14- 18, 1962, in Sukabumi, Indonesia* (Rangoon: Rangoon Gazette), 1963.

116. All Africa Churches Conference, *Drumbeats from Kampala: Report of the First Assembly of the All Africa Conference of Churches held at Kampala April 20-30, 1963* (London: Lutterworth Press, 1963), p. 54.

117. *Ibid.*

118. *Ibid.*, p. 55.

119. *Ibid.*, p. 58.

120. James H. Cone, "Reflections from the Perspective of U.S. Blacks: Black Theology and Third World Theology," *Irruption of the Third World: Challenge to Theology*, Virginia Fabella and Sergio Torres, eds. (Maryknoll: Orbis Books, 1983), p. 238, points out the importance of the independent usage of "liberation" in the late 1960s. As we have seen, the term had theological usage already in an Asian context in 1952 by Russell Chandran, and then in African discussions at Ibadan, 1958, and at Kampala, 1963.

121. See D. T. Niles, "A Church and its Selfhood," *A Decisive Hour for the Christian Mission: The East Asian Christian Conference and the John R. Mott Memorial Lectures*, Norman Goodall et al (London: SCM Press, 1960); and

Africa in Transition, p. 83f.

122. *Drumbeats from Kampala,* p. 43.

123. See Devasahayam, et al, *Rethinking Christianity in India,* pp. 36-38 for instance.

124. See *Ecumenical Press Service* 41/15-17, June 1974, for text. The *International Review of Missions* 64/254 (1974), covered the discussion as well. Adrian Hastings, *African Christianity: An Essay in Interpretation* (London: Geoffrey Chapman, 1976), p. 35, however, labeled the idea of a missionary moratorium "essentially an irrelevance," arguing that missionary control of the church was already marginal.

125. Shoki Coe, "In Search of Renewal in Theological Education," *Theological Education* 9/4 (1973).

126. Shoki Coe, "Across the Frontiers: Text and Context of Mission," *Christian Action in the Asian Struggle,* [Singapore: Christian Conference of Asia, 1973], p. 71. Coe's explicit use of *missio Dei* and extensive references to the missiological discussions within the IMC and the WCC intentionally relate his paradigm to that of the ecumenical movement centered around the North Atlantic.

127. Coe, "Across the Frontiers," p. 78. Coe, "Across Frontiers," p. 76, wrote: "Speaking from the point of view of the Younger Churches, we owe our Christian faith to Modern Missions. The existence of the Younger Churches is an undying tribute to this missionary enterprise of the last 150 years." Viewed in light of his subsequent discussion of *missio Dei not* originating in the church, his remark can only be seen as ironic.

128. Coe, "In Search of Renewal in Theological Education," p. 242.

129. *Ibid.*

130. Reports and papers from the first seven EATWOT conferences have been printed in Sergio Torres and Virginia Fabella, eds., *The Emergent Gospel: Theology from the Underside of History* (Maryknoll: Orbis Books, 1978); Kofi Appiah-Kubi and Sergio Torres, eds., *African Theology en Route* (Maryknolll: Orbis Books, 1979); Virginia Fabella, ed., *Asia's Struggle for Full Humanity: Towards a Relevant Theology* (Maryknoll: Orbis Books, 1980); Sergio Torres and John Eagleson, eds., *The Challenge of Basic Christian Communities* (Maryknoll: Orbis Books, 1981); Virginia Fabella and Sergio Torres, eds., *Irruption of the Third World: Challenge to Theology* (Maryknoll: Orbis Books, 1983); and Virginia Fabella and Sergio Torres, eds., *Doing Theology in a Divided World* (Maryknoll: Orbis Books, 1985); and K. C. Abraham, ed., *Third World Theologies: Commonalities and Divergences* (Maryknoll: Orbis Books, 1990).

131. Torres and Fabella, eds., *The Emergent Gospel,* p. 1; see also Fabella and Torres, eds., *Irruption of the Third World,* p. 217. EATWOT sponsored several conferences of Third World Women during the 1980s; see Virginia Fabella and Mercy Amba Oduyoye, eds., *With Passion and Compassion: Third*

World Women Doing Theology (Marynoll: Orbis Books, 1988); and Virginia Fabella and Sun Ai Lee Park, eds., *We Dare to Dream: Doing Theology as Asian Women* (Hong Kong: Asian Women's Resource Center for Culture and Theology), 1989.

132.   Orlando Costas, *Christ Outside the Gate: Mission Beyond Christendom* (Maryknoll: Orbis Books, 1982), p. 189.

133.   Ayandele, *African Historical Studies*, p. 230. For a similar perspective from an Asian context, see Aloysius Pieris, *An Asian Theology of Liberation* (Maryknoll: Orbis Books, 1988), p. 45f.

134.   Ayandele, *African Historical Studies*, p. 234.

135.   *Ibid.*, p. 211.

136.   *The Jerusalem Meeting of the IMC, Volume IV: The Christian Mission in the Light of Race Conflict* (New York: IMC, 1928), p. 7.

137.   See Ans J. van der Bent, ed., *Breaking Down Walls: World Council of Churches Statements and Actions on Racism 1948-1985* (Geneva: WCC, 1985).

138.   *Bangkok Assembly 1973: Minutes and Reports of the Assembly of the Commission on World Mission and Evangelism* (Geneva: 1973). Philip Potter, in his Report to the CWME in Bangkok, noted the fears of some Christians regarding the new programme on Dialogue with Living Religions (p. 63). Section I of the Bangkok Assembly Report (p. 78f.) affirmed dialogue with other living faiths. Strong recommendations from this Section were made concerning racism, colonialism and imperialism; however, no recommendations were made in regard to inter-religious dialogue.

139.   *Your Kingdom Come: Mission Perspectives: Report of the World Conference on Mission and Evangelism at Melbourne, Australia, 12-25 May 1980* (Geneva: WCC, 1980).

140.   See Jean Stromberg, ed., *Missions and Evangelism: An Ecumenical Affirmation, A Study Guide* (Geneva: WCC, 1983).

141.   *Ibid.*, p. 18.

142.   *Ibid.*, p. 40

143.   Wilson, *The San Antonio Report*, p. 70

144.   *Ibid.*, p. 140.

145.   *Ibid.*, p. 126.

Chapter 5:

Continuing the Dialogue

The household is a place for conversation, and the members of the household a community of communication. Dialogue between members of the household is not a method, a means to an end, but the most basic expression of their relationship. A household where the members no longer talk to one another is dead and decaying. -- Konrad Raiser

At any moment in the development of the dialogue there are immense, boundless masses of forgotten contextual meanings, but at certain moments of the dialogue's subsequent development along the way they are recalled and invigorated in renewed form (in a new context). Nothing is absolutely dead: every meaning will have its homecoming festival.
    --Mikhail Bakhtin[1]

1. Multiple Trajectories within the World Council

It was over half a century ago now that Archbishop William Temple of the Church of England first called the ecumenical movement "the great new fact of our time." And indeed has been an enduring fact, permanently changing Christians on every continent. The opening of the Roman Catholic Church to dialogue with its spiritual siblings and neighbors in the wake of Vatican II; the emergence of new networks and organizations for global fellowship among Christians communities in all continents of the world; and the growing appreciation for racial-cultural diversity, and for the rights and ministry of women in churches all over the world all have to some degree been the legacy of the modern ecumenical movement. Over the course of the last century new ways of interacting have become common among Christians from different traditions. New levels of awareness and appreciation have been attested to among Christians belonging to diverse communities around the world. In some places previously separated Christians have even begun to worship together.

Over the past half century the World Council of Churches in particular has institutionally fostered dialogue and mutual understanding among members of diverse Christian communities. The result has been a significant increase in the respect Christians from different historical and cultural traditions now show one another. But at the same time the dialogue has encouraged Christians whose unique cultural and theological gifts have not yet been fully appreciated within the wider world community to claim for themselves a voice of their own. The ecumenical movement has characteristically enabled churches and communities of faith to move toward one another in a greater unity of faith. But it has also facilitated the development and articulation of new expressions of Christian faith and practice, especially from beyond the traditional theological boundaries of European Christendom. The World Council has been a forum in which peoples from diverse situations and contexts have met and worked together. It has been a vehicle for the development of new expressions of faith and practice more adequate for a post-colonial and post-modern world.

Protestant and Orthodox member churches from both Northern and Southern hemispheres have found in the WCC a forum for interaction and exchange across the multiple boundaries that separate them -- cultural, confessional, historical, political and geographical. But even those churches that are not members of the WCC, most notably the Roman Catholic Church, but also Conservative Evangelical and Pentecostal communities, have found themselves responding beyond their own boundaries of faith on account of the work of the World Council. Willingly or unwillingly, they have found themselves engaged in ecumenical dialogues that more often than not were being fostered within the institutional arena of the WCC. Even for communions that are not members, the WCC has served to open a wider and more diverse horizon of faith. In the case of Faith and Order, churches which do not belong to the WCC have responded to specific reports and texts that representatives from their own communions or traditions have participated in producing. In other cases churches or individuals have found themselves responding critically or positively from specific ecclesiological perspectives that are self-consciously located outside the main currents of the ecumenical movement. In both cases, however, churches find themselves compelled to respond to imperatives that originate beyond their own boundaries. In doing so they participate in (re)building the framework for a still-wider ecumenical movement.

If rebuilding the ecumenical framework is an on-going task, if not the very essence, of the movement itself, it is incumbent upon us to attend to the accomplishments of the ecumenical movement in this century which provide the basis upon which we can rebuild. We do well to attend to those issues, themes, and trends that have emerged from the ecumenical conversations thus far. The image of the ecumenical movement as an on-going conversation is one I have utilized throughout this book, for it is an image that reflects the fundamentally discursive nature of the ecumenical enterprise. What individual representatives of churches, councils, and agencies have primarily done in the ecumenical movement is to engage in dialogue and conversations, in meetings, conferences, and assemblies, but also through publications, reports, and correspondences. As with any good conversation, unexpected turns and developments have taken us by surprise, opening up new moments for our common renewal. At their best, ecumenical conversations have significantly contributed to the "edification" (*oikodome* in Greek) of the churches involved.[2]

From this perspective itis clear that 'conversation' is more than a passing verbal moment, or merely an exchange of words. It is a discursive mode of intercourse or interaction that permanently changes those who participate in it.[3] Borrowed from the Latin term *conversari*, meaning 'to keep company with, to live with,' 'conversation' and 'converse' (Latin: *conversus*) share a common root (*convertere*) with the modern English words, 'conversion' and 'convert.' A conversation is at its best truly a moment of conversion, of turning toward and turning around. It is not a simple affair, for it always already involves multiple voices and perspectives in dialogue. It is not a trivial affair, but is structuring of human life at its deepest levels. All true conversations contain within themselves their own critical moments or breaks (conversion). Authentic conversations are always moments (however minute) of real transformation. The ecumenical conversation is, in the richest sense of the word, an instance of conversion, or *metanoia* in the midst of the *oikoumene*, directed toward the *oikodome* of the church, (I Cor. 14.4).

There is a sense then in which the ecumenical movement as a whole can be understood as a new form of conversation taking place among churches and ecclesial communities. Whatever else its accomplishments (insofar as church unions, new institutional structures, new programs, doctrinal advances, articulation of new theologies, or moments of solidarity) they have been first of all brought forth through a *praxis* of conversation/conversion. The conversation has been rich and multifaceted, and has resulted in many cases in a permanent change or conversion in the life of the communities engaged in the ecumenical movement. Its inscribed traces, composed of a primary body of collectively produced records, reports, and statements from conferences, consultations, and assemblies; and of the secondary publications and responses that surround them as a body of commentary, have likewise been complex and changing. The published records and texts of the ecumenical movement document the conversation that has been carried out over the course of the past century, revealing significant instances of renewal and newness in the lives of the churches. But these publications have also been part of the on-going conversation, carrying it forward at times or serving as the basis for further face-to-face conversations and dialogue.

In this regard sharp distinctions between oral and written forms of dialogue prove to be a hindrance to understanding the character of the ecumenical conversation over the course of the past century.[4] The very *praxis* of the ecumenical movement, of bringing representatives of churches together across the multiple boundaries that separate them as communities, has cut across the frontier that has divided oral and written forms of utterances as well. Inscribed in the official reports and statements from ecumenical conferences and meetings are numerous moments of face-to-face dialogue. The disputes, misunderstandings, or agreements that took place in personal dialogical encounter among representatives and participants often find their way into the published texts that emerge from the events. At the same time the published texts of earlier conferences and assemblies, the historical or theological studies authored and edited by individual scholars, and even the official statements and responses issued by particular churches or ecclesial organizations enter the oral conversations of the movement in numerous and diverse ways. The ecumenical movement offers a sustained experience of what literary critics now call 'intertextuality,' as earlier texts find their way into later texts and later texts uncover new meanings in earlier texts, substantially altering how they can thereafter be read. The multitude of written and oral expressions of the ecumenical movement have reflected a multitude of diverse voices in this conversation. Indeed it is the central thesis of this book that the ecumenical movement over the last century has fostered more options for diversity in and among the churches than it has succeeded in achieving the unity of the churches of the world. Certainly the unity of the churches has been one of the ecumenical movement's central pursuits, but it is precisely because unity has been *one* of its pursuits that my thesis has been advanced: the unity of the churches has been one of several goals and objectives that have been central to the ecumenical movement. When unity is one of several competing objectives, then diversity is the more descriptive term.

For the purposes of this particular study of the ecumenical movement I have focused methodologically on the official statements and records of the assemblies, conferences, and programs of the World Council of Churches. I have examined the body of texts that have been produced by the conversations and programs that take place under the umbrella of the WCC, reading them as dialogical moments in an on-going conversation taking place over time and crossing multiple historical and cultural boundaries. In doing so I have sought to interpret along several narrative trajectories the major theological issues that have emerged from the ecumenical conversations occurring within the World Council of Churches. These trajectories are closely related, but not confined, to the major programmatic focal points of the World Council. In other words, they are the trajectories belonging to the three major streams of the movement, concerning doctrinal unity, the *praxis* of the churches in the world, and missions. Along each of these trajectories I have sought to locate the major points of dialogue that have taken place, and I have found two major axes for conversation and action: one is an axis whose poles are unity and mission, the other an axis whose poles are solidarity and contextualization.

In reading the texts and the trajectory of the Faith and Order movement I uncovered several contending voices concerning the meaning of unity, and of the diversity of experience in the churches today. Faith and Order has maintained its essential focus on issues relating to doctrine and ecclesiastical order, but has engaged in the study of particular issues insofar as they are significant to what is perceived to be the scandal of Christian disunity, symbolized above all else by the failure of churches to meet in eucharistic communion. To this end the work of Faith and Order has not directly engaged questions regarding doctrinal or confessional truth, nor has it sought a theological reductionism of a 'least common denominator' type of approach to Christian unity. It has explored both christological and ecclesiological questions related to the practice of sacraments and ministry, and the historical factors that impinge upon the current disunity of Protestant, Orthodox, and Roman Catholic churches.

Implicitly at first, and then explicitly following the 1963 Faith and Order Conference in Montreal, the discussion of christological and ecclesiological issues affecting unity has focussed on the nature of tradition. Specifically the perplexing question of the relation of the multiple traditions to something called the Tradition occupied Faith and Order in a search for what could be called the essence or kernel of Christian truth, hidden among the non-essential (non-theological) husks of the multiple traditions. Faith and Order's pursuit of the relationship of tradition and traditions to the Tradition inevitably led in an historical direction to the theological invocation of the memory of a united church contained in the Nicene Creed. The political and cultural dimensions of the Nicene Creed, and of the Tradition that is associated with it, have essentially been ignored in this discussion within Faith and Order, as have the grand narratives of Byzantine and Latin Christendom which have been invoked in its memory. I have argued that the search for Christian unity has been a search for the renewal of a theological tradition of dominance (the Tradition), and a renewal of a cultural memory of Christendom.

But this is only part of the story, or better, one set of voices in the dialogue. I have found that the conversation of Faith and Order has been more complex than has often been perceived, and that inscribed within the Faith and Order movement's documents have been voices which engage more critically with the dominant voices of the Tradition. These other voices, located often on the margins and in the footnotes of Faith and Order earlier in the century, became more pronounced in the decades after 1948. The voices of those from churches outside the dominant European/American community, and of women, have not sought a different center which would move the dominant churches and creeds to new margins. They have instead opted for a de-centered faith and practice, challenging the churches to be renewed in the diversity of their historical, cultural, and theological traditions. These voices have turned the Faith and Order dialogue in the direction of the plurality of contexts in which Christians live in the world. Rather than seeking convergence upon a common memory, these other voices in the Faith and Order dialogue have opened up the plurality of memories and traditions for the churches of the world, and have led to new models of reconciled diversity for Christian communities of women and men.

Since 1970 the various voices in the Faith and Order dialogue have been structured through the three major on-going study projects of the Commission, concerning sacraments and ministry, the apostolic tradition, and unity and renewal. The very manner in which these separate study projects, employing different methodologies and directed toward different (and at times seemingly contradictory) goals, have been conducted together within one Commission suggests a more dialogical understanding of Faith and Order than an isolated reading of the texts and responses of any one study would suggest. But even a cursory reading of the texts and documents of the various studies themselves, *Baptism, Eucharist and Ministry* for instance, reveals dialogical aspects of convergence and divergence, of differences that remain while reconciliation is pursued.

The manner in which dialogue presupposes differences and divergences provides an important insight into the very nature of the ecumenical movement today. The contemporary ecumenical dialogue has revealed significant social, cultural, and theological differences among the churches and ecclesial communities of the world. But it is precisely through the interaction of these churches and communities with one another in the ecumenical movement that critical ethical and theological understanding have emerged. Critical understanding and even change have more often resulted from ecumenical exchanges among communities of divergent perspectives or beliefs than from shared perspectives or consensus. From the "material interaction of different communities" a sharper, more critical ecumenical understanding of has emerged dialogically, pointing the way toward a new meaning of reconciliation.[5] The experiential basis for reconciliation that affirms and even celebrates difference has for the Faith and Order movement been discovered in the *praxis* of solidarity.

Ada Maria Isasi-Diaz has argued that solidarity "is grounded in 'common responsibilities and interests,' which necessarily arouse shared feelings and lead to joint action."[6] The mutuality of common responsibilities and interests that is characteristic of authentic solidarity demands commitment to action, or *praxis*, while *praxis* is at the same time the enabling condition for the mutuality of friendship or *koinonia*.

But solidarity does not lead to the eradication of difference, the erasure of local memories, or the subordination of particular traditions to the Tradition. It is an enabling mutuality which affirms differences in *koinonia*, providing in a critical yet limited way an eschatological glimpse of the reality known from Christian scriptures as what Isasi-Diaz calls the "kin-dom" of God.[7] The solidarity of the *koinonia* of God celebrates the multiplicity of human community. It embraces memories and traditions commonly identified as Christian, but it also opens up to the renewal of memories and traditions which lie beyond the historical domain of the Christian religion. Furthermore solidarity does not represent an uncritical embrace of memories and traditions, but rather it calls for discernment of the liberative dimensions of both.

Commitment to the *praxis* of solidarity has not been an exclusive discovery of the Faith and Order Commission in the World Council of Churches. It has emerged in other programs of the World Council as well, and throughout the larger ecumenical movement. As a broadly defined *praxis* intended to transform existing ecclesiastical, social, political, and cultural structures that variously define human experiences of community today, solidarity has provided the critical basis for ecumenical *koinonia* in many different forms. In the various programs and agencies of the WCC itself the *praxis* of solidarity represents the ground from which a vital and coherent ecumenical theology can eventually grow. The *oikoumene* in which this *praxis* of solidarity is taking shape is one marked by centuries of domination and oppression, however. At the same time, the ecumenical response to the social and political structures and practices of domination has been hampered by the lingering commitments in some sectors of the ecumenical movement to the memory of the cultural synthesis of Western European Christendom. This, we have seen, has been evident in the discussions and controversies of the WCC surrounding issues of Church and Society.

The Life and Work movement initially emerged within the horizon of a collapsed Western civilization following the First World War (or better, First All-European War) of 1914-1917. Its primary goal was the search for a unified witness on the part of a number of European and North American Protestant and Orthodox churches in response to the social problems of modern Western civilization, a witness the churches had not had at least since the division of East and West in the eleventh century and the further fracturing of the Western (Latin) churches of the sixteenth century. Issues such as industrialization, economic life, and race relations were on the agenda of Life and Work as it took shape over the first quarter of the twentieth century.

Ironically several of the social and technological developments that were identified by Life and Work as problems to be addressed were themselves factors that enabled the rapid development of the ecumenical movement on a global scale during this century. The development of rapid transportation by steamship and rail, of communication technologies such as the telegraph, and of new technologies for dissemination of information through mass media, did much to bring churches into more direct and intimate contact with one another. Despite the role such technological developments played in the emergence of the ecumenical movement in the twentieth century however, their larger social framework of modern capitalism and industrialization and the concomitant cultural development of secularization presented a challenge that drew Protestant and Orthodox churches together for deliberations and common action.

While the Life and Work movement did not produce significant solutions to the problems of industrialization, race relations, or economic unemployment, it did enable representatives from the dominant Protestant churches of North America and Western Europe to begin to rediscover a common ecclesial identity as church, reflected in the Oxford Conference's rallying cry in 1937, "let the church be the church!" At the same time, along with Faith and Order, Life and Work provided delegates representing Protestant communions an opportunity to work together with Orthodox church leaders from Western Europe and the Eastern Mediterranean countries. These experiences in Life and Work in particular were to prove to be especially important during the early years of the World Council of Churches, for in the formation of the World Council the concerns of Life and Work were programmatically dispersed throughout its structure. Faith and Order maintained a relative autonomy within the World Council as a whole, operating under its own constitution and electing its own members. Life and Work on the other hand disappeared into the overall structure of the WCC. The major programmatic concerns of the World Council, including its work in governmental relations, interchurch service, and refugee relief, but also its study divisions on Church and Society and on the Cooperation of Women and Men, continued through the 1950s to operate primarily within a horizon that had characterized Life and Work as much as Faith and Order: the horizon of Western society.

This was generally true for the WCC as a whole, for the social and political issues confronting Christian communities which were not within the horizon of Western civilization were not to emerge in a decisive way for the World Council until the end of the 1950s. The major turning point often pointed to in the life of the World Council is the 1966 Geneva study conference on Church and Society. Yet as we have seen above the Geneva Conference did not represent a radical break with the agenda of Western social and political life so much as it represented the emergence in the social and political discourse of the WCC of alternative voices articulating the revolutionary situations confronting the churches in the world beyond Western societies. If we assess the break in the dominant Eurocentric horizon of the WCC in terms of ecumenical *praxis* then we would better mark the inauguration of the Programme to Combat Racism in 1969 and the 1974 Berlin Consultation on Sexism as the major turning points in the WCC, and perhaps by extension in the ecumenical movement as a whole.

In the Program to Combat Racism we encountered a strategic project intending to engage the WCC in a *praxis* of solidarity with communities who have suffered the effects of racism and who are struggling against it. The PCR has represented not only a *praxis* of solidarity among communities of racial difference within the WCC. It has intentionally sought to express and achieve the solidarity of the WCC as a whole with communities that have experienced racial oppression in the modern world. As an expression of solidarity the PCR has at the same time implicitly acknowledged the boundary that exists between the WCC as a whole, and the communities of racially oppressed peoples in the world today. The PCR has revealed the World Council's structural reproduction of, and participation in, European racial domination; at the same time it has signified the World Council's intentional commitments to transforming these structures, and instituting new forms of mutuality within the larger ecumenical community.

In a similar manner, although admittedly often with a lesser degree of visibility, the WCC program on Women in Church and Society has sought to reveal the structural oppression of sexism among and within the churches and communities of the WCC. The problems and issues of sexism only began to be addressed in the World Council in the 1970s, beginning notably with the 1974 West Berlin conference. The *praxis* of solidarity between women and men that emerged in the "Community of Women and Men" joint project of the Sub-Unit on

Women in Church and Society and the Commission on Faith and Order in the late 1970s and early 1980s pointed toward new forms of mutuality in human community. As Sun Ai Lee Park has pointed out, the emergence of the two "great movements" within the ecumenical community, "the women's movement and the movement of various peoples in grass-roots contexts," marks a "new phase" in the ecumenical movement as a whole.[8]

What is new in the ecumenical movement's response to social and political life is not only the emergence of voices other than those of Western Christian white men. A new commitment to joint action and struggle, among peoples of diverse experiences of exclusion and oppression, but also eventually encompassing those Western Christian white men who respond to the ecumenical call to solidarity, has become the mark of the *praxis* of this new phase. The *praxis* of solidarity that has characterized the ecumenical struggle against sexism in the 1980s has not sought to isolate women's oppression from other forms, nor to reduce sexism, racism, classism, and other oppressions to a single form or a common source. In a similar manner the PCR has become more explicitly concerned with the interconnections between sexism and racism, and has paid specific attention to the struggles of women against racism. Recognizing the multiple dynamics of racism, classism, and sexism, the ecumenical struggle for solidarity in the 1980s has become characterized by mutual and multiple modes of *praxis* concerning these different experiences.

The mode of community generated through solidarity amidst differences, especially in experiences of suffering and oppression, suggests a more dialogical understanding of solidarity and community than the WCC has yet come to embody. It still remains a hope and a vision for the WCC, and for the ecumenical movement as a whole. Nor is it yet a hope and vision that is shared by all sectors of the ecumenical movement, or even by all within the World Council of Churches. It remains in most instances an imperative that has emerged from beyond the ecumenical horizon of European social and cultural patriarchy and racism. Nevertheless it is a call to new community issued to all people of faith, embodying says Annie Nachisale Musopole the Tumbuka proverb, "Kawepano nkhatonse," or "What falls here is for us all."

The ecumenical movement is called to be a lamp shining to show that in Jesus Christ there is neither male nor female, neither poor nor rich, neither black nor white. The ecumenical movement is called to be a global village wherein all God's people live with and for one another. "What falls here is for us all."[9]

The vision of unity that will be embodied in this new ecumenical community is one that no longer upholds the boundaries that separate Western from non-Western Christian communities. That is to say, the coherence and vitality of the ecumenical movement lie beyond the boundaries constructed originally by the Christendom-mission lands dichotomy. As we have seen above in considering the third stream of the modern ecumenical movement, institutionalized in the International Missionary Council and later in the WCC's Commission on World Mission and Evangelism (and to a lesser extent in the sub-unit on Dialogue with People of Living Faiths and Ideologies), the ecumenical movement cannot be understood apart from the emergence of Protestant missions in the modern era.[10] In particular the relationship between Protestant (and to a lesser extent Roman Catholic) missions and European colonialism during what Stephen Charles Neill calls "the Vasco de Gama era" between 1492 and 1947 must be reckoned with in any accounting of missions and the ecumenical movement.[11] As the "new event," the ecumenical movement continues to contain inscribed within it the memory of that over against which it is the new, that is, the memory of European missions and their close relations to European colonialism.

The word 'missions,' then, contains within it the historical context of Western Christendom's ambiguous response to the European Enlightenment, and its affinities with European colonialism. Modern missions, as we have seen, served both to demarcate and to extend the boundaries of Western Christianity; they were as much an expression of the anxieties concerning Christendom's loss of vitality and coherence as they were a response to the boundary-breaking imperatives of the Gospel. But we have also seen that this is not the only context that is inscribed within the memory of missions from the modern era. The memory and experiences of those who responded in faith to the proclamation of the story of Jesus Christ, the multiple origins and dynamics of the formation of Christian communities of faith and churches amidst peoples outside Western Christendom, the intentions and purposes that came to expression in the experiences of conversion of those not seeking to revitalize a Western Christian tradition, are equally part of the context inscribed in the word. 'Missions' has contained within it these various contexts, and their relationship is dialogical.[12] Thus it is open to new meaning, and to the new paradigm that the ecumenical movement has sought to become.[13]

The theological point at which the dialogue became effective within ecumenical discourse was at the Willingen IMC conference in 1952. Willingen marks a theological turning point and the emergence of what became a quiet revolution within the discourse and *praxis* of missions. Considering mission as belonging first to God, and then assessing the plural missions of the churches that live in response to God's one Mission in the world, Willingen laid a foundation for a clearer articulation of their dialogical. By the end of the 1950s a de-centered conception of mission and a new awareness of the intrinsic relationship between mission and church heralded the end of the IMC as a separate institution and its integration into the WCC at New Delhi in 1961. In the decades that followed the New Delhi Assembly the new Commission on World Mission and Evangelism sought to define the meaning of missions and of evangelism in a post-colonial church and world. The attempt has not always been successful, for the dialogue has often remained one-sided and only partially open to new directions.

Where the new paradigm has emerged successfully has been in the movements for contextualization and liberation. Wilbert Shenk has pointed out that the shift in missions associated with the term "contextualization" has led to a poly-centric view of history and a new balance between profound commitments to the locality of missions and an awareness of their global dimensions.[14] Contextualization, as it has been articulated in its theological and missiological dimensions, is perhaps better described as the dialogical interaction between the texts of the biblical and theological past, and the multiple living contexts of social, political, cultural, and religious life today. The result of contextualization has been a multiplicity of Christian theologies, and the development of a more radical pluralism than has been known to Christian communities in the past. Contextualization has opened up new avenues for faith which in previous eras might well have come under the suppression of the dominant ecclesiological powers as being heterodoxical. The close relationship which has emerged between contextual and liberation theologies suggests that the interaction between ecclesiological and political power in missions that were characterized by domination is beginning to give way to new forms of mission through solidarity and local initiatives.

In one critical aspect in particular the problematic character of the incomplete dialogue of missions has revealed itself in ecumenical conversations that have followed from Edinburgh 1910. Uncertaintly and even uneasiness concerning dialogue with persons of other faiths have continued to show up in WCC discussions. The continuing tension such dialogue generates for traditional Western understandings of mission and evangelism suggests that the new paradigm dialogue has not yet been completely realized, even within the WCC. The possibility of such dialogue, and the fuller realization of community open to churches living beyond the failures of Western missions, has emerged as an imperative in particular for Christian communities in Africa and Asia. But the call to living in community with peoples of other faiths is equally an imperative for North Atlantic churches today, one which is integral to the full emergence of the new paradigm for missions.

Wesley Ariarajah has explored the ecumenical quest for relationship in community with people of other faiths by focussing on the history of ecumenical dialogue in the WCC between Christians and Hindus.[15] Ariarajah's commitment to full community across boundaries of religious difference excludes by definition those missionary practices of that seek to eradicate religious beliefs of other communities. Such missionary practices I have termed 'religiocide,' for they are closely related to both the ethnocide and genocide practiced by modern Western European powers in the modern era. Ariarajah criticizes not only the exclusive conceptions of theological truth that undergird the practice of religiocide, but he challenges the 'inclusive' christological approaches such as those advocated by Karl Rahner ('anonymous Christians') and Raimundo Panikkar (the 'unknown' or 'hidden Christ'). Over against these two ways of relating the Christian religion to non-Christian religions, Ariarajah opts for a third way which he acknowledges is not yet completely coherent, but which will emerge not out of a theoretical consideration of religious truths but out of the living experiences of Christians and Hindus in relationships together.

Aspects of the theological outline of this third way are discernable among a number of contemporary voices concerning mission, unity, and religious pluralism. Ariarajah suggests several elements necessary for a Christian theology in a religiously plural context, among them a renewed awareness of the Trinitarian mystery which is at the heart of Christian faith; an awareness of inherent limitations of any human language, thought, or intentionality in relation to the transcendence of this mystery; and a renewed commitment to the enrichment of living in dialogical relationships amidst the pluralism of the world.[16]   The

Trinitarian and eschatological dimensions of mission as dialogue become visible in his consideration of inter-religious relationships. The manner in which such dialogue is eschatologically open to the fullness of community which is in the future, and which is realized through the mission of the Holy Spirit, offers a critical ecumenical direction for a theology of missions.[17]

In all of these ecumenical streams that have flowed within the World Council of Churches we can discern a multiplicity of voices and projects. In some the dialogue has been clearer, in others more difficult to hear. At times there have been attempts at suppression, and at times the dialogue has even seemed one-sided. But when the whole experience is considered, across the multiple trajectories of ecumenical history, distinctive dialogical voices can be heard and have been inscribed within the texts of ecumenical history. In general, we have discerned across the three ecumenical streams in the World Council the struggle between voices recalling the memory (or the myth) of a united church in Europe's past on the one hand, and the multiple memories of peoples and communities beyond Christendom on the other. At times it has been difficult to discern the dialogue which is taking place on account of the monologue of Western patriarchal and racial domination. Carlos Abesamis has pointed out that at times "a bracketing off" of Western theological discourse is necessary, in order to hear the dialogical voices of the counter-stories and counter-theologies that are being articulated despite the monologue of Western domination.[18] Nevertheless the theology that is emerging from such dialogue, from the living encounter of concrete human communities, is opening up a new future in faith even for the Western churches that have practiced domination and exclusion.

2. Multiple Trajectories beyond the World Council

For the most part in this book I have attended to the dialogues that have taken place within the arena of the World Council of Churches, and have only occasionally alluded to those ecumenical projects beyond it. Yet a fuller understanding of the contemporary ecumenical movement must at least recognize some of the dimensions of ecumenism beyond the World Council. Perhaps the most significant ecumenical work which falls outside the domain of the WCC today is that which has emerged from the context of the Roman Catholic Church, especially in the wake of Vatican II. Here it is only possible to sketch the ecumenical trajectories that have emerged from Vatican II, primarily in relationship to the World Council of Churches. The major statement of Vatican II impinging upon ecumenical relationships, *Unitatis Redintegratio* (The Restoration of Unity), commonly called the "Decree on Ecumenism," spells out the fundamental principles the Catholic Church has maintained in its inter-ecclesiastical relations over the last several decades, although other documents of Vatican II have also proven to have significant ecumenical effects.[19]

Unitatis Redintegratio placed before the Roman Church guidelines within which Roman Catholics could respond to the call to ecumenism emerging from among the "separated" brothers and sisters in other churches. Reasserting as a fundamental ecumenical principle the preeminence of the See of Peter, and the Apostolic unity secured by "the bishops with Peter's successor at their head," the Decree nevertheless went on to affirm that those who have come to faith in Christian communities other than the Roman Catholic Church cannot be charged with the sin of separation.[20] Furthermore, certain the elements of ecclesial grace can exist among these churches outside the boundaries of the Catholic Church, and the Spirit has used them as effective means of salvation. Recognizing a different ecumenical situation between Catholic relations with Orthodox and with Protestants (the Decree affirmed the distinctive apostolic heritages handed down in Eastern Orthodox churches while raising concerns about the preservation of the eucharistic mystery and the absence of the sacrament of orders among other Western Protestant churches) *Unitatis Redintegratio* invited ecumenical dialogue with both Orthodox and Protestant communities, opening up a new era in Roman Catholic ecumenism.[21]

In the years immediately following Vatican II Rome entered into a series of bilateral dialogues with other communions, East and West. New initiatives between the Roman Catholic Church and the World Council of Churches were undertaken as well, most notably the establishment of the Joint Working Group and the Committee on Society, Development and Peace (Sodepax) in the late 1960s. Roman Catholic participation in the Faith and Order Commission since 1967 has likewise proven to be a significant ecumenical development. Despite such efforts, however, Rome did not move toward an organic relationship with the World Council, and since 1980 there has been little in the way of new initiatives between the Roman Catholic Church and the World Council of Churches. The barriers that remain between Rome and the WCC are significant, entailing both matters of ecclesiology (most notably the issue of Petrine supremacy, but more generally of the apostolic nature of the church) and of ecumenical responses to social issues.[22] The result has often been a frustration on the part of those who live amidst the imperatives for ecumenical dialogue between, but also initiatives that are taken on local or regional levels of ecumenism and which point toward the ecumenical future.[23]

The other major ecumenical Christian trajectories that have remained predominantly outside the domain of the WCC have been those of Conservative Evangelical Protestantism and of Pentecostalism in this century. Conservative Evangelical and Pentecostal communities have generally regarded the basis for membership in the World Council too doctrinally loose, and some of the Protestants churches represented in the ecumenical movement as being too liberal (or modernist). Dispensationalist -- those anticipating the imminent secret return of Christ for the faithful, and the inauguration of the final tribulation of human history depicted in apocalyptic biblical passages -- have seen in the World Council the contours of a world religious system under the "false prophet" serve the totalitarian purposes of a single world ruler, the "anti-Christ" (see esp. Rev. 13:11-18, 19:20).[24] The most important criticisms voiced recently by Conservative Evangelicals have concerned the diversity that is contained within the WCC, and what appears to many Evangelicals at least to be the demise of traditional exclusionary conceptions of mission and evangelism.[25] Consequently it has not been uncommon to find Protestantism (Anglo-American Protestantism in particular) divided into 'Evangelical' vs. 'Ecumenical' camps this century, this despite repeated and continuing invitations from the WCC to greater Evangelical participation in its structures and programs.

Too often the more conservative streams of Anglo-American Protestantism have been lumped together into the general category of the Evangelicals, obscuring some of the critical differences and debates that have been occurring among these more traditional communities. Divisions among Conservative Evangelical, Holiness, Pentecostal, and Charismatic communities can be as severe as those that characterize churches in the WCC. There have been important recent initiatives from among sectors of the Holiness and Pentecostal communities toward the WCC, in North and Latin America in particular.[26] Holiness and Pentecostal churches have shared many of the concerns for social

problems and the united witness of the churches that have been on the
ecumenical agenda this century.   On the other hand, Evangelical,
Holiness, and Pentecostal streams of Protestantism in North America,
and since the 1960s in the larger global context, have converged to form
a distinctive ecumenical expression of their own this century, often
standing over against the WCC and its programs.

The more extreme manifestations of this "evangelical ecumenism"
were manifested in the formation of the International Council of
Christian Churches (ICC) in 1948 also in Amsterdam, largely under the
inspiration of the U.S. Fundamentalist leader, Rev. Carl McIntire of
Collingswood, NJ.[27] Churches in the ICC generally represented what
they called "Protestant Orthodoxy," upholding strict doctrinal adherence
to the standards of the Reformation and in generally rejecting what they
perceived to be the general accommodation of Protestantism to the spirit
of the modern era.   While many of these churches shared earlier
ecumenical commitments to foreign missions, they perceived the
development of the ecumenical movement in the twentieth century to be
a heretical corruption of the Protestant faith. The World Council was
especially the target of vehement attack by the ICC and other radical
Fundamentalists of this period, for it was perceived not only as
embracing modernism, but as collaborating with communism.

The ecumenical movement's embrace of the heterodoxy of what
Fundamentalists called "Barthianism," and its openness to the Catholic
character of Eastern Orthodoxy, called into question the commitment of
the Protestant churches of the WCC to the historical Protestant faith as
far as the ICC was concerned. Where the WCC did offer any form of
doctrinal standard, notably in its basis, it appeared to be lax in enforcing
conformity to an orthodox interpretation, or worse, to willingly embrace
some who denied the authority of Jesus Christ in spite of the WCC
basis. The admission of the Russian Orthodox Church into the WCC
in 1961 at New Delhi was a sign to in particular to the ICC of the
apostasy of the WCC, for it had admitted a church that was believed to
be communist controlled (since it was a recognized church from a
communist country).[28] The sinister aims of the ecumenical movement
appeared to the ICC to be similar to the aspirations to world-domination
that it perceived in communism and Roman Catholicism. In place of
one world church this form of Orthodox Protestantism maintained a
radically individualistic notion of salvation, strict adherence to what it
perceived to be essential standards of Protestant faith, and a minimally
functionalist ecclesiology. Despite its vehement attack on ecumenism,

however, the manner in which the ICC followed (and even parodied) the WCC in its organization and activities suggests that it can only be understood as an expression of counter-ecumenism among radical Protestant Fundamentalism.

The emergence of neo-evangelicalism in North America in the middle of the 1940s brought with it an alternative form of evangelical ecumenism, expressed institutionally in such organizations as the National Association of Evangelicals (NAE). Unlike the WCC for whom the task of calling the churches to visible unity in faith and communion has been central, the NAE was not intended to be a movement for denominational union, nor has it encouraged visible unity among the churches that belong to it. The NAE is a voluntary fellowship among conservative Protestant and Pentecostal Christian churches and denominations expressing common interests and serving as an instrument for common tasks such as evangelism.

While the NAE has not held to many of the extreme views of the ICC, it shared with the ICC a commitment to strict adherence to what was perceived to the essential doctrines of conservative Protestant Christianity, such as the inspiration and infallibility of the Bible, the Trinity, the deity of Jesus Christ, vicarious atonement, bodily resurrection, and, concerning the unity of the church, belief in the spiritual unity of believers in Christ. Membership in the NAE has from the beginning been open to denominations, organizations, and local churches or groups of churches which accepted these beliefs. Nevertheless, the essential separatism of the NAE found expression in its early provision that no denomination belonging to its fellowship could at the same time belong to the Federal Council of Christian Churches in America (the ecumenical body of the 1940s preceding the formation of the National Council of Churches USA), although individual churches of those denominations could join the evangelical movement.[29]

The 1960s witnessed major developments among North American and European evangelicals cooperating in missions and evangelism, a movement which reached significant world-wide proportions with the formation of the Lausanne Committee for World Evangelisation and the holding of the Lausanne consultation in 1974.[30] The Lausanne movement has also broadened the range of evangelical concerns to embrace issues of social justice that had been more commonly identified with the ecumenism of the WCC. At the same time, despite doctrinal differences and continued evangelical criticisms of the WCC,

Conservative Evangelicals have made significant contributions to the WCC throughout its existence. In recent years there have been more active dialogue and cooperation in several areas, most notably in missions and evangelism.[31]   Evangelicals participating in these discussions have themselves come under criticism from other conservative Protestants on account of their involvement in the ecumenical movement.[32] Ecumenical leaders on the other hand have, as Michael Kinnamon points out, welcomed the "larger ecumenism" of Evangelical-Ecumenical dialogue.[33]

The dialogue Pentecostal and Charismatic communities of the world have carried on with the WCC has unfolded in a manner similar to that of Evangelicals and the WCC. The person who more than any other individual represented the Pentecostal presence within the ecumenical movement earlier this century was David du Plessis.[34] For the most part, however, Pentecostalism has remained outside the ecumenical arena of the WCC, save for those few Pentecostal churches that have chosen to become members of the World Council. While the relationship of Pentecostal churches to the WCC remains minimal, a more active interest in ecumenism has appeared among Charismatics, many of whom are often within traditions that have been represented in the major streams of ecumenical movement.[35] Within the WCC the call for greater ecumenical engagement with Pentecostal churches has been issued repeatedly, with signs in recent years of it becoming more of a reality.[36]

In addition to these major trajectories in Roman Catholic, Conservative Evangelical, and Pentecostal traditions numerous other local or regional ecumenical trajectories could be sketched, and local or regional ecumenical movements delineated. The on-going work of renewal among communities of women and men is a sign of the renewal of the Holy Spirit which continues to break through the racial, cultural, ideological, and doctrinal barriers that separate individuals and communities from one another. The work of renewal has brought together members of different communities for moments of intense interaction in the transit lounge. Often it has meant significant breakthroughs in understanding and new openness to a common future; but just as often the ecumenical encounters that have taken place *en route* have made differences clearer, sharper, more exacting. At times is has appeared that the ecumenical Spirit has succeeded in driving individuals and communities further apart rather than closer together.

Even such moments of ecumenical dissonance and distancing remain essential moments of dialogical encounter however. Quite often they provide the starting point for future episodes of the dialogical *praxis*. We have seen that in the case of Roman Catholic and Conservative Evangelical refusals to participate fully within the WCC, the ecumenical movement cannot be reduced to the World Council even though the World Council remains a primary expression (or privileged instrument) of the larger movement. At the same time we have seen the dialogical character of the WCC, and of its various streams and programs, is itself more complex than any one perspective of the dialogue can represent. Its 'truth' is shared among diverse perspectives and communities, and remains irreducible to one point of view or definition. Over the course of almost a century of life the ecumenical movement has not narrowed differences among Christians, nor has it reduced the number of distinctive ecclesial and ecclesiastical identities in the world; quite the contrary, as I have pointed out, the ecumenical movement has served to intensify and enable the development of a greater number of differences among churches. Yet this is not a sign of ecumenical failure. Progress toward uniformity and sameness, or the totality of a singular Tradition, is not more representative of the Gospel than is progress toward alterity, solidarity, and community amidst difference.[37]

3. Ecumenical Memories and the Ecumenical Future

We are left to conclude then that alterity and difference are as much signs of vitality in the ecumenical movement today as are consensus and convergence. As the crossroads among churches and ecclesial communities the ecumenical movement is also the place where alterity and otherness are experienced and embodied through dialogical relationships. The ecumenical movement has played an important role for change and for generating the 'New' among churches of the world. At the same time, one of its significant outcomes has been the creation of a common experience and a common memory for the churches engaged in it. Over the course of the century churches in the ecumenical movement have forged a common body of discourse, a tradition, through projects, conferences, assemblies, and written texts. Equally significant however has been the diversity of experiences within the ecumenical movement, and the manner in which it has exposed churches and communities to ecclesial memories other than their own. The ecumenical memory that has been generated by the movement over the course of this century has not been characterized by its closure, but rather by its opening up to what is beyond the provence of any one community or perspective on the movement as a whole.

In recent years there have been concerns in the World Council of Churches in particular for what has been called 'a common ecumenical memory.' As new participants have come into the various arenas of ecumenical life, and as new voices have begun to be heard around the common tables of ecumenical discourse, concerns about a common historical memory have emerged. On the one hand the plea for a common memory has resulted from the realization that without a sense of shared history and identity the contemporary ecumenical movement is in danger of succumbing to absolute difference which is chaos. On the other the concern for a common memory has represented the need for a sense of direction and purpose on the part of many within the movement today. In both cases, the call to remember the particular historical experiences which have given shape to ecumenical discourse and *praxis* represents a call to remember a singular ecumenical narrative, running from Edinburgh, 1910 to today.

However much we may call for and even achieve a common ecumenical memory, the contents of that memory will remain plural and characterized by difference. For no matter how narrowly we define the various streams of the ecumenical movement through the greater part of this century, the experiences and events which have taken place have involved participants from different perspectives and contexts, holding to different (and even contradictory) understandings of the meaning of these experiences and events. The conferences, assemblies, consultations, and studies which form the body of ecumenical history this century have by design and definition been representative of different contexts, perspectives, and ecclesial memories. The very nature of the experiences and events composing the history of the ecumenical movement requires us to recognize the irreducibly pluralistic and open character of the ecumenical memory.

The manner in which these different contexts and perspectives meet and collide within the ecumenical movement can be seen in events at the recent WCC Assembly held in Canberra, Australia in February of 1991. As the Seventh WCC Assembly, Canberra 1991 stood within a continuous ecumenical stream that runs from Edinburgh 1910, through

Amsterdam 1948 to the present. At the same time, as the controversy over Korean theologian Chung Hyun-Kyung's address on the main theme of the Assembly revealed, discontinuity and disjunction continue to characterize this ecumenical memory as well. Not only the words of Chung's address delivered on the second day of the Assembly, but her actions that accompanied her words, and the ensuing debates which continued in their wake during the remainder of the Assembly and beyond, reveal a more complex memory and identity than can fitted into a simple framework of Christian ecumenical memory.

Removing her shoes in recognition of the Aboriginal Holy Ground on which she stood in Canberra, and inviting the rest of the Assembly to join her in this Asian ceremony of preparation for encountering the Spirit of God, Chung proceeded to open her address by invoking the spirits of the victims of human history. Her invocation called upon the spirit of Hagar, Uriah, Jephthah's daughter, and the innocents of Bethlehem of biblical memory; the spirit of indigenous peoples who suffered under the genocide of European colonialism and Christian missions; the spirit of Mahatma Ghandi, Steven Biko, and Martin Luther King, Jr.; the spirit of the creation; the "spirit of the Liberator, our brother Jesus, tortured and killed on the cross."[38] She then offered up her list of names as a burning offering of those who have suffered, letting the ashes drift to the sky.

Her invocation drew a wider circle of memory than that often associated with Christian history, but a circle which she identified from her own context of Korea, "the land of spirits full of *Han*," that is, full of anger, resentment, bitterness, grief, and broken-heartedness.[39] It is through the *Han*-ridden spirits that we can hear the Holy Spirit, she asserted, recognizing the *Han*-ridden spirits to be "ikons" of the Holy Spirit. Through them the churches are being called to repentance, to a new life-centeredness. Chung identified the Holy Spirit not only iconically with the spirits of those who have suffered oppression, torture, and genocide, but positively with what is known in North East Asian culture as *Ki* (the life energy), or in East Asian women's religiosity as *Kwan In* (the Buddhist bodhisattva, "Goddess of compassion"). It was this identification more than anything else in her address which became the focus of controversy in the following days during the Assembly. Immediate negative responses to Chung's address as being "syncretism and paganism" came from Orthodox delegates as well as from delegates from Western Protestant churches. And while other Western delegates spoke in favor of her address to the Assembly, it was clear that the divisions that arose were due to differing contexts and historical experiences of Christian faith.[40]

The context Chung spoke out of was that of women of the Third World and of Asia, a post-colonial generation shaped by the history of Western ecclesiological compliance with colonial regimes. Her context is one in which Christians continue to seek what it means for them to live in community with peoples of other faiths, and to share a common ancient religious and cultural heritage. Chung acknowledged the risk of asserting her tradition, and the risk of syncretism. But she accepted the risk, noting that the churches elsewhere have drawn upon resources from their culture contexts in expressing its faith. At Canberra the most visible immediate response came from Orthodox theologians whose concerns for the uniqueness of Jesus Christ and for the need for discerning the spirits led them to question the presentation by Chung. While it was pointed out that the Orthodox tradition is itself an example of the successful contextualization or syncretism (of Christian faith and ancient Hellenistic culture) Orthodox theologians asserted that there are limits to cultural contextualization, noting the refusal in the early Christian era to acknowledge the other divinities of the Greco-Roman world as being equal to Jesus Christ for instance.

On the surface this debate that was begun during the two weeks at Canberra and is still being carried on appears to pit one set of contextual concerns for orthodoxy and apostasy over against another set of ethical concerns for the dispossessed who struggle against the ecclesiastical and political establishments of our day. On a deeper level, however, it is a debate that has brought together one memory of the Christian tradition from the context of an ancient church that successfully resolved its conflict between faith and culture in the first several centuries after the apostles, with another memory of the Christian tradition from a post-colonial Asian context in which Christians continue to struggle for justice and liberation. The two different memories resist being easily reconciled or harmonized; their ecumenical character is in fact located precisely in their difference, or more specifically in the manner in which they exist together as two unreconciled memories in one ecumenical assembly of churches.

That the spirits Chung Hyun-Kyung invoked are remembered by many in the churches today, by those who are Christian and who also remember Jesus Christ, requires us to include them within the circle of ecumenical memories, despite concerns regarding the dangers they pose to the faith. The concerns are legitimate -- they need to be raised again and again for all contexts where the dangers of cultural accommodation threaten to swallow up the authentic voices of faith, not least of all in the middle-class world of white North Atlantic Protestant Christianity today. But the presence of so many spirit-voices from beyond Eurocentric Christendom is one of the signs of ecumenical life, not death, today. There are memories of Christian experience beyond the lives of Western Christendom, memories and experiences which belong to those whose histories are outside the boundaries of Christendom.

Chung took off her shoes at the beginning of her address in order to show her respect for the Holy Ground of Aboriginal peoples on which she stood. This seemingly simple act was an expression of solidarity, not one centered around a common Christian identity, but an act of Christian solidarity centered around a common Asian identity. Admittedly it was on the Holy Ground of orthodox traditions that she walked in her shoelessness. The Holy Ground on which she danced was visibly contested ground, that is, ground on which was taking place a calling to witness, or testifying (Latin: '*contestari*'). The contestation which took place on these ecumenical grounds recalls the story of Jacob, who wrestled not only with the visitor but for the tradition as well, who witnessed to a new memory, and who received a blessing through being wounded (Gen. 32.24-30). The WCC Assembly at Canberra found with Jacob that the place of difference is a place of hope precisely because it is a contested terrain. The negative responses by some, the affirmative responses by others, and the continuing discussion of events at Canberra represent the on-going witnessing to, the contesting of, memory, tradition, and faith through dialogue.

The charges of syncretism and paganism that have been made in the course of this intense debate reveal again the distance that remains between various communities within the ecumenical movement. They have raised anew the problems of division and schism. Yet even if the visible fellowship were to be broken, and particular churches were to remove themselves from the WCC, these would be further acts in the contested dialogue of the ecumenical movement. Churches might withdraw from the WCC in protest (as has happened at times in its short history). But the memory of the dialogue which has already taken place, the expectations of dialogue which will yet occur, and the manifold ways in which churches find the means of continuing dialogue outside the structures of visible fellowship, will not be erased. And it is such common memories, even of differences and divisions, that will keep this contested movement alive. The ecclesiastical transformations which have taken place will continue to bear the marks of the dialogue that produced them. Whatever its future shape might be, the ecumenical movement will remain important in the lives of the churches and ecclesial communities of the world who will continue to be affected by the experiences of others outside of themselves, and will continue to be called to respond although they will be changed.

At the same time, the churches and ecclesial communities which have been, and continue to be, engaged in ecumenical dialogue will continue to hold different and perhaps even contradictory understandings of the meaning, purpose, and achievements of the ecumenical movement. As there are as many understandings of the meaning of a dialogue as there are participants engaged, so one could speculate that there are as many meanings to the ecumenical movement as there are communities and churches in it. The presence of the multiple and different contexts that participants bring to the dialogue and from which they speak suggests a multiplicity of meanings and understandings brought around a common table. The common words, statements, and actions that we share around the common table carry along their multiple meanings and contexts, carried by the multiple trajectories and pasts over which we have travelled to arrive at the common table of our present. The character of these contexts remains irreducibly multiple, the content of these memories different.

This again was evident in the events at Canberra surrounding the address by Chung Hyun-Kyung. The words she used were, as are all words, received from others and filled with the voices of the past. The intertextual character of these words, as Bakhtin would have pointed out, carries them along from context to context, infusing them with new meaning but also realizing the old. The dialogue moves along from text to text, across boundaries of time and cultural location. In their dialogical capacity even our simplest words and utterances remain filled with the past.[41] The movements of our bodies, the *praxis* of our communities are filled with social and individual memory.[42] The written and performed text of Chung's presentation at Canberra was a moment at the crossroads of intertextual meanings, drawn from several histories. Occurring in a context in which the historical memory of imperial Christendom remains alive, her traditional Christian words and actions were intertextual with a different history, a different memory --

those of Asian religious identity, of colonialism, and of women's oppression. For many who heard her at first these appeared to be outside the domain of their own Christian memory, in some sense heretical or 'pagan.' Yet by responding, even in anger, they begin to incorporate them into this other Christian memory, making them intertextual with the memory of Christendom.

Her words and actions took on meaning that neither she nor others necessarily intended. The new meaning which emerges in the ecumenical moment is a collective product, born from the plural. "Meaning (communication) implies community," notes Tzvetan Todorov; "the interlocutor participates in the formation of the meaning of the utterance, just as the other elements -- similarly social -- of the context of uttering do."[43] Chung's words and actions, and other's responses, were not absolutely incommensurable, for they were the content of dialogical interaction through controversy and debate. Those who agreed and those who disagreed (her interlocutors) together participated in a dialogue (admittedly heated). Through this dialogue new meaning is created, not one in which the previous meanings of the past are overcome or subsumed but one which opens up a fuller memory and fuller participation in community. It is only eschatologically that the dialogue is ever complete; but it is also eschatologically true that no memories, no meanings, are ever lost. As Bakhtin said, and Chung Hyun-Kyung demonstrated, every memory, every meaning, will have its homecoming festival.

The dialogue of the ecumenical movement is one important meeting place in preparation for this homecoming festival. It is a welcome table set for all who gather in memory of Jesus of Nazareth. It is at the same time a crossroads, a place where those who remember Jesus meet and bring together their other memories and meanings that will also receive some day their homecoming festival. At the crossroads of the ecumenical movement each becomes a 'transgredient' to the other through dialogue, although none is reduced to another. The (mono)-logics of our separate theo-logics become dialogic when they interact concretely in the ecumenical arena. Through the ecumenical movement theology thus becomes concrete, that is, literally it grows together (*concrescere*). The complex blending and weaving of ecumenical 'texts,' 'contexts,' and 'intertexts' -- woven fabrics of meaning all -- is a critical dialogical *praxis* in which representatives of diverse communities no longer speak of one another but to one another.

In this critical dialogical *praxis* the historical differences and disjunctions that exist among churches are not so much eliminated as they are presupposed, and from the plenitude of ecumenical dialogue is provided their homecoming.

Anthony Ugolink has recently pointed out that the incarnational sense of values and mystery informing Mikhail Bakhtin's understanding of dialogue was derived from Bakhtin's own deeply grounded Orthodox Christian faith.[44] From his Orthodox tradition Bakhtin understood the materiality of the word, and the manner in which for the Christian faith meaning is always already incarnate. Similarly, the mutuality and reciprocity which characterize dialogue are reflective of the Orthodox understanding of the nature of the Holy Trinity. Ugolink notes the Trinitarian origins of Bakhtin's conception of the plurality of consciousness which emerges from dialogue. That is to say, the 'communal personhood' of the Orthodox doctrine of the Holy Trinity is itself the basis for the dialogical existence that I have found becoming concretely realized in and through the ecumenical movement.[45] Dialogue is perhaps the best descriptive method we could offer for the 'reciprocal definition' of the *perichoresis* (the 'interdwelling,' or 'dancing together') among the Father, Son, and Holy Spirit that is at the heart of the Orthodox Christian faith.[46] The 'reciprocal definition' of 'dancing together' is at the very heart of the ecumenical community and movement, I would go on to say.[47]

Ugolink suggests that in the Orthodox tradition liturgy is a divine-human dialogue which likewise reflects the reciprocal definition of Trinitarian life. "Liturgy constitutes that dialogic arena within which the Word 'comes to mean.' It creates a context.... Liturgy is a dialogic act, an expression of our mutuality as Christians."[48] For the Orthodox tradition the divine liturgy of the Eucharist is the culmination rather than a means of visible and doctrinal unity, and thus it represents not only the fullness of divine-human reciprocity but the fullness of ecclesiological (human-human) reciprocity as well. The Orthodox tradition continues to remind the ecumenical movement as a whole of that Welcome Table which still lies in its future, and of the fullness of dialogue which is yet to come.

But even at that Table the dialogue will not end. The on-going dialogue of eucharistic liturgy and of the perichoretic *praxis* of solidarity, in worship and work, will continue to bring us together and open us to new and unfinalizable futures in the infinite abundance of

God's 'New.' Along the way to our new futures the ecumenical dialogues in which we are engaged will continue to re-center and de-center us, to move us together and send us apart, so that through the ecumenical movement we will perhaps come to realize more clearly the Trinitarian mystery of the Holy Spirit who eternally proceeds from the Father, but brings all things to their own unique eschatological fulfillment. If it is the work of the Spirit to make us one in Christ, this is not according to Vladimir Lossky a oneness which suppresses the uniqueness of each one's personhood. The human persons renewed in Christ are not themselves suppressed. "Within the Church the Holy Spirit imparts to human hypostases [persons] the fullness of deity after a manner which is unique, 'personal', appropriate to every man [sic] as a person created in the image of God."[49] "Thus," Lossky asserts, "the work of Christ unifies; the work of the Holy Spirit diversifies."[50] Diversity is still the work of the Spirit amidst ecumenical life today. It is the work of the Spirit bringing each community and person to their fullness and perfection. It is the work of the Spirit preparing every meaning its own homecoming. Diversity is the risk of ecumenical life today; it is the also the challenge for the ecumenical future.

Notes

1. Konrad Raiser, *Ecumenism in Transition: A Paradigm Shift in the Ecumenical Movement?* (Geneva: WCC, 1991, p. 106; and Mikhail M. Bakhtin, *Speech Genres and Other Late Essays*, Vern W. McGee, trans., Caryl Emerson and Michael Holquist, eds. (Austin, Tx: University of Texas Press, 1986), p. 170.

2. Paulos Mar Gregorius, *The Meaning and Nature of Diakonia* (Geneva: WCC, 1988), pp. 21-24.

3. Melanie A. May, *Bonds of Unity: Women, Theology, and the Worldwide Church* (Atlanta: Scholars Press, 1989), has fruitfully explored this aspect of the meaning of ecumenical conversation, providing a demonstration of the multiple conversations that surrounded the "Community of Women and Men" study of the WCC.

4. Gayatri Chakravorty Spivak, *In Other Worlds: Essays in Cultural Politics* (New York: Routledge, Chapman and Hall, Inc., 1988), pp. 123f, and 212f, has undertaken a critique of "phonocentrism." On the problematic character of maintaining rigid theoretical boundaries between written and oral texts of speech see Bakhtin, *Speech Genres and Other Late Essays*, pp. 132ff.

5. See Sharon D. Welch, *A Feminist Ethic of Risk* (Minneapolis: Fortress Press, 1990), p. 124.

6. Ada Maria Isasi-Diaz, "Solidarity: Love of Neighbor in the 1980s," *Life Every Voice: Constructing Christian Theologies from the Underside*, Susan Brooks Thistlethwaite and Mary Potter Engel, eds. (San Francisco: Harper and Row, Publishers, 1990), p. 33.

7. *Ibid.*, p. 304 n4.

8. Sun Ai Lee Park, "A New Phase in the Ecumenical Movement: One Woman's Perspective on Asian Activities," in *Women and Church: The Challenge of Ecumenical Solidarity in an Age of Alienation*, Melanie A. May, ed. (Grand Rapids: Wm. B. Eerdmans Publishing Co. / New York: Friendship Press, 1991), p. 155.

9. Annie Nachisale Musopole, "Toward a New Ecumenical Movement: A Malawian Perspective," in May, ed., *Women and Church: The Challenge of Ecumenical Solidarity in an Age of Alienation*, p. 151.

10. David J. Bosch, *Transforming Mission: Paradigm Shifts in Theology of Mission* (Maryknoll: Orbis Books, 1991), pp. 262-341 provides an overview of the historical emergence of Protestant missions in the modern era, and discusses the impact of the European Enlightenment's rationalism, concepts of historical progress, and objectivization of "others" had on missions.

11. Stephen Charles Neill, *Colonialism and Christian Missions* (NY: McGraw-Hill Book Co., 1966), p. 7. See also Bosch, *Transforming Mission*, pp. 302-313. As Bosch points out on p. 462, the ecumenical movement can be

understood as the "new" in relationship to the paradigm of missions that emerged in the period of European colonialism and the Enlightenment.

12. Tzvetan Todorov, *Mikhail Bakhtin: The Dialogical Principle*, Wlad Godzich, trans. (Minneapolis: University of Minnesota Press, 1984), p. 41. Bakhtin wrote in "Discourse in the Novel": "Every word smells of the context and contexts in which it has lived its intense social life; all words and all forms are inhabited by intentions." (*The Dialogic Imagination: Four Essays*, Michael Holquist, ed. [Austin: University of Texas Press, 1981], p. 360.)

13. The emergence of this new ecumenical paradigm has been noted by a number of missiologists. It is the main focus of Bosch's study, *Transforming Mission*.

14. Wilbert R. Shenk, "Mission in Transition: 1972-1987," *Missiology: An International Review* 15/4 (Oct. 1987), p. 429.

15. Wesley Ariarajah, *Hindus and Christians: A Century of Protestant Ecumenical Thought* (Amsterdam: Editions Rodopi/ Grand Rapids: Wm. B. Eerdmans Publishing Co., 1991).

16. *Ibid.*, p. 213.

17. See Jose Comblin, *The Holy Spirit and Liberation* (Maryknoll: Orbis, 1988).

18. Carlos Abesamis, "Doing Theological Reflection in a Philippine Context," *The Emergent Gospel: Theology from the Underside of History*, Sergio Torres and Virginia Fabella, eds. (Maryknoll: Orbis Books, 1978), p. 119; see also Suh, Nam-dong, "Historical References for a Theology of Minjung," *Minjung Theology: People as the Subjects of History* (Maryknoll: Orbis Books, 1983), p. 167.

19. For the text of *Unitatis Redintegratio* see Austin Flannery, ed., *Vatican Council II: The Conciliar and Post Conciliar Documents* (Northport, NY: Costello Publishing Co., 1980), pp. 452-470. The trajectory that led to the ecumenical awakening in Vatican II is sketched by Paul M. Minus, Jr., *The Catholic Rediscovery of Protestantism: A History of Roman Catholic Ecumenical Pioneering* (New York: Paulist Press, 1976). Concerning the ecumenical importance of other documents from Vatican II see Margaret Nash, *Ecumenical Movement in the 1960s* (Johannesburg: Ravan Press, 1975), pp. 93-165.

20. *Ibid.*, p. 454.

21. See also the "Reflections and Suggestions Concerning Ecumenical Dialogue," issued by the Vatican's Secretariat for the Promotion of the Unity of Christians in 1970, in *ibid.*, pp. 535-553.

22. See Hans Küng, ed., *Apostolic Succession: Rethinking a Barrier to Unity (Concilium*, Vol. 34) (New York: Paulist Press, 1968); Heinrich Stirnimann and Lukas Vischer, *Papsttum und Petrusdienst* (Frankfurt am Main: Verlag Otto Lembeck, 1975); Heinrich Fries and Karl Rahner, *Unity of the Churches: An Actual Possibility* (Philadelphia: Fortress Press / New York:

Paulist Press, 1985); John J. McDonnell, *The World Council of Churches and the Catholic Church* (Lewiston, NY: The Edwin Mellen Press, 1985); and Thomas Sieger Derr, *Barriers to Ecumenism: The Holy See and the World Council of Churches on Social Questions* (Maryknoll: Orbis Books, 1983).

23. See in particular Walbert Bühlmann, *With Eyes to See: Church and World in the Third Millennium* (Maryknoll: Orbis Books, 1990), esp. pp. 50-62.

24. Examples of this dispensationalist response to the WCC abound in the popular literature, but I site one statement in particular, in one of the most popular religious books of the modern era: Hal Lindsey, in *The Late Great Planet Earth* (Grand Rapids: Zondervan Publishing, 1970), writes on p. 104-105, "We believe that the joining of churches in the present ecumenical movement, combined with this amazing rejuvenation of star-worship, mind-expansion, and witch-craft, is preparing the world in every way for the establishment of a great religious system, one which will influence the Antichrist."

25. Harvey T. Hoekstra, *The World Council of Churches and the Demise of Evangelism* (Wheaton, Ill: Tyndale House, 1979) accuses the World Council of having abandoned missions and disregarded the mandate for evangelism.

26. Donald W. Dayton, "Yet Another Layer of the Onion: Or Opening the Ecumenical Door to Let the Riffraff in," *Ecumenical Review* 40/1 (Jan. 1988, pp. 87-110, has explored problems and possibilities in Wesleyan Holiness tradition and the WCC. Harold D. Hunter reports on recent Pentecostal ecumenical initiatives in "Brighton 91: A Pentecostal Perspective," *Ecumenical Trends* 21/4 (April 1992), pp. 51-54. Prospects for convergence between Roman Catholic base communities and Pentecostal communities in Latin America are explored by Charles E. Self, in "Conscientization, Conversion, and Convergence: Reflections on Base Communities and Emerging Pentecostalism in Latin America," *Pneuma: The Journal of the Society for Pentecostal Studies* 14/1 (Spring 1992), pp. 59-72.

27. See Carl McIntire, *Modern Tower of Babel* (Collingswood, NJ: Christian Beacon Press, 1949).

28. See Major Edgar Bundy, "Moscow-Directed Subversion in the Churches," in *Jesus Christ the Same Yesterday, and To Day and For Ever: Messages Given at the Fifth Plenary Congress of the International Council of Christian Churches* (Collingswood, NJ: Christian Beacon Press, 1962), pp. 133-154.

29. See *Evangelical Action: A Report of the Organization of the National Association of Evangelicals for United Action* (Boston: United Action Press, 1942); and James Deforest Murch, *Cooperation Without Compromise: A History of the National Association of Evangelicals* (Grand Rapids: Eerdmans, 1956).

30. Developments in evangelicalism's world mission theology are discussed in Rodger C. Bassham, *Mission Theology, 1948-1975: Years of Worldwide*

Creative Tension, Ecumenical, Evangelical and Roman Catholic (Pasadena: William Carey Library, 1979); proceedings of what is perhaps the most important evangelical mission conference of the 1960s, held in Wheaton, Illinois, in 1966, are found in Harold Lindsell, ed., *The Church's Worldwide Mission: An Analysis of the Current State of Evangelicals and a Strategy for Future Activity* (Waco, Tx: Word Books, 1966). On the Lausanne movement see J. D. Douglas, ed., *Let the World Hear His Voice: International Congress on World Evangelization. Lausanne, Switzerland, Official Reference Volume* (Minneapolis: World Wide Publications, 1975); and Edward R. Dayton and S. Wilson, ed., *The Future of World Evangelization: The Lausanne Movement* (Monrovia, Ca: MARC, 1984). It should be pointed out that while other ecumenical organizations such as the NAE, the NCCC, and the WCC are constituted by member churches and organizations, the Lausanne Committee for World Evangelization is composed of individual Christians who have signed the Lausanne Covenant.

31. Orlando E. Costas, *Christ Outside the Gate: Mission Beyond Christendom* (Maryknoll: Orbis Books, 1982), engages evangelical and ecumenical themes in creative dialogue concerning contemporary missions. A more systematic study of the convergences and contrasts in mission theologies is James A. Scherer, *Gospel, Church, and Kingdom: Comparative Studies in World Mission Theology* (Minneapolis: Augsburg Publishing House, 1987).

32. A recent fundamentalist attack on the ecumenical movement and the WCC by Homer Duncan has included a warning to evangelicals engaged in dialogue with the ecumenical community. So he writes: "The intentions of the evangelicals in the [Ecumenical Movement] are good, but they have been deceived by Satan when they think it is the will of God for them to cooperate with Christ-rejecting Protestants, and with Roman Catholics who have made the Word of God of none effect by their own traditions." *The Ecumenical Movement in the Light of Holy Scriptures*, Revised Edition, (Lubbock, Tx: Missionary Crusader, 1976), p. iii. A more moderate evangelical critique of the WCC is provided by Hoekstra, *The World Council of Churches and the Demise of Evangelism*.

33. Michael Kinnamon, *Truth and Community: Diversity and its Limits in the Ecumenical Movement* (Grand Rapids: Wm. B. Eerdmans, 1988), p. 98f.

34. See David du Plessis' autobiography, written with Bob Slosser, *A Man Called Mr. Pentecost* (Plainfield, NJ: Logos International, 1977); as well as his book, *The Spirit Bade Me Go*, Revised edition (Plainfield: Logos International, 1970).

35. One of the more important recent expressions of "charismatic ecumenism" is found in Peter D. Hocken, *One Lord, One Spirit, One Body: The Ecumenical Grace of the Charismatic Movement* (Gaithersburg, Md: The Word Among Us Press/ Flemington Markets, Australia: Paternoster Press, 1987). Hocken speaks of the renewal of the Holy Spirit being experienced in

the contemporary charismatic movement as "a transcendent ecumenical grace" bringing divided churches to unity (p. 87). See also Arnold Bittlinger, ed., *The Church is Charismatic* (Geneva: WCC, 1981); and the two editions of the *International Review of Missions*, 75/297 (January 1986) and 75/298 (April 1986).

36. See in particular *Pneuma: The Journal of the Society for Pentecostal Studies*, 9/1 (Spring 1987) which examines the current state of dialogue among Pentecostals and Charismatic communities with others in the ecumenical movement.

37. See Emmanuel Levinas, *Time and the Other [and Additional Essays]*, Richard A. Cohen, trans. (Pittsburgh: Duquesne University Press, 1987).

38. Chung Hyun-Kyung, "Come Holy Spirit, Renew the Whole Creation," *Signs of the Spirit: Official Report Seventh Assembly Canberra, Australia, 7-20 February 1991*, Michael Kinnamon, ed. (Geneva: WCC / Grand Rapids: Wm. B. Eerdmans, 1991), p. 39.

39. *Ibid.*

40. The debate was carried on in the daily Assembly newsletter, *Assembly Line*; see, for instance, nos. 2, 3, 5, and 9.

41. Tzvetan Todorov, *Mikhail Bakhtin: The Dialogical Principle*, Wlad Godzich, trans. (Minneapolis: University of Minnesota Press, 1984), p. 48. For an excellent introduction to the practice of intertextuality, see Danna Nolan Fewell, ed., *Reading Between Texts: Intertextuality and the Hebrew Bible* (Louisville: Westminster/John Knox Press, 1992), esp. the "Introduction" and "Glossary," and introductory essay by Timothy K. Beal, "Ideology and Intertextuality: Surplus of Meaning and Controlling the Means of Production," pp. 11-39.

42. On the performative character of memory, and the relationship between inscribed and incorporated memory, see Paul Connerton, *How Societies Remember* (Cambridge: Cambridge University Press, 1989).

43. Todorov, *Mikhail Bakhtin*, p. 30. In a similar manner but different context Franz Rosenzweig came to the notion of "speaking-thinking" during the first decades of the twentieth century, arguing for a distinction between "logical" and "grammatical" thinking similar to the distinction made here between logical and dialogical. Rosenzweig wrote: "In the old philosophy, 'thinking' means thinking for no one else and speaking to no one else (and here, if you prefer, you may substitute 'everyone' or the well-known 'all the world' for 'no one'). But 'speaking' means speaking to some one and thinking for some one. And this some one is always a quite definite some one, and he [sic] has not merely ears, like 'all the world,' but also a mouth." (Nahum N. Glatzer, *Franz Rosenzweig: His Life and Thought* [New York: Farrer, Straus, and Young, 1953], p. 200.

44. Anthony Ugolink, *The Illuminating Icon* (Grand Rapids: Wm. B. Eerdmans, 1989), p. 162.

45. *Ibid.*, p. 163.

46. Barbara Brown Zikmund, "The Trinity and Women's Experience," *Christian Century*, 104/72 (April 15, 1987), pp. 354-356, acknowledges the problems of patriarchal terminology that inhere in traditional Trinitarian dogmas, especially concerning the "Father" and "Son," but goes on to discuss the importance of the meaning of *perichoresis* within a feminist theological context. Concerning the problem of patriarchy and the doctrine of the Trinity, see also Catherine Mowry LaCugna, "The Baptismal Formula, Feminist Objections, and Trinitarian Theology," *Journal of Ecumenical Studies* 26/2 (Spring 1989), pp. 235-250.

47. F. Eboussi Boulage, in *Christianity Without Fetishes: An African Critique and Recapture of Christianity* (Maryknoll: Orbis, 1984), p. 194, writes: "Thus understood, the doctrine of the Trinity could prescribe a mode of thinking, or better, a mode of conducting oneself and existing, a mode of living in society." See also Leonardo Boff, *Trinity and Society*, Paul Burns, trans. (Maryknoll: Orbis Books, 1986), pp. 118-119; Catherine Mowry LaCugna, *God For Us: The Trinity and Christian Life* (San Francisco: HarperCollins, 1991); Mercy Amba Oduyoye, *Hearing and Knowing: Theological Reflections on Christianity in Africa* (Maryknoll: Orbis, 1986), pp. 141-145; and Maria Clara Bingemer, "Reflections on the Trinity," in *Through Her Eyes: Women's Theology from Latin America*, Elsa Tamez, ed. (Maryknoll: Orbis, 1989).

48. Ugolink, *The Illuminating Icon*, pp. 171-172.

49. Vladimir Lossky, *The Mystical Theology of the Eastern Church* (Crestwood, NY: St. Vladimir's Seminary Press, 1976), p. 166.

50. *Ibid..* p. 167.

Index